American Language Hub

CB081787

LEVEL 4A
Student's Book

LOUIS ROGERS

macmillan education

Contents

Welcome

GRAMMAR

The passive voice

A **Complete the sentences with the passive voice form of the verbs in the box.**

arrest cancel destroy kill release take

1 Apparently, over 700,000 people ______________________ by mosquitos every year.
2 A decision ______________________ by the management board later in the week.
3 Three men ______________________ in connection with an attempted robbery in Soho last week.
4 The band's debut album ______________________ on August 27, 1991.
5 'We regret to inform passengers that the 7:36 flight to San Diego, California ______________________.'
6 Over 600 homes ______________________ in the forest fires that hit the area last month.

Zero, first and second conditionals

B **Choose the correct options (a, b or c) to complete the conditional sentences.**

1 If you don't hurry up, ___ the beginning of the movie.
a we'll miss **b** we'd miss **c** we'd have missed
2 Let me know if ___ any help with anything.
a you'll need **b** you need **c** you'd need
3 If ___ the fire alarm, leave the building by the nearest exit.
a you'll hear **b** you'd heard **c** you hear
4 I can't help you unless ___ me what's wrong.
a you'd tell **b** you tell **c** you'd have told
5 If I had the money, ___ all my food there.
a I'll buy **b** I'd buy **c** I'd have bought
6 If ___ Emily, I'll tell her to give you a call.
a I see **b** I'll see **c** I'd see

VOCABULARY

Word formation

A **Complete the sentences with the correct form of the words in parentheses.**

1 I thought that was a really ______________ (*product*) meeting actually.
2 Just relax. Try not to ______________ (*think*) it.
3 That reminds me, I need to ______________ (*new*) my passport.
4 Sorry, but I think you may have ______________ (*understand*) the question.
5 There's simply no ______________ (*science*) evidence to support that.

Collocations

B **Choose the correct options to complete the collocations.**

1 We're sorry to announce that there are ***serious* / *severe*** delays on the central line.
2 Many new business owners find it difficult to ***make* / *create*** a profit in their first year.
3 I'm finding it really difficult to ***stay* / *remain*** motivated right now.
4 LeBron James has ***made* / *given*** the decision not to renew his contract with the Cleveland Cavaliers.
5 Scott seems pretty confident that his team will ***reach* / *make*** their target by June.
6 My brother-in-law actually ***does* / *runs*** a small business from home.
7 The government has ***launched* / *released*** a new campaign focusing on mental health.
8 Annoyingly, we got stuck in ***serious* / *heavy*** traffic on our way back.

C **SPEAK** **Work in pairs. Discuss the questions.**

1 What can you do to help stay motivated at work and in your studies?
2 Do you know anyone that runs a successful business? What do they do?
3 What's the most difficult decision you've ever made?

PRONUNCIATION

Intonation

0.1 **A** **Draw arrows in the parentheses to show whether the intonation rises (↗) or falls (↘) at each point in the sentences. Then listen and check.**

1 Oh, really? ( ) Wow! That sounds great! ( )
2 It's a formal dinner, ( ) so it's important that you look nice. ( )
3 You've been to New York before, ( ) haven't you? ( )
4 Hmm … I'm not sure really. ( ) Maybe tomorrow afternoon? ( )
5 OK. ( ) I'll speak to Alicia and get back to you. ( )

Silent consonants

0.2 **B** **Underline the silent consonants in each word. Then listen and check.**

1 dishonest
2 listen
3 designer
4 climbing
5 muscle
6 knowledge

1 CONNECTIONS

> Friends show their love in times of trouble, not in happiness.
>
> Euripides

Women in a minimalist photo shoot in Copenhagen, Denmark.

OBJECTIVES

- talk about reactions and feelings
- design and present a meet-up group
- compare, contrast and summarize short biographies
- talk about people that have influenced you
- give your opinion on the role of inherited ability in success
- write a formal letter asking for information

Work with a partner. Discuss the questions.

1. Read the quote. Do you agree with Euripides? Why/Why not?
2. Can online relationships ever be as close as face-to-face relationships? Why/Why not?
3. What are the most important relationships in your life? Why?

S skimming for the main ideas V feelings G question forms P intonation in *yes/no* and *wh-* questions

READING

A SPEAK Work in groups. Discuss the questions.

1 What qualities make someone a hero?
2 What type of people would you describe as 'everyday heroes'? Why?
3 Have you ever done anything heroic?

B SKIM FOR MAIN IDEAS Skim read *Inspiring stories of everyday heroes*. Choose the best summary (a or b) for each story. Use the information in the box to help you.

Skimming for the main ideas

Many modern articles, particularly those online, are presented in multiple short paragraphs to make them easier to read in a short amount of time. We can usually understand the main ideas in this kind of article by quickly skimming the text.

1 a A man jumped onto the train tracks to save his baby.
  b A man jumped onto the train tracks to save a woman's baby.
2 a A young couple was saved from a forest fire that broke out in the fields they were driving through.
  b A young couple saved a family from a forest fire that spread to their house.
3 a A group of heroic pedestrians helped pull a schoolgirl out from under the car that had just hit her.
  b A driver heroically pulled a young schoolgirl out from under his car after an accident.
4 a Despite not being a strong swimmer, a young man was able to rescue his dog from strong currents in the ocean.
  b A passerby was able to rescue a dog that had been swept out to sea.

C READ FOR DETAIL Read the article again and answer the questions. Underline the parts of the text that give you the answers.

1 What caused the stroller to start rolling toward the train tracks?
2 Was Jonas Neff in any real danger?
3 How did the fire develop so rapidly?
4 How did the children escape the burning building?
5 What had Becca Edwards been doing before the accident?
6 How did the driver react after the accident?
7 Why couldn't the dog get back to the beach?
8 Why was the rescuer so sure he could help?

D SPEAK Work in pairs. Discuss the questions.

1 How do you think you would react in the situations described in the article? Why?
2 Do you agree with Jonas Neff that he isn't a hero because 'anyone would do the same'? Why/Why not?
3 Why was Becca Edwards lucky that her accident happened on a main road?

Inspiring stories of EVERYDAY HEROES

BY EMILY FISCHER | OCT 15, 2018

In an age dominated by movies about superheroes, it's good to know that we can all be heroes in the right context. To inspire you to do something next time you see someone in trouble, here are four real-life stories of normal people who jumped into action without a second thought.

BACK ON TRACK

Reactions are vital in everyday situations. Mother-of-one Christine Thomas was waiting on a crowded platform for her train home, when her phone rang. Expecting an important call, Christine rooted through her bag, not noticing that the brake on her child's stroller had failed and it was rolling toward the platform edge. She looked up, **horrified**, to see the stroller fall off the platform and onto the tracks below. Everyone on the platform froze, too **tense** to move, except Jonas Neff. Jonas jumped down quickly and lifted the stroller and child onto the platform, before pulling himself up just in time to avoid the oncoming train. Interviewed later by local radio, Jonas said, 'I'm not a hero. Anyone else would do the same.' Maybe a little too modest considering that everyone else had been too shocked to move!

ESCAPING THE BLAZE

Everyone can be brave no matter how young or old they are. In the dry heat of the summer, a fire started burning slowly in a farmer's field. As the winds became stronger, the fire spread quickly, surrounding the Sanchez family home. Trapped inside were a grandmother and her two young grandchildren. Spotting the danger as they were driving past, local residents Maria and Javier Hernandez stopped and got out to help. Maria later told local reporters '… I was so **impressed** by the character of such young children. They didn't know who we were but trusted us to catch them as they jumped from the top window. Once they were out, the grandmother jumped too.' The family was clearly upset to lose their home but equally **relieved** to all be alive.

THE STRENGTH OF MANY

Sometimes what you need is a whole group of heroes. **Thrilled** at having just won a local soccer tournament, 10-year-old Becca Edwards was riding her bike home from school one evening when she was hit by a car that had driven through a red light. The car stopped, trapping Becca underneath. **Devastated** by what had happened, the driver could do nothing as Becca screamed for help. Luckily for her, the accident took place on a busy main road. Nine pedestrians ran to help, working together to lift the car up just enough for a tenth hero to pull the schoolgirl out from underneath. Mark Benson, the first paramedic at the scene, said Becca was lucky to be alive and praised the quick response of the passers-by.

DANGER AT THE BEACH

Michael was happily throwing sticks into the ocean for his dog, Linus, when suddenly it all went wrong. Strong currents dragged poor Linus out to sea and he wasn't able to swim back to shore. Terrified that Linus might die, but not a particularly strong swimmer, Michael stood helpless and **frustrated** on the beach. All of a sudden, a man came running past and dived into the water. After a brief struggle, he managed to pull Linus back to the shore where he was met with a huge round of applause from the crowd of onlookers that had gathered. 'Initially, I felt kind of **awkward** on the beach because I didn't know what to do' said the young hero. 'But I'm pretty confident in the water, so I just jumped in. I'm glad I could help out, but I wouldn't recommend swimming in such dangerous currents unless you're confident you can get back. A person's life is much more important than a dog's!'

VOCABULARY

Feelings

A Scan the article again. Complete the definitions with the adjectives in bold.

1. ______________ feeling happy because something bad has stopped or hasn't happened
2. ______________ feeling nervous, worried and not able to relax because of what might happen
3. ______________ feeling embarrassed and not relaxed
4. ______________ feeling very shocked and upset
5. ______________ feeling very shocked or frightened
6. ______________ feeling very happy and excited
7. ______________ feeling admiration for someone because of an unusually good achievement, quality or skill
8. ______________ feeling annoyed or impatient because you can't do or achieve what you want

B Complete the sentences with adjectives from Exercise A.

1. I felt a little ______________ at first because I wasn't wearing a suit like everybody else.
2. I was just really ______________ because the police wouldn't let me help.
3. It'd been a horrible flight and I was pretty ______________ when the plane finally landed.
4. Firefighter Mark Cox was ______________ to receive an award for bravery after the incident.
5. You couldn't help but be ______________ by how quickly he reacted to the danger.
6. The crowd grew ______________ as they waited to see if firefighters would reach the child in time.
7. I was ______________ to hear that my grandmother had died because we were very close.
8. We were all ______________ as the elevator fell 15 floors toward the ground.

C Go to the Vocabulary Hub on page XVI.

D SPEAK Work in pairs. When was the last time you felt any of these emotions? What happened?

SPEAKING

SPEAK Work in groups. Read the scenarios (1–3) and discuss what you would do in each and why.

1. You're on a busy train when the woman in front of you suddenly falls over. Her eyes are closed and she doesn't appear to be breathing.
2. You're walking home late at night when you see a group of men shouting at a terrified businessman. You think they might attack him.
3. A fire breaks out in the house across the street. The elderly woman that lives there has difficulty walking and has poor hearing.

LISTENING

A SPEAK Work in pairs. Read the information about Get Together and discuss the questions.

1. What is the purpose of Get Together?
2. What kind of groups are available?
3. Do you think this is a good idea? Why/Why not?

Get Together

Home About us Contact Login Sign up

Get Together helps connect millions of people with similar interests around the world. The basic idea is simple – find people in your local area that share your passion and form a group. Meet regularly to play together, learn new skills or just make new friends.

Our members have rediscovered their passion for reading, trained for triathlons, even changed their careers – the possibilities are endless. Whatever you're interested in, you're sure to find a group that suits you.

Members	Groups	Countries
25 million	185,967	148

1.1 **B LISTEN FOR MAIN IDEAS Listen and match the conversations (1–3) to the pictures (a–c).**

Conversation 1 ___ Conversation 2 ___ Conversation 3 ___

1.1 **C LISTEN FOR DETAIL Listen again. Are these sentences true (T) or false (F)? Correct the false sentences.**

1 a Both speakers at the ukulele group regularly go to meet-ups. T / F

b They have played the ukulele for the same amount of time. T / F

2 a The man's apartment is in a convenient location. T / F

b The man has done a 10K race before. T / F

3 a Martin needs to return the registration form as soon as possible. T / F

b Martin and Yumi both enjoyed the Haruki Murakami novel *Norwegian Wood*. T / F

D SPEAK Work in groups. Discuss the questions.

1. What are the benefits of joining a group like this?
2. Do you think this is the best way to meet new people in your area? Why/Why not?
3. What Get Together groups would you like to join in your area? Why?

GRAMMAR

Question forms

1.2 **A Listen to extracts from the conversations again. Complete the questions.**

1 **Sarah:** Yeah, same really. It just seemed like a fun thing to do. Anyway, ____________ ____________ the group tonight?

Mark: Uh, Lucy, I think. She's actually a professional musician, so we're in good hands.

2 **Fyodor:** Well, I like Rochester, but my apartment is a really long way from the train station and I don't really get along with my roommates.

Alana: Fair enough. ____________ ____________ like them?

Fyodor: Well, one of them works night shifts so he always comes home really late and the other just spends all his time in his room.

3 **Fyodor:** I suppose so. Who ____________ ____________?

Alana: A couple of friends I've known since college. They can definitely be annoying sometimes, but I wouldn't want to live with anyone else.

4 **Martin:** Excuse me, ____________ ____________ where I sign in for the book club Get Together?

Yumi: Uh, yeah, right here actually. I'm running the group tonight. Can I take your name, please?

B WORK IT OUT Choose the correct options to complete the rules.

Question forms

Indirect questions

We use indirect questions when we want to be more polite. They usually start with phrases like *Could you tell me …?, Do you know …?* and *Would you mind …?* In indirect questions, we use the same word order as a statement (i.e. [1]***verb + subject / subject + verb***) and we don't use the auxiliary *do*.

Questions with prepositions

If a verb is followed by a preposition, the preposition comes at the [2]***beginning / end*** of the sentence.

Subject questions

When we ask about the subject of a sentence, we use the same word order as a statement, and the question word (e.g. *when, who, what, which,* etc) replaces the [3]***subject / object***.

Negative questions

When we ask negative *wh-* questions, we [4]***use / don't use*** the auxiliary verb, even in subject questions.

C Go to the Grammar Hub on page VI.

D PRACTICE Reorder the words to make questions.

1 would / most like to meet / which / you / famous person

_______________________________________?

2 is / can / ask / your earliest memory / I / what

_______________________________________?

3 think / you / is more important / diet or exercise / do

_______________________________________?

4 English / you / why / are / studying

_______________________________________?

5 your job / what / like about / you / don't

_______________________________________?

E SPEAK Work in pairs. Discuss the questions in Exercise D.

PRONUNCIATION

Intonation in *yes/no* and *wh-* questions

A 1.3 Listen to the questions from the conversations. Draw arrows to show whether the intonation rises (↗) or falls (↘) at the end of each question.

1 Have you been playing long? ___

2 Where were you living before? ___

3 Who do you live with? ___

4 Have you had time to finish the book yet? ___

B 1.4 Circle the arrows to predict which intonation will be used in each question. Then listen and check.

1 Is there an application fee? [↗] / [↘]

2 What kind of event could we run? [↗] / [↘]

3 How often does the group meet? [↗] / [↘]

4 Do you need any special equipment? [↗] / [↘]

5 Is everyone happy with that? [↗] / [↘]

SPEAKING HUB

A PLAN Work in groups. Brainstorm a list of things you like doing or are interested in.

B PREPARE Choose one of your ideas from Exercise A to use as the focus of a new meet-up group. Write notes about:

- what you'll actually do at the meet-ups
- where / how often you'll meet
- what special events you might organize
- how much members will need to pay and why

C PRESENT Present your ideas to the class. Ask other groups follow-up questions to get more information.

D DISCUSS As a class, discuss which meet-up groups would work best in your area and why.

- Talk about reactions and feelings
- Design and present a meet-up group

1.2 Who we are

- Compare, contrast and summarize short biographies
- Talk about people that have influenced you

G – tense review
V – personality adjectives; noun suffixes
L – listening for the main ideas
P – connected speech: final consonant and initial vowel

READING

A SPEAK Work in groups. What do you know about the people in the article below?

B READ FOR GIST Read *The long road to success* and choose the sentence (1–3) that best describes the connection between the two people.

1 famous people that had difficult childhoods
2 famous people that overcame challenges to succeed
3 famous people that failed in college

C SCAN Scan the article again and check (✓) the person that each sentence is about.

Which person …	Stephen Hawking	Vera Wang
1 had an unusual childhood?		
2 didn't meet their academic potential?		
3 had a significant change in their career?		
4 was inspired to start a new business?		
5 lived much longer than people expected?		
6 is very rich and successful today?		

The long road to success

It's easy to think that the rich and famous have always lived a privileged life, but many have overcome great adversity to get to where they are today. When life presents us with challenges, how we react can determine how successful we become.

Stephen Hawking

What was his early life like?

Keeping bees in the basement of their crumbling St. Albans home, making fireworks in the greenhouse and driving around in a former London taxi, the Hawking family was certainly a little eccentric. In fact, they frequently ate dinner in silence [1]while each of them was reading a book.

Was he always a gifted academic?

At school, Hawking was thought of as bright but not brilliant. In his first year of high school, [2]he was the third worst student in the class. He also admitted to being a lazy student at Oxford University, only spending about an hour a day studying.

When did his condition develop?

Hawking first recognized something was wrong when he started to occasionally trip and fall while studying for a PhD at Cambridge University. At 21 years old, he was diagnosed with amyotrophic lateral sclerosis (ALS), and given just two years to live.

How did this affect him?

Hawking said that before he was diagnosed with ALS, he had been bored with life. Being told that he would not live to complete his PhD encouraged the young physicist to focus on his studies.

What made him famous?

Hawking is most famous for his research into black holes. By his early thirties, he had won many awards and went on to publish numerous papers and books, including *A brief history of time*. He was still proposing groundbreaking ideas about space and time until his death 50 years later.

Glossary

ALS (n) amyotrophic lateral sclerosis is a serious disease that affects nerve cells and causes muscles to become smaller and weaker

Vera Wang

Did she always want to work in fashion?

From the age of eight years old, Wang wanted to become a professional figure skater. After years of training and competing, she realized that no matter how hard she trained, she would never make the Olympic team. She gave up figure skating and moved to Paris to study Art History. It was there in the French capital that Wang realized she wanted to pursue a career in the fashion industry. After [3]she had completed her year in another country, Wang moved back to the US where she worked as a sales person at Yves Saint Laurent. It was at this point she met *Vogue* fashion director Frances Stein, who told Wang to give her a call when she graduated. A year and a half later she did, and spent the next 17 years working as an editor at the magazine.

How did she get into fashion design?

Wang left *Vogue* in 1982 and lived in Paris for several years before taking a position as design director at Ralph Lauren in New York. When planning her wedding in 1989, she was so disappointed by the lack of fashionable wedding dresses that she decided to design her own. A year later, she opened her own bridal shop, from which [4]she has built a fashion empire worth millions. [5]Today, she is worth over $600 million and is considered one of America's most successful self-made millionaires. Her clothes are worn by everyone from Michelle Obama to Kim Kardashian. She remains heavily involved in her company and is known for working long hours and holding frequent meetings to ensure she knows [6]exactly what's happening.

D READ FOR DETAIL Read again. Complete the sentences with no more than two words from the article.

1. Stephen Hawking was considered a ________________ student at Cambridge University.
2. Before finding out about his illness, he only studied for ________________ each day.
3. He was told he would live for just ________________ more years.
4. He was given a lot of ________________ for his early work.
5. Vera Wang gave up her dream of becoming a professional ________________ after realizing she would never make the Olympic team.
6. She worked as a ________________ before joining Vogue shortly after graduation.
7. She left Vogue in 1982, after ________________ working as an editor.
8. Her personal fortune is thought to be more than ________________.

E SPEAK Work in pairs. Can you think of anyone else that has overcome huge challenges in order to succeed?

GRAMMAR
Tense review

A Scan the article again. Match the highlighted sentences (1–6) to the tenses below.

__ simple present	__ past progressive
__ simple past	__ present progressive
__ past perfect	__ present perfect

B WORK IT OUT Complete the rules with the tenses in Exercise A.

Tense review

We use the [1] ________________ to talk about past states or completed actions in the past.

We use the [2] ________________ to talk about things happening now or around now.

We use the [3] ________________ to talk about a state or action that started in the past and is still happening now.

We use the [4] ________________ to talk about something that is generally true.

We use the [5] ________________ to talk about an action in the past that was in progress when something else happened.

We use the [6] ________________ to talk about a past action that occurred before another past action.

C Go to the **Grammar Hub** on page VI.

D PRACTICE Complete the text with the correct form of the verbs in parentheses.

Saroo Brierley

Saroo Brierley [1] ________________ (*be*) born in Ganesh Talai, a suburb in Khandwa, India. His family was poor and regularly had to beg for food and money. When he was five, Saroo [2] ________________ (*take*) a train with his older brother, Ghuddu, from Khandwa to the city of Burhanpur, where Ghuddu had a job cleaning trains at night. By the time they arrived, Saroo was so tired he fell asleep on the platform. Ghuddu told him to wait there but when he [3] ________________ (*not return*), Saroo grew impatient and got on a train that [4] ________________ (*wait*) at the platform. He fell asleep and when he woke up, he realized that he [5] ________________ (*travel*) to Kolkata by mistake – 1,500 km away from home.

After living on the streets for three weeks, he was placed in a local orphanage. An Australian family adopted him and he [6] ________________ (*spend*) the next 25 years living in Australia. Saroo wanted to find his family. Using his memories and Google Earth, Saroo eventually [7] ________________ (*find*) his hometown in India.

Before his story was turned into an internationally successful book and movie, Saroo [8] ________________ (*help*) his dad run a business. Now he [9] ________________ (*work*) as a motivational speaker until he decides what to do next. Since living in Australia, Saroo [10] ________________ (*have*) a happy life and always feels lucky.

E SPEAK Work in pairs. Discuss the questions.

1. What challenges do you have in your life right now?
2. What is the biggest challenge you have ever faced? How did you deal with it?

SPEAKING

A PREPARE Student A – Go to the **Communication Hub** on page XX. Student B – Go to the **Communication Hub** on page XXII.

B SPEAK Tell your partner about the person you read about.

C DISCUSS Work in groups. Discuss the questions.

1. What are the similarities between the two people you read about?
2. Who do you think had bigger challenges to overcome? Why?

LISTENING

A SPEAK Work in pairs. Tell your partner about your closest friends. How are they similar/different? Is it important to have different types of friends? Why/Why not?

1.5 **B LISTEN FOR MAIN IDEAS Listen to an interview about friendship, personality and success. Put the following topics in the order they are discussed. Use the information in the box to help you.**

> **Listening for the main ideas**
>
> Talks, speeches and interviews usually contain multiple main ideas, based around one central theme. Speakers frequently introduce each new idea or point with phrases such as *the next is*, *another one is*, *the last is*, etc. Identifying these phrases can help you focus on the key information that follows.

___ a work colleague who makes you laugh
___ a complete opposite of you
___ a best friend you can rely on
___ a very honest friend who tells you the truth
___ a neighbor in your community
___ a friend who is not afraid

1.5 **C LISTEN FOR DETAIL Listen to the interview again. Choose the correct options (a, b or c) to complete the sentences.**

1. According to research, we can only maintain a friendship group of …
   a several hundred people.
   b no more than 50 people.
   c no more than 20 people.
2. Open-minded adventurers are people who …
   a are always making new friends.
   b don't find new situations stressful.
   c like habit and routine.
3. It's important to have a friend who …
   a will constantly praise you.
   b is very flexible.
   c will be brutally honest with you.
4. Moving a lot affects our relationships with …
   a our neighbors.
   b our colleagues.
   c our relatives.
5. Successful people …
   a prioritize work over everything else.
   b work longer hours than their colleagues.
   c feel part of a group.

D SPEAK Work in groups. Discuss the questions.

1. What positive and negative effects does social media have on our relationships?
2. How well do you know your neighbors/colleagues/classmates? Do you consider any of them friends?

VOCABULARY

Personality adjectives

1.6 **A Complete the extracts with the personality adjectives in the box. Then listen and check.**

> arrogant down-to-earth easy-going loyal
> open-minded self-centered stubborn witty

1. We all need a ________________ best friend. Someone who will support us no matter what happens.
2. This person is an ________________ adventurer. They always force us into new and different situations.
3. They are ________________ and open to new ideas, cultures and activities. None of these things stress them out.
4. No, these people aren't ________________. They just have a lot of self-belief.
5. They'll tell you when you're being ________________ and should think about others more.
6. Or they'll tell you you are being ________________ and need to be more flexible.
7. She's very ________________. She just does everything in this very sensible, practical way. I guess she is a helpful person to have around!
8. Having no ________________ people to have a laugh with would make work very boring.

B Choose the correct adjectives to complete the sentences.

1 My neighbor is really ***easy-going / open-minded***. He's always willing to consider new ideas or opinions.

2 In a difficult situation, she stays calm. She's so ***loyal / down-to-earth*** and knows exactly what to do.

3 She never gets stressed. She's so ***easy-going / witty***.

4 I find her really ***arrogant / self-centered***. It's like she thinks she is better than everyone.

5 Even when I've done stupid things, she has always been ***loyal / down-to-earth*** and supported me.

6 There's no point arguing with him. He's just so ***stubborn / arrogant*** and won't change his mind.

7 I think she's really ***easy-going / witty*** actually. She's always making relevant jokes.

8 Stop being so ***self-centered / stubborn***. Try to think about other people for once!

C Go to the **Vocabulary Hub** on **page XVII**.

D Complete the personality quiz.

What kind of person are you?

Rate yourself on a scale of 1–5.
1 = Strongly disagree 5 = Strongly agree

You find it easy to stay focused even when you are under pressure.	1 2 3 4 5
You usually start conversations.	1 2 3 4 5
You rarely do something just out of curiosity.	1 2 3 4 5
You feel more important than other people.	1 2 3 4 5
Getting what you want is more important than keeping others happy.	1 2 3 4 5
Making other people laugh is important to you.	1 2 3 4 5
You try to win arguments even when you might be wrong.	1 2 3 4 5
You don't believe in hiding your feelings to keep people happy.	1 2 3 4 5

E SPEAK Work in pairs. Describe your partner's personality using their answers to the quiz in Exercise D. Do you agree with their description of you?

PRONUNCIATION

Connected speech: final consonant and initial vowel

1.7 **A** Listen to the sentence and draw (‿) between any words that link together.

Most people spend at least 50 percent of their waking hours at work.

B Work in pairs. Look at the example in Exercise A and discuss the questions.

1 Does the first word end in a consonant or a vowel sound?

2 What sound does the next word begin with?

1.8 **C** Read the sentences. Draw (‿) to predict which words are connected. Then listen and check.

1 They are open-minded and friendly.

2 She achieved a lot despite having a difficult childhood.

3 He built a successful business at a young age.

4 We spent a lot of our time together going for walks in the country.

5 We hung out at the beach, went out at night and played games online together.

VOCABULARY

Noun suffixes

We use the following suffixes to change adjectives to nouns:

-ion (e.g. *ambitious* > *ambition*)

-ity/-ty (e.g. *flexible* > *flexibility*)

-ence (e.g. *different* > *difference*)

-ness (e.g. *stubborn* > *stubbornness*)

-ism (e.g. *pessimistic* > *pessimism*)

Complete the sentences with the noun form of the adjectives in parentheses. Use the information in the box to help you.

1 I think what I value most in a friend is ______________ (*loyal*).

2 ______________ (*optimistic*) is a great quality for a close friend to have.

3 Her ______________ (*determined*) to succeed had a great influence on me.

4 Frankly, I was amazed by his ______________ (*arrogant*).

5 She took ______________ (*responsible*) for her actions.

6 He always gave me the ______________ (*confident*) to try new things.

SPEAKING HUB

A PREPARE Make a list of people that have had a big influence on you (e.g. a teacher, your best friend, a grandparent, etc).

B PLAN Choose one of the people in Exercise A to tell your partner about. Use the following questions to write notes:

1 What was their personality like?

2 Why did they have such an influence on you?

3 What things did you do together?

C SPEAK Work in pairs. Use your notes from Exercise B to talk about the person you chose. Ask follow-up questions to find out more about them.

D DISCUSS As a class, discuss the types of people that influenced you. What personality traits do they share?

Compare, contrast and summarize short biographies

Talk about people that have influenced you

1.3 Keeping it in the family

A– idioms: family S– developing and introducing new topics

The Special Olympics

COMPREHENSION

A **Work in pairs. Successful athletes are usually not the only person in their family to compete at the highest level. Why do you think this is?**

B **Watch a news report about a competitor at the Special Olympics. The report focuses on this person because …**

1 he is competing at the highest level in his sport.
2 his great grandfather was also a successful athlete.
3 he is competing in multiple events.

C **Watch again. Complete the sentences with no more than three words from the report.**

1 Daniel Wolff won the ________________ event at the Special Olympics in 2015.
2 His great grandfather won a ________________ at the Berlin Olympics in 1936.
3 Daniel's grandfather describes his achievement as '________________'.
4 This year's Special Olympics has drawn crowds of ________________ people.
5 ________________ people in Daniel's family have come to watch him compete.

D **Are these sentences true (T) or false (F)? Correct the false sentences. Then watch the report again to check.**

1 Daniel's grandfather believes that sporting ability is genetic. *T / F*
2 Daniel was confident before the event that he would win. *T / F*
3 The reporter believes Daniel had a good level of support at the event. *T / F*
4 His father didn't think it was fair to leave his children at home. *T / F*
5 The 400 meters is the only event Daniel is taking part in. *T / F*

AUTHENTIC ENGLISH

A **Work in pairs. Read the extract from the report. What do you think the expression in bold means?**

Daniel Wolff crosses the line to win the 400 meters and shows that athletic success really can **run in the family**.

B **Read the information in the box and check your answer to Exercise A. Why is this idiom appropriate for the report?**

> **Idioms: family**
>
> Idioms are a group of words whose meaning is different from the meaning of the individual words. Since this can make them difficult to remember, one way to record new idioms is to group them by topic. Some common idioms in English are connected to the topic of family:
>
> *You have to choose your brother. Remember –* ***blood is thicker than water!*** (= used to say that family relationships are always more important than any others)
>
> *Athletic ability* ***runs in the family*** *– both he and his father played for their country.* (= if an ability, quality, disease, etc runs in the family, many family members have it)

C **Read the sentences (1–3) and try to guess the meaning of the idioms in bold.**

1 His grandfather was also a famous author – writing must **be in the blood**.
2 She **followed in her** mother's **footsteps** and trained to become a doctor.
3 He **is the spitting image of** his father at that age.

D **Work in pairs. Discuss the questions.**

1 Do you think any of your skills, abilities, etc are in your blood?
2 Have you followed in the footsteps of anyone in your family?
3 Have you ever been told you are the spitting image of someone?

Family matters

SAM MALCOLM AMANDA HARRY EMILY

A Work in pairs. What job do you have now or want to have in the future? What makes you particularly suitable for it?

B Watch the video. What runs in Harry's family? What runs in Sam's family?

SPEAKING SKILL

A Watch the video again and complete the extracts from the conversation.

Sam: And I must remember to get the paper towels for the toilets. ¹ ______________, did the hand soap arrive in the delivery?

Sam: I'm just so excited about getting this new café off the ground – I don't want to forget anything. Anyway, how are you getting on?

Sam: Oh really? You're not going to blame your upbringing are you?

Harry: ² ______________ because untidiness really does run in my family. I mean, you should have seen the state of our house when I was growing up!

Sam: ³ ______________ things that run in the family, I actually saw this really heartwarming story on the news …

B Work in pairs. Discuss the questions. Then read the information in the box to check your answers.

1. What is the function of the phrases you wrote in Exercise A?
2. What is different about *anyway*?

Developing and introducing new topics

Developing topics

During a conversation, a speaker may say something that reminds us of relevant information or a related topic. To introduce our idea, we can use the following expressions:

Speaking/Talking of which …, Talking of [topic] …, Actually, that reminds me of …, Strange you should mention that (because) …

Introducing new topics

We use *anyway* to introduce a completely unrelated topic.

Anyway, I think we should …

C Work in pairs. Student A – Talk about one of the topics below. Student B – Listen and either develop or change the topic. Then swap roles.

- a movie that you saw recently
- a news item you read recently
- a restaurant you went to recently
- an interesting thing that happened to you recently
- a trip you went on recently
- an athletic event you saw recently

SPEAKING HUB

A PREPARE Work in pairs. Brainstorm a list of factors that affect our abilities and skills.

B PLAN Work in two groups. You are going to debate the following:

Practice has no effect on ability – we inherit our abilities from our parents.

Group A – You agree with the idea above.

Group B – You disagree with the idea above.

Plan your arguments. Think about how to support your position, as well as what the other group might say.

C SPEAK Hold your debate.

D REFLECT Which group put forth the more persuasive argument? Which side do you agree with?

Give your opinion on the role of inherited ability in success

➤ Turn to page XXIV to learn how to write a formal letter asking for information.

Unit 1 Review

VOCABULARY

A Choose the correct options (a, b or c) to complete the sentences.

1. They were ___ to arrive at the airport just in time for their flight.
   a relieved **b** devastated **c** furious
2. I was completely ___ when we lost the World Cup final on penalties.
   a thrilled **b** relieved **c** devastated
3. Louis was ___ to find out his daughter had been offered a place at Yale University.
   a disgusted **b** thrilled **c** horrified
4. I'm pretty ___ by your lack of enthusiasm.
   a frustrated **b** impressed **c** relieved
5. Everyone sat in ___ silence as I broke the bad news.
   a relieved **b** disgusted **c** stunned

B Complete the sentences with the adjectives in the box.

easy-going	loyal	optimistic	sensitive	stubborn	witty

1. Why does he have to be so ________ all the time? Not everything in life is good!
2. This girl I met at the party was so ________. I was laughing all night!
3. I don't think I've ever seen him get stressed or upset. He's so ________.
4. The team has a lot of ________ fans. They're still buying tickets – even at $120 a game!
5. Stop being so ________ and just admit that you're wrong!
6. How can we break the news to her? She's such a ________ person.

C Complete the text with the correct form of the words in parentheses.

Perfectionism

Do you find it hard to live up to your own [1]________ (*expect*)? Do you experience [2]________ (*frustrate*) when you work with lazy people? If so, you might be a perfectionist. The positive thing about working with a perfectionist is their [3]________ (*reliable*), [4]________ (*dedicate*) and [5]________ (*professional*). However, if you are a perfectionist, don't assume everyone will want to work with you because of these characteristics. Your constant criticism of other people can affect their [6]________ (*confident*). Your [7]________ (*stubborn*) and inability to admit you might be wrong are not attractive either. You probably won't be worried about that, though, because you're likely to be convinced of your own [8]________ (*superior*).

GRAMMAR

A Choose the correct options to complete the sentences.

1. Could you tell me ***where is the reception desk / where the reception desk is***, please?
2. So why ***didn't you / you didn't*** like the movie?
3. Really? So, ***what was happening / what happened*** then?
4. Who ***Javier is meeting / is Javier meeting***?
5. Which candidate ***are you going to vote for / are you going to vote***?
6. Why ***you don't come / don't you come*** out this evening?
7. ***You haven't / Haven't you*** finished the homework yet?
8. Do you mind telling me ***how old you are / how old are you***?
9. Can I ask what you think ***you are doing / are you doing?***
10. Why ***you are so / are you so*** worried about it?

B Complete the conversations with the correct form of the words in parentheses.

1. **A:** ________ (*you / ever / be*) to Japan?
   B: Yes, I actually ________ (*teach*) English in Tokyo for three years after college.
2. **A:** ________ (*you / know*) Yara?
   B: Yes, I ________ (*know*) her since college.
3. **A:** Why ________ (*be / you*) at work today? I thought you had an important meeting.
   B: I ________ (have) a tough week, so I decided to take a day off.
4. **A:** What ________ (*you / do*) when you heard the news?
   B: I ________ (*just / put*) Mia to bed when my brother called.
5. **A:** ________ (*you / find*) a new job yet?
   B: Maybe. I actually ________ (*have*) an interview last week.
6. **A:** Where ________ (*you / go*) when you had the accident?
   B: I ________ (*drive*) to work.
7. **A:** Oh no! My yoga class ________ (*start*) in five minutes and I can't find my mat!
   B: Calm down. Try to think. Where ________ (*you / last / see*) it?
8. **A:** I kept getting lost when I ________ (go) to Berlin last week.
   B: It's difficult to learn your way around a place you ________ (*never / go*) to before.

2 LIFESTYLES

Underwater view of a boy jumping into a swimming pool.

OBJECTIVES

- talk about health and lifestyle choices
- plan and conduct a lifestyle survey
- conduct an interview about lifestyle changes
- debate the impact of smartphones
- give your opinion on food choices
- write an article giving advice

Work with a partner. Discuss the questions.

1 Read the quote. What do you think Goethe means? Do you agree with him? Why/Why not?
2 Do you dive into the unknown or do you play it safe?
3 What is most important to you in life?

2.1 A full life

- Talk about health and lifestyle choices
- Plan and conduct a lifestyle survey

V – health and fitness
G – present perfect and present perfect progressive
L – listening for reasons
P – connected speech: present perfect progressive

VOCABULARY

Health and fitness

A SPEAK Work in pairs. Brainstorm a list of things that have positive or negative effects on our health.

B Complete the definitions (a–f) with the words in bold.

1 A lack of healthy lunch options has led to worrying levels of childhood **obesity**.
2 Drinking a lot of coffee can cause **anxiety** and negatively affect sleep.
3 Fatty foods like butter and cheese can increase levels of **cholesterol**.
4 She suffered from **depression** after losing her job.
5 There are around 500 **calories** in an average slice of chocolate cake.
6 My husband's been under a lot of **stress** at work recently.

a ________ (n) a unit for measuring how much energy you get from food
b ________ (n) a type of fat in the blood that can cause heart disease if you have too much
c ________ (n) a condition in which someone is too fat in a way that is dangerous for their health
d ________ (n) a medical condition in which a person is so unhappy they cannot live a normal life
e ________ (n) pressure or worry caused by problems in everyday life
f ________ (n) the feeling of being very worried that something bad is going to happen

C Complete the sentences with words from Exercise B.

1 I suffer a lot from ________ in the winter. I'm much more positive in the summer months.
2 Keeping your diet low in fatty foods can help lower ________.
3 Nuts have more ________ in them than you might think.
4 ________ is a huge problem in my country. Almost a quarter of the population is dangerously overweight.
5 ________ is one of my biggest issues. I worry so much about everything.
6 I worry about my ________ levels. I'm under too much pressure at work.

D Go to the **Vocabulary Hub** on **page XVII**.

E SPEAK Work in pairs. What effects do the following have on our health?

- junk food
- smoking
- lack of exercise
- poor work–life balance

READING

A PREDICT Work in pairs. Look at the pictures (1–6) and the corresponding sub-headings in the article. Discuss how you think each of these things might help people to live longer.

B SCAN Read *Six ways to live longer* and check your predictions from Exercise A.

C READ FOR DETAIL Read the article again and answer the questions. Underline the parts of the text that give you the answers.

1 Why might owning a pet be good for your physical health?
2 What is different about the Japanese diet?
3 Why do people who think about details tend to live longer?
4 What charitable activity can help you live longer?
5 What does singing reduce?
6 What don't negative people pay attention to?

D SPEAK Work in pairs. Discuss the questions.

1 Why do you think owning a dog might reduce the risk of heart disease?
2 Why do you think 'smaller plates' have a positive effect on Japanese health?
3 Which of the suggested lifestyle changes in the text would you be happy to make? Why?
4 What other changes could you make to improve your overall health?

SIX WAYS TO LIVE LONGER

For the first time, people are expected to live a shorter life than their parents. Higher levels of obesity, a reliance on processed foods and more sedentary lifestyles are all taking their toll. If we want to live longer and healthier lives, there are many things we can do to slow the aging process and it doesn't just involve eating more healthily and going to the gym.

1 GET A PET

If exercise isn't your thing, then maybe you should consider getting a pet. Scientists in Sweden found that people who owned a dog had a much lower risk of various heart diseases and other illnesses. Dogs obviously need walking but having a pet is also good for many mental health issues such as lowering stress, fear and anxiety.

2 MOVE TO JAPAN

A dramatic solution would be to move to a new country. The Japanese lifestyle is arguably much healthier than in many other countries. First, they eat a lot less fat and lower their cholesterol by eating less dairy and swapping red meat for fish. They also make healthier food choices by eating seaweed, a lot of vegetables and by eating fewer **processed foods**. They use smaller plates and have a lower **calorie** intake than most other countries. Therefore, Japan has a very low obesity rate, with just under 4% of the population considered obese.

3 THINK OF THE DETAILS

People who think carefully about everything and pay a lot of attention to detail tend to live longer. Those who are careful with money, put everything in its right place and focus on details don't comfort eat as much as other people, and sleep better. People who carefully think things through deal better with stress and generally see the positives in most situations. They also have less risky lifestyles.

4 HELP OTHERS

In general, having strong social ties is a good predictor for living a longer and healthier life. People who take care of others are much more likely to make and keep friends throughout their life. Not only will you feel better if you help others but you will also live longer. A study in the US found that people who volunteer regularly in their lifetime live significantly longer than those who don't.

5 SING

People who regularly sing, especially in groups, tend to have a longer life expectancy. Researchers at Harvard and Yale universities in the US found that singing in a choir makes you happier and healthier than others. Singing can reduce stress levels and also helps to improve your immune system so that you are better able to fight illnesses.

6 DON'T COMPLAIN

Positive people live longer. If you're an optimist, then you are likely to live 12 years longer than a pessimist. Researchers at the US Mayo Clinic found that pessimists are more likely to get viral illnesses and they are much less likely to check their own physical health. Positive people also have a lower risk of suffering from heart disease and are better able to cope with stress.

SPEAKING

A DISCUSS Work in groups. Discuss the questions.

1. Why do you think so many people continue to do things that are widely known to be harmful to their health?
2. Do you think it is more important to focus on your physical or mental health? Why?
3. What can be done to reduce the risk of obesity, heart disease and other illnesses that are all associated with modern lifestyles?
4. What could be done to increase life expectancy in your country?

B PRESENT Present the main conclusions of your discussion to the rest of the class. Explain your reasoning.

LISTENING

A SPEAK Work in pairs. Look at the pictures (a–f) and discuss the questions.

1 Which of these things would you find difficult to give up? Why?

2 What are some of the potential benefits of giving these things up?

3 What other things do people typically try to give up?

4 Have you ever tried to give anything up? How successful were you?

B PREDICT People frequently decide to give things up at the start of a new year. How successful do you think they are? What percentage of people do you think break their New Year's resolution after:

a a month? **b** a year?

2.1 **C LISTEN FOR GIST** Listen to the first part of a radio show about lifestyle changes and check your predictions from Exercise B.

2.2 **D LISTEN FOR MAIN IDEAS** Listen to the next part of the radio show. Match the speakers (1–5) to the things that they have given up from Exercise A. There is one more option than you need.

Speaker 1 ______________

Speaker 2 ______________

Speaker 3 ______________

Speaker 4 ______________

Speaker 5 ______________

2.2 **E LISTEN FOR REASONS** Listen to the interviews again. What reason(s) does each speaker give for their lifestyle change? Write notes. Use the information in the box to help you.

Listening for reasons

In interviews, speakers are frequently asked to explain their reasons for a particular action or belief. Reasons are usually signaled with:

- **Fixed words and expressions** (e.g. *because (of), since, that's why, due to the fact that, in order to, etc*). ***Since** my family still lives in the area, we decided to move back there.*
- **Infinitives of purpose** *I stopped eating red meat **to help** reduce my blood pressure.*

However, speakers don't always explicitly state their reasons for something. Sometimes we need to guess the implied meaning from context:

I just remember reading a lot of articles about the impact smoking can have, not only on your health, but on the health of everyone around you. I quit last summer, and I feel much, much healthier.

(= We can guess from the context that the speaker stopped smoking because of the articles they read.)

GRAMMAR

Present perfect and present perfect progressive

A **Work in pairs. Read the extracts from the radio show and answer the questions.**

1 Which sentence describes a finished action? Which describes an unfinished action?

a Yeah, I've actually given up coffee.

b We've been spending more time together as a family.

2 Which sentence focuses on the present effect and which focuses on the action itself?

a I've managed to lose a little weight.

b We've been living without smartphones and tablets for six months now.

3 Which sentence is a temporary action and which is permanent?

a My car's in the garage right now, so I've been riding my bike to work for the past two weeks.

b Well, this is going to sound weird, but I stopped using shampoo.

4 Which sentence focuses on frequency? Which focuses on duration?

a I've only had three chocolate bars this month!

b I've been living without coffee for months now.

B WORK IT OUT Choose the correct options to complete the rules.

Present perfect and present perfect progressive

a finished vs unfinished
We use the present [1]*perfect / perfect progressive* for finished actions with a present effect, and the present [2]*perfect / perfect progressive* for unfinished actions.

b result vs action
We use the present [3]*perfect / perfect progressive* to emphasize the result of an action, and the present [4]*perfect / perfect progressive* to highlight the action itself.

c temporary vs permanent
We use the present [5]*perfect / perfect progressive* to suggest that something is permanent, and the present [6]*perfect / perfect progressive* to suggest something is temporary.

d frequency vs duration
We use the present [7]*perfect / perfect progressive* to say how much / many times something has happened, and the present [8]*perfect / perfect progressive* to say how long something has continued to happen for.

C Go to the Grammar Hub on page VIII.

D PRACTICE Complete the sentences with the present perfect or present perfect progressive of the verbs in parentheses. If both are possible, use the present perfect progressive form.

1 I ________________ (*stop*) working 12 hours a day.
2 She ________________ (*try*) to spend less time on social media but she's finding it hard.
3 I ________________ (*work*) at a restaurant to pay my college fees.
4 I ________________ (*be*) to the gym five times this week.
5 I ________________ (*exercise*) all morning. I can't wait for lunch.
6 I ________________ (*give up*) junk food and now I feel great!

E SPEAK Work in pairs. Use the prompts to ask and answer questions in the present perfect or present perfect progressive.

1 How many times / you / check / social media today?
2 What / you / give up / in the last ten years? Why?
3 What / you / do / recently in order to be healthier?

PRONUNCIATION

Connected speech: present perfect progressive

A 2.3 Listen to three extracts from the radio show. Is there a pause between the words in bold? Is the strong or weak form of *been* used?

1 **We've been spending** more time together as a family.
2 Absolutely! **I've been living** without coffee for months now.
3 **I've been riding my bike** to work for the past two weeks.

B 2.4 Listen and complete the sentences.

1 ________________ working really hard recently.
2 ________________ using my phone too much lately.
3 ________________ eating less junk food.
4 ________________ spending more time together.
5 ________________ going to the gym a lot lately.

C 2.4 Listen again and repeat the sentences.

SPEAKING HUB

A PREPARE What have you been doing too much of recently? What have you not been doing enough of recently? Write notes about:

- use of technology
- exercise
- diet
- family

B PLAN Work in pairs. Write six questions you could ask other students about their habits. Use your notes from Exercise A to help you.

1 What unhealthy foods have you been eating too much of?
2 How often have you seen your family this month?

C SPEAK Ask other students in the class your questions. Try to give each other advice on changes you could make.

A: How often have you seen your family this month?
B: I haven't seen them at all! I'm just so busy all the time.
A: Well maybe you could try calling them once a week? You don't need to talk for long, but it's important to stay in touch.

- Talk about health and lifestyle choices
- Plan and conduct a lifestyle survey

2.2 Change

- Conduct an interview about lifestyle changes
- Debate the impact of smartphones

G *used to, would, get used to, be used to*
S identifying assumptions
P catenation: *used to*
V adverbs of stance; adverb + adjective collocations

LISTENING

A SPEAK Work in pairs. You're going to listen to an interview with a family that has moved from the city to a remote island. What do you think would be the advantages and disadvantages of such a move?

2.5 **B LISTEN FOR GIST** Listen to the interview. Which members of the family are happy with the move? Which aren't?

2.5 **C LISTEN FOR DETAIL** Listen to the interview again. Choose the correct options (a, b or c) to complete the sentences.

1 Frank made the decision to leave New York because …
   a he found his job too demanding.
   b he found his lifestyle uneventful.
   c he couldn't afford to live there.
2 Since moving to the island, the family …
   a largely eats food that is home-grown or caught.
   b has to spend a lot of money at the local store.
   c generally has a much better diet than before.
3 Frank says that the family's new lifestyle …
   a was surprisingly easy to adapt to.
   b is less physically demanding.
   c has tested them financially.
4 Katie cannot stream media on the island because …
   a the mountains affect her phone signal.
   b the internet connection is terrible.
   c the family cannot afford the internet.
5 Katie is homeschooled by her mother because …
   a there isn't a good school on the island.
   b she is planning to take US exams.
   c it gives her more time to gather food.
6 Frank thinks his son enjoys life on the island because …
   a there are lots of young children to play with.
   b he's allowed to play outside all day.
   c he hated growing up in New York.

D SPEAK Work in pairs. Imagine moving to a small island far away from where you live. What would you miss? What would you be happy to leave behind?

GRAMMAR

used to, would, get used to, be used to

A Work in pairs. Match the extracts from the interview (1–4) to their meaning (a–d).

1 I **used to work** long hours and it was stressful.
2 I'**m used to getting up** at 6 o'clock every day…
3 Financially, it has also been much harder but we'**re getting used to** it.
4 Back in New York **he'd complain** about his job constantly.

a This situation is still strange, but it's becoming more familiar.
b This habit was true in the past but isn't true now.
c This situation was true in the past but isn't true now.
d This was strange at first but is normal for me now.

B WORK IT OUT Complete the rules with the words in the box.

be used to | get used to | used to / didn't use to | would

used to, would, get used to, be used to

We use [1] ________________ + base form to talk about finished habits and states: things that were true in the past but aren't true now.

We can also use [2] ________________ + base form to talk about finished habits and routines, but not to talk about states.

We use [3] ________________ to talk about something that was unfamiliar but is not unfamiliar now.

We use [4] ________________ to talk about something that is still unfamiliar and not a current habit.

C Go to the Grammar Hub on page VIII.

D PRACTICE Complete the sentences with *used to*, *would*, *be used to* or *get used to* and the verbs in parentheses.

1 I ________________ (*look*) very different when I was younger.
2 I ________________ (*not / like*) mornings but now I enjoy getting up early.
3 When I was a teenager, I ________________ (*eat*) a lot of junk food.
4 I ________________ (*work*) long hours now. I've done it for years.
5 I am ________________ (*cook*) for myself but I'm still not great at it.
6 When I was younger, I ________________ (*play*) video games for hours.
7 I ________________ (*not / drive*). I only passed my test recently.
8 I've decided to cut down on sugar. I ________________ (*eat*) less but it's a little boring!

E PRACTICE Rewrite the sentences in Exercise D so they are true for you.

F SPEAK Work in pairs. Discuss your sentences from Exercise E. Ask follow-up questions for more information.

PRONUNCIATION

Catenation: *used to*

2.6 **A** Listen to these extracts from the interview. Do we pronounce the final /d/ in *used to*? Do we use the strong or weak form of *to*?

1 I used to dream of living a quieter and more peaceful life.
2 I'm getting used to being isolated from everyone.
3 I guess I'm not used to it yet.

2.7 **B** Listen and repeat the sentences.

1 She used to have long hair.
2 Have you gotten used to living on your own?
3 I'm used to getting up early every day.
4 I actually used to drink a lot of coffee.
5 Don't worry, he's used to it by now.

SPEAKING

A PREPARE Think about how your life has changed in the last ten years. Make a list of positive changes in these areas:

- where you live
- family
- work
- education
- free time
- health

B PLAN Write notes about the three biggest changes in Exercise A. Use these questions to help you:

- What prompted the change?
- How has the change affected your life?
- Are you used to the change yet?

C SPEAK Work in groups. Take turns explaining your changes. Ask follow-up questions for more information.

READING

A SPEAK Work in groups. What are some of the positive and negative effects of social media?

B SCAN Read *The big debate* quickly. Which of your ideas from Exercise A are discussed?

C READ FOR GIST Read the article again. Choose the most appropriate debate question (1–4) for the article.

1 Should social media be banned?
2 Have relationships in society gotten worse?
3 Has social media made us less social?
4 Should we reconnect with the people around us?

THE BIG DEBATE

PETE LOMAS, PSYCHOLOGIST

Admittedly, the internet is pretty much the greatest invention of all time. However, I'd argue that social media is the worst invention to appear in this internet era. It seems to me that despite being 'in contact' with more and more people, we are in fact losing contact – meaningful contact – with most people in our lives.

[a]Beyond question, we're less comfortable in social settings than we once were. **Sadly**, we have all sat around a table where no one is really talking as they skim through their social media. Research by Ofcom has found that 51% of adults and 65% of teenagers have used their smartphone while socializing. **Frankly**, this is going to have a negative impact on our relationships. In fact, in some countries, groups of friends now have a rule – if you check your phone during dinner in a restaurant, then you have to pay for everyone. Are we really in a position where we need to fine people to get them to pay attention to us?

[b]Unfortunately, it's not just affecting how we interact but it is also making us feel worse, not better. **Naturally**, constant communication transforms how you feel, especially if you monitor emails, text messages and status updates. There is even an acronym for this phenomenon: FOMO – 'fear of missing out'. [c]As I see it, anything social should make us feel involved but social media is clearly making some people feel left out rather than part of something.

Social media should be renamed anti-social media. [d]In an already isolated world, social media is cutting us off from the world around us even further.

AMY DAY, APP DEVELOPER

From my perspective, social media has **undoubtedly** enhanced our relationships with others. It is true that not all of our online relationships are as close as our face-to-face connections but, on the other hand, it has allowed us to reconnect with lost friends, maintain connections and build new ones.

[e]From my point of view, modern life had already made us all fairly isolated individuals. We work long hours. We commute long distances. We move to cities where we know nobody, just for work. Our families all move around, not just in the country we live in, but also to different countries. I'm sure that social media has **simply** emerged from the pressures of modern life and our desire to connect with others despite these obstacles.

Apparently, we are giving up face-to-face relationships with people in favor of less personal social media ones. In all honesty, I don't think this could be further from the truth. According to research by Marketing Charts using data from Nielsen, in the space of five years, TV viewing by 18–24 year olds has fallen from 25 hours a week to **merely** 12. Those aged over 50 still watch over 40 hours a week and this figure isn't declining. Young people are clearly giving up anti-social activities in favor of other ways of interacting.

People who argue that social media has made us less interactive with the world around us clearly have the image in their mind of people on a train with their heads down looking at their phones. These people aren't choosing to be antisocial. [f]Far from it – they are choosing to interact with the people they deem important in their own lives.

D IDENTIFY ASSUMPTIONS **Read the article again. Match the sentences in the text (a–f) with the assumptions (1–6). Use the information in the box to help you.**

Identifying assumptions

Writers frequently make assumptions about what groups of people think or the opinions of others. These are signaled with phrases such as *As we all know …*, *Without a doubt …* and *Beyond question …*, which are used to try to convince the reader of a certain point of view.

The assumption can also be implied rather than stated directly. For example:

It seems to me that despite being 'in contact' with more and more people, we are in fact losing contact, meaningful contact, with most people in our lives.

(= assumes that online contact is not meaningful.)

1. Previous generations were all good at socializing. ___
2. Nobody that uses social media feels like they're part of a group. ___
3. Social media makes nobody feel positive. ___
4. The world was disconnected before social media. ___
5. Everyone on their phone is using social media. ___
6. Everyone in the modern world felt disconnected anyway. ___

E SPEAK **Work in groups. Which of the assumptions in the text do you agree with? Which do you disagree with? Why?**

VOCABULARY

Adverbs of stance

A **Scan the article again. Complete the definitions with the adverbs in bold.**

1. ______________ used to say that something is true even though it may weaken your argument
2. ______________ based only on what you have heard, not on what you are certain is true
3. ______________ used to emphasize that you are about to give your honest opinion, even though the person you are talking to might not like it
4. ______________ used to emphasize that something is small or unimportant
5. ______________ in the way that you would expect
6. ______________ used to say that something is certainly true or is accepted by everyone
7. ______________ used to show that you think something is bad or wrong
8. ______________ used to emphasize that you are saying something in a plain and straightforward way

B **Choose the correct options to complete the sentences.**

1. ***Naturally / Sadly***, all new developments come with both advantages and disadvantages.
2. ***Merely / Admittedly***, I see less of my friends in person now.
3. ***Frankly / Apparently***, we have a weaker sense of community than we used to, but I'm not sure I agree.
4. Social media is ***merely / apparently*** another method of communication.
5. ***Simply / Frankly***, I think social media enhances relationships.
6. The internet has ***undoubtedly / apparently*** enhanced many aspects of our lives. I don't think anyone could question that.
7. I think many people regret the breakdown of communities. ***Sadly / Naturally***, many communities are not as close as they once were.
8. It's very ***simply / merely*** the best solution to the problem.

VOCABULARY

Adverb + adjective collocations

Some adverbs and adjectives are commonly used together. For example, we say *strongly opposed* NOT ~~*deeply opposed*~~ or ~~*utterly opposed*~~. Learning these collocations will help make your language sound more natural.

Complete the sentences with the adverbs in the box.

absolutely bitterly deeply highly ridiculously

1. It is ______________ likely that more and more of our relationships will be conducted using phones.
2. It is ______________ ridiculous to say that smartphones have been negative for relationships.
3. I think society should be ______________ concerned about the negative impact of smartphones.
4. Smartphones make it ______________ easy to stay in touch with people.
5. I was ______________ disappointed when my friend started checking her phone during dinner.

SPEAKING HUB

A PLAN **Work in pairs. How do you use technology to support your relationships?**

B PREPARE **Work in two groups. You are going to debate the following:**

Smartphones have had a negative impact on our personal relationships.

Group A – You agree with the statement above.

Group B – You disagree with the statement above.

Plan your arguments. Think about how to support your position, as well as what the other group might say.

C SPEAK **Hold a class debate.**

Conduct an interview about lifestyle changes

Debate the impact of smartphones

Café Hub

2.3 Clean eating

A– adding emphasis   S– backchanneling and lexical repetition

Ella's story

COMPREHENSION

A **Work in groups. Look at the picture and discuss the questions.**

1 You are going to watch a video about clean eating. What do you think this term means? Why?

2 Do you pay close attention to your diet? Why/Why not?

3 Who or what influences the food you eat?

Glossary

gluten (n) a natural, sticky substance found in some foods (e.g. wheat)
vegan (n) someone who doesn't eat anything made from animals or fish, including eggs, milk and cheese

B **Watch the interview with Ella Mills and answer the questions.**

1 Why is Dr. Yeo interviewing Ella Mills for the program?

2 What do all of Ella's recipes have in common?

3 What made Ella decide to change her diet?

4 What did Ella give up as part of her change in diet?

C **Watch the interview again. Are these sentences true (T) or false (F)? Correct the false sentences.**

1 Ella's first cookbook wasn't very successful when it was originally published. *T / F*

2 Ella decided to become a vegetarian more than ten years ago. *T / F*

3 Ella felt that her original medical treatment wasn't working effectively. *T / F*

4 Ella was initially doubtful that a change in diet could improve her condition. *T / F*

5 The fact that many others could identify with her experience encouraged Ella to continue sharing her story online. *T / F*

D **Work in groups. Discuss the questions.**

1 Because Dr. Yeo refers to 'Professor Google' in the video, what do you think his attitude is toward seeking medical advice online?

2 Do you think it's a good idea to search for medical advice online? Why/Why not?

AUTHENTIC ENGLISH

A **Work in pairs. Read the extracts from the interview (1–4). Underline the words and phrases used to make the sentences more emphatic.**

1 … and her debut cookbook was the fastest-selling ever in the UK.

2 I was the least vegetarian person you would have ever met in your life.

3 … and I came across lots of stories of people who'd used a change in diet and lifestyle to help manage all kinds of conditions, which I was, to be honest, incredibly skeptical of …

4 Her story of how she changed her diet to change her health has proved hugely influential.

B **Read the information in the box and check your answers to Exercise A. How else can you make what you say more emphatic?**

Adding emphasis

In informal spoken English, speakers frequently use superlatives, adverbs of degree, *ever/never* and expressions like *in your life* to exaggerate or make their sentences more emphatic. Doing so helps maintain the interest of the listener or highlight the importance of what's being said.

C **Work in pairs. Take turns talking about the following topics. Use the techniques in Exercise B to make your descriptions more emphatic.**

1 a terrible meal you once had

2 an amazing movie you've seen

3 a terrifying experience

The worst meal I've ever had was when I was on vacation in Thailand. I was with my …

You are what you eat

SAM MALCOLM AMANDA HARRY EMILY

A Work in pairs. Discuss what you had for breakfast and what you think your partner's choices say about them.

B Watch the video. What are the differences between Emily and Malcolm's attitudes toward food?

SPEAKING SKILL

A Watch the video again. Complete the box with examples from the conversation.

Backchanneling and lexical repetition

Backchanneling

Giving signals to show we are interested in what the other speaker is saying is called backchanneling.

To show interest, we say things like *I see* or just make noises like [1]__________, __________.

To show surprise, we say single words like [2]__________, __________, __________.

Lexical repetition

Another way to show we're engaged is lexical repetition. Sometimes this means using the same words as someone else. For example, when Emily first talks about clean eating, Malcolm starts his next turn by saying *clean eating* to show that he is following the topic. Another form of lexical repetition is to rephrase what has been said.

Emily: *For me, it's about eating mindfully – I mean, really thinking about what you're putting into your body and how your body uses the energy.*

Malcolm: *I see. So it's just about trying to eat* [3]______________________________?

Emily: *Yeah, making sure your body is getting* [4]______________________________.

B Work in pairs. Student A – Make a comment about one of the topics below. Student B – Rephrase your partner's comment to show you're engaged. Then swap roles.

- the weather today
- a type of food you like
- a movie you like
- a country you've been to
- a city you know
- what you are wearing
- a singer or band

A: It's nice and sunny today.
B: Oh, it's beautiful, isn't it?

SPEAKING HUB

A PREPARE Brainstorm a list of the advantages and disadvantages of becoming a vegan.

B PLAN Do you think you could become a vegan? Why/ Why not? Use your ideas from Exercise A to write notes.

C DISCUSS Work in pairs. Discuss whether or not you would be prepared to become a vegan. Explain your reasoning.

A: I don't think I could ever be a vegan. I enjoy eating meat too much.
B: But what about the health benefits? A lot of people believe that vegans have a much longer, healthier life.

Give your opinion on food choices

➤ Turn to page XXV to learn how to write an article giving advice.

Unit 2 Review

VOCABULARY

A Match the causes (1–6) to their effects (a–f) to form full sentences.

1 High-**calorie** diets …
2 Regular **physical** exercise …
3 Strong friendship groups can **reduce the risk of** …
4 A low-calorie diet may **slow the aging process** …
5 Eating heavily **processed foods** may result in …
6 Maintaining a good **level of fitness** could be positive …

a can result in reduced levels of **stress**.
b **depression** occurring.
c a person's **cholesterol** levels rising.
d could lead to higher levels of **obesity**.
e for a person's **mental health**.
f and lead to a longer **life expectancy**.

B Replace the words in italics with adverbs from the box.

admittedly apparently frankly merely naturally sadly simply undoubtedly

1 I didn't say you had to do it, I *only* suggested you might want to.
2 Have you heard about Mark and Emily? *I'm not sure, but I was told* they're having a baby!
3 That's *just* not true! We sent them multiple emails asking for more time.
4 Tom didn't get the job. *As you'd expect*, he's pretty disappointed, but I'm sure he'll get over it.
5 *It's obvious that* stress has played a large part in her decision.
6 *To be honest*, I think you need to spend more time with your family.
7 *It's true that* I don't exercise enough.
8 *I'm disappointed that* we can't go on vacation this summer.

C Choose the best adverbs to complete the collocations.

1 I'm ***bitterly / deeply*** concerned about his mental health right now.
2 You should try the 'couch to 5K' running plan. It's ***highly / ridiculously*** easy.
3 This diet is ***absolutely / deeply*** terrible. I don't see how anyone can stick to it.
4 I was ***bitterly / absolutely*** disappointed when I heard I didn't get the job.
5 It's ***ridiculously / highly*** likely that she'll pass the exam and get into the university.
6 It was ***bitterly / deeply*** cold outside and I'd forgotten my winter coat.
7 Have you ever seen *The Shining*? It's ***highly / absolutely*** terrifying!
8 The actor admitted he was ***deeply / ridiculously*** ashamed of his behavior.

GRAMMAR

A Complete the conversations with the present perfect or present perfect progressive form of the verbs in the box.

decorate have live reply send travel

1 **A:** We must be almost there by now – we ____________ for hours!
B: Don't worry, not long to go!
2 **A:** Have you managed to get in touch with Andy yet?
B: No! I ____________ him half a dozen emails, but he still ____________.
3 **A:** Where are you staying right now?
B: I ____________ with my parents while I look for a new apartment.
4 **A:** What are you working on?
B: The same thing! I ____________ the same house for weeks now!
5 **A:** Do you want to go out for coffee?
B: No, I'd better not. I ____________ three already this morning.

B Complete the letter with *used to, would, be used to* or *get used to* and the correct form of the verbs in the box.

arrive be (x2) drive go know live run

Before the internet

In the past, if someone 'followed' you, then you [1] ____________ quickly in the opposite direction. 'Going viral' [2] ____________ a bad thing and 'trolls' were only toys and not unpleasant people. Arguments [3] ____________ on for a long time because no one could quickly find the answer on their phone. People [4] ____________ everyone's phone numbers by heart. If you wanted to meet your friends, they [5] ____________ on time, otherwise it was impossible to find them later. Today, people [6] ____________ without a map and never having to plan their trips. We all seem to have [7] ____________ in a world where people speak to their devices as if they're human! I have to say that of all these changes – one thing I'll never [8] ____________ is these devices spying on me!

Richard Solomon

Cleveland, Ohio

C Work in pairs. Discuss the questions.

1 What did you used to look like when you were younger?
2 What's something that you used to hate, but now love?
3 Do you think you're used to speaking in English yet?
4 What would someone have to get used to if they lived in your country?

3 SURVIVAL

Nearing the summit of the Totem Pole in Tasmania, Australia.

OBJECTIVES

- create a collaborative story
- tell a personal anecdote
- discuss priorities in a survival situation
- talk about fears and offer advice
- describe a trip or journey
- write a short story

Work with a partner. Discuss the questions.

1 Read the quote. What do you think Plato means?

2 Look at the picture. What would you be afraid of if you were alone in this place?

3 What skills and strengths do you have to survive a challenging situation?

3.1 Staying alive

- Create a collaborative story
- Tell a personal anecdote

S – following the sequence of a narrative
V – descriptive verbs
G – narrative tenses
P – dramatic storytelling techniques

READING

A SPEAK Work in pairs. Discuss how you might survive in the following situations.

1 Your plane crashes in the jungle and you're lost without a phone.

2 On a climb in the Alps, you trip and break your ankle.

3 Your boat sinks, but you manage to swim to a desert island.

4 While driving through the Sahara, your jeep breaks down, miles from any towns.

5 There's a fire in your office building and you're on the top floor.

B READ FOR GIST Read *Nigerian cook survives for three days in an underwater air bubble* and answer the questions. Write notes.

1 Who is the main focus of the story?

2 What happened to the Jascon-4?

3 How did the ship's cook survive for three days?

4 What happened to the other crew members?

5 How was the cook eventually rescued?

C FOLLOW THE SEQUENCE OF A NARRATIVE Read the article again. Put the events in the order they happened. Use the information in the box to help you.

Following the sequence of a narrative

Articles describing the sequence of past events don't always present the information in chronological order. To help you identify the order in which things happened, look for:

Time expressions

Writers use a combination of specific time expressions (e.g. *at 5 am, on May 26th*, etc) and phrases (e.g. *24 hours later, over the next three days*, etc) to highlight key points in the narrative.

Tenses

Identifying which tense has been used and why (e.g. past perfect to show that one action happened before another) will also help you to understand when events happened in relation to each other.

___ He woke up and went to the bathroom.
___ He found some equipment.
___ He gave the divers a huge shock.
___ He thought he heard sharks outside.
___ He stopped the water coming in.
___ The boat was turned over by a powerful wave.
___ He opened the door and went into the passageway.
___ He knocked on the wall with a hammer.
___ He spent two days recovering.

Nigerian cook SURVIVES for THREE DAYS in UNDERWATER AIR BUBBLE

Harrison Okene was trapped 30 meters below the surface in freezing waters.

Harrison Okene was a happy young man who was about to get married in a few days. At the time, he was working as a cook on a boat and before getting married, he had to go on one last trip. Unfortunately, it quickly turned into a nightmare.

The events started to unfold at 5:00 am on May 26th. The crew of the Jacson-4 had been sleeping while the boat was resting 20 miles off the Nigerian coast. While a violent storm was raging, Okene got up to go to the bathroom. As he was standing in the bathroom, a huge wave hit the boat. It turned over and plunged 30 meters below the surface, with Okene and the rest of the crew still inside. Water quickly began to fill the cabin, blocking the bathroom door as the boat sank into the ocean. Using all his strength, Okene forced open the door and headed out into the passageway. Wearing nothing but pajamas, he waded through the passageway in total darkness toward the only light he could see. Quickly he grabbed a drink and a few tools and made it to the light.

Stuck in a small pocket of air, he blocked the sides with furniture to keep the water out. Unknown to Okene, all of his crewmates had already drowned. With hardly any air to breathe, time was running out. Hungry, cold and tired, Okene thought he could hear sharks circling the boat and started to lose hope. However, his luck was about to change.

When a rescue crew arrived, they assumed everyone had died since the boat had been resting on the seabed for 60 hours. Realizing the sounds he had heard were human, Okene started banging on the wall with a hammer. Thinking he wouldn't be discovered, he jumped into the water and began swimming through the ship. Seeing a rescue diver swim past him, Okene reached out to touch the man on the shoulder. Although initially terrified, the diver realized he'd found a survivor and called for support. Shortly afterward, Okene was strapped to diving equipment and taken back to the surface where he spent two days in a decompression chamber.

GRAMMAR

Narrative tenses

A Complete the sentences with the correct form of the verbs in parentheses. Then scan the article again to check your answers.

1 At the time, he ________________ (*work*) as a cook on a boat.

2 While a violent storm ________________ (*rage*) outside, Okene got up to go to the bathroom.

3 It ________________ (*turn*) over and plunged 30 meters below the surface, with Okene and the rest of the crew still inside.

4 Unknown to Okene, all of his shipmates ________________ (*already / drown*).

5 When a rescue crew arrived, they assumed everyone had died, as the boat ________________ (*rest*) on the seabed for 60 hours.

B WORK IT OUT Choose the correct tenses to complete the rules in the box.

Narrative tenses

We use the [1]*simple past / past perfect* for completed actions that are the main events in a story.

We use the [2]*past progressive / simple past*:

- for actions in progress at a particular point in time.
- when a longer action is interrupted by a shorter action.
- to set the scene of a story.

We use the [3]*past perfect / past perfect progressive* for completed actions that happened before the main event.

We use the [4]*past perfect / past perfect progressive* for longer actions that started before other events and continued up to these events.

C Go to the Grammar Hub on page X.

D PRACTICE Complete the text with the correct form of the verbs in parentheses.

NEWS SPORT CULTURE LIFESTYLE SEARCH

7-YEAR-OLD JAPANESE BOY SURVIVES FOR OVER A WEEK ALONE IN THE WOODS

FAMILY DAY OUT TURNS TO DISASTER

A family day out looking for wild vegetables quickly turned to disaster when a boy's parents decided to punish his bad behavior. Yamato Tanooka [1] ________________ (*throw*) stones at cars as he waited for his parents. Spotting his behavior, his father quickly [2] ________________ (*become*) very angry and [3] ________________ (*yell*) at him. To punish their son, Mr. and Mrs. Tanooka [4] ________________ (*leave*) him on the side of the road and [5] ________________ (*drive*) a few hundred meters away. By the time they [6] ________________ (*drive*) back to the spot, Yamato [7] ________________ (*already / leave*). His father [8] ________________ (*call*) the police and [9] ________________ (*say*) he [10] ________________ (*become*) separated from his son while they [11] ________________ (*pick*) wild vegetables. In the meantime, Yamato [12] ________________ (*walk*) off into the woods, upset that his father [13] ________________ him ________ (*tell off*). When the army finally [14] ________________ (*find*) Yamato, he [15] ________________ (*live*) for six days on his own in woods that are home to brown bears. Yamato told reporters that he[16] ________________ (*walk*) for five hours through the woods when he found an old army cabin. Afraid of the dark, he decided to hide there and wait for his parents to find him.

E PRACTICE Work in groups. Write the first sentence of a dramatic story. Pass your sentence to the student on your right. Add another sentence to the story you have just received. Keep doing this until your story is complete.

SPEAKING

A PREPARE Go to the Communication Hub on page XX.

B PRESENT Choose one person to tell your story to the class. Listen to the other stories and ask questions about the details.

LISTENING

A Label the pictures (1–6) with the activities in the box.

bungee jumping | free running | free climbing | potholing | skydiving | whitewater rafting

B SPEAK Work in pairs. Discuss the questions.

1 Which of these sports do you think is the most dangerous? Why?

2 Why do you think some people enjoy doing dangerous sports like these?

3 Have you ever done any of these sports? Would you like to? Why/Why not?

3.1 **C LISTEN FOR GIST** Listen to a radio talk show about extreme sports and answer the questions. Write notes.

1 Which of the sports from Exercise A do the speakers talk about?

2 How many of the speakers have been injured while doing their sport?

1 ____________________

2 ____________________

3 ____________________

4 ____________________

3.1 **D LISTEN FOR DETAIL** Listen again and choose the correct options (a, b or c) to complete the sentences.

1 Paul started free climbing when he was …
   a 10 years old. b 17 years old. c 27 years old.

2 Paul thinks climbing without safety equipment …
   a is a terrible idea.
   b is a good challenge.
   c allows him to go higher.

3 Paul was most scared when …
   a he was caught in strong winds during a climb.
   b the bridge he was crossing on broke.
   c a snake shot out of a crack in a rock.

4 Hayley thinks that …
   a potholing is more challenging than rock climbing.
   b rock climbing is too challenging.
   c potholing is more like walking than climbing.

5 Hayley was lost underground for …
   a a few minutes. b a few hours. c a few days.

6 Lee started free running …
   a because his friends were doing it.
   b because he saw a video of people doing it.
   c because he wanted something more challenging than gymnastics.

7 Lee most enjoys …
   a the physical challenge of free running.
   b the way free running makes you look at a city.
   c the risks involved in free running.

8 Lee says that …
   a you should push yourself beyond your limits.
   b you need to be very competitive to be good at free running.
   c you should only do what you know you are capable of.

E SPEAK Work in groups. Discuss the questions.

1 Who do you think had the most frightening experience. Why?

2 Which of the sports would you like to try? Why?

VOCABULARY
Descriptive verbs

A **Work in pairs. For each extract, choose the option that makes the same sound as the verb in bold.**

1 I can still remember the snow **crunching** under our feet as we walked together.
  a old leaves under your feet
  b your feet in an empty hospital hallway
2 Sometimes the wood **groans** under your weight, which can be a little scary, but so far none have ever actually broken!
  a grass under your feet
  b floorboards under your feet
3 I am terrified of snakes, so I just froze as it started to **hiss** and arch backwards.
  a the wind closing a door
  b air slowly escaping from a tire
4 It can be silent for just a few minutes and all you can hear is water **trickling** around you.
  a a slow-running tap
  b a large, powerful river
5 I can still hear my ankle **snap** as I landed.
  a a branch breaking
  b a window breaking

B **Complete the sentences with the correct form of the verbs in Exercise A.**

1 The snake ________________ and slithered back into the undergrowth.
2 The leaves were ________________ under our feet as we crept slowly through the forest.
3 I could hear the branch of the tree ________________ under my weight before it ________________ and I fell to the ground.
4 Every time it rained, I could hear water ________________ down the wall behind my bed.

C **Go to the Vocabulary Hub on page XVIII.**

D SPEAK **Work in pairs. Use descriptive verbs to make this story more interesting.**

I was walking through the forest with fallen leaves under my feet. The trees were blowing in the wind. Suddenly, I heard a branch break behind me. I turned to see a huge dog running toward me.

5 ________________

PRONUNCIATION
Dramatic storytelling techniques

3.2 **A** **Listen to this extract from the talk show. Mark the pauses with (/) and underline any words that are emphasized.**

Well, a few years ago I was in South Africa with a few of my friends and we'd almost finished the first part of an all-day climb. I was just pulling myself up when I saw a huge snake right in front of me. I am terrified of snakes, so I just froze as it started to hiss and arch backwards. I waited for another few minutes, not moving, and then it just seemed to get bored and slithered back into a crack in the rock. It was the most terrifying moment ever and it had nothing to do with climbing!

3.2 **B** **Listen to the story again. When does the speaker speed up and slow down? Why do you think he does this?**

C **Read the story extract. Predict where you think the pauses will be, which words the speaker will stress and when they will speed up.**

So a few months ago I was staying at my parents' house when this strange thing happened. We were all enjoying the warmth of the crackling fire as the trees creaked in the wind outside. Suddenly, we heard glass smashing upstairs and something heavy banged on the floor. We rushed upstairs to find that a huge branch had crashed through the roof of the house.

3.3 **D** **Listen and check your answers to Exercise C. Then, practice telling the story with a partner.**

SPEAKING HUB

A PLAN **Think of the most amazing, terrifying or embarrassing moment in your life. Write notes about:**

- where you were
- who you were with
- what happened

B PREPARE **Work in pairs. Tell your stories and work together to make them more dramatic or exciting.**

C PRESENT **Work in small groups. Tell your stories as dramatically as you can. Ask questions to get more information.**

6 ________________

- Create a collaborative story
- Tell a personal anecdote

3.2 Fear and danger

- Discuss priorities in a survival situation
- Talk about fears and offer advice

G – alternatives to *if* in conditionals
S – listening for definitions, examples and explanations
P – intonation in conditional sentences
V – phrasal verbs to describe problems; dependent prepositions: adjectives

READING

A SPEAK Work in groups. Discuss what you would do in the following situations.

1 You're caught in some quicksand in the desert. As you're sinking you see a large stick nearby.
2 You're attacked by a swarm of killer bees in the woods. There's a house in the distance and a lake a few meters away.
3 You're doing parachute jump, but your parachute fails. If you stretch out, you could probably reach your friend.

B READ FOR GIST Complete the interview with the questions (a–d).

a Is that in your show this time?
b Can we expect any dangerous animals this year?
c Are you feeling excited about your new series starting next week?
d What can viewers expect from this series?

C READ FOR DETAIL Read again. Choose the correct options (a or b) to complete the sentences.

1 Chuck advises carrying a stick in the desert …
 a to move quicksand away from your body.
 b to stop yourself sinking into quicksand.
2 When you are in quicksand, Chuck suggests …
 a moving quickly to escape.
 b getting out carefully.
3 Chuck says that hitting killer bees …
 a is the first form of defence against them.
 b is likely to make the situation worse.
4 If you follow his advice, Chuck says you may break your arm when …
 a your friend's parachute opens.
 b your parachute opens.

D SPEAK Work in groups. Has anyone you know ever been in a life-threatening situation? How did they survive?

CHUCK ADAMS:

SURVIVE THE WILD

In the office of *Live, Play, Work Magazine*, we're all very excited to see the return to TV of Chuck Adams and his series *Survive the Wild*. Tom Wood caught up with Chuck to ask him about surviving in the desert, killer bees and why breaking your arm is sometimes the best thing to do …

Tom: **It's great to see you again, Chuck! 1___**

Chuck: I am. The first series was incredibly popular and we're taking viewers into some even more exciting situations in the new series.

Tom: 2___

Chuck: Well, we look at how to survive dangerous situations in different locations. From mountains to deserts to the Arctic. For example, in the desert or along the coast, always carry a stick in case you need it. Quicksand is really dangerous! As soon as you start to sink, put the stick on the surface of the sand and lie on it. If you do this, it will stop you from sinking. Once you stop sinking, you need to crawl, climb and almost swim out. You'll be OK as long as you move slowly out of the sand. If you move too quickly, you'll sink.

Tom: **Sounds like hard work! Last series you looked at surviving crocodile attacks and shark attacks. 3___**

Chuck: Definitely! We have all sorts, including killer bees! People sometimes freeze when they see a bee, but this won't stop it from stinging you. And definitely don't try to hit them – this just makes them angrier. If bees fly around you, try to find shelter as quickly as possible. Provided you can get into a building, or shelter in long grass, you'll be fine. A lot of people jump into water to get away. Don't do this. The bees will just be waiting for you when you come up!

Tom: **That sounds horrible! What about surviving accidents? 4___**

Chuck: Of course! People usually do parachute jumps with other people. If your parachute doesn't open, grab the person near you, lock your arms together and hold onto each other. When your friend opens their parachute you will survive, but you will also probably break your arm – so be prepared for some pain!

Tom: **I feel a little sick at the thought of breaking my arm!**

Chuck: Maybe, but unless you lock arms, you won't survive!

Tom: Well we can't wait for the show to return next week! Thanks for speaking to us today.

GRAMMAR

Alternatives to *if* in conditionals

A **Work in pairs. Read the extracts from the interview and choose the correct meaning.**

1 … in the desert or along the coast, always carry a stick in case you need it.
   a Take a stick because you will definitely need it.
   b Take a stick because you might need it.

2 As soon as you start to sink, put the stick on the surface of the sand and lie on it.
   a When you start sinking, use the stick immediately.
   b When you start sinking, use the stick when you can.

3 You'll be OK as long as you move slowly out of the sand.
   a It's the only way to get out of the sand.
   b It's one way to get out of the sand.

4 Provided you can get into a building, or shelter in long grass, you'll be fine.
   a You will only be fine if you get into a building or shelter in long grass.
   b You will be fine whatever happens.

5 Maybe, but unless you lock arms, you won't survive!
   a Don't do this and you might survive.
   b Do this or you won't survive.

B WORK IT OUT **Complete the rules with words and phrases in the box.**

as long as | as soon as | in case | provided (that) | unless

Alternatives to *if* in conditionals

We use [1] ____________ to mean *if … not*.

We use [2] ____________ and [3] ____________ to mean *only if*.

We use [4] ____________ to talk about doing something now to prepare for a possible situation.

We use [5] ____________ to mean in the shortest time possible.

C Go to the Grammar Hub on page X.

D SPEAK **Work in pairs. Give advice about the following situations using conditional conjunctions.**

1 You're in the middle of a field when a thunderstorm begins.
2 You're swimming in the ocean when you see a shark swim by.
3 You're lost in the country when your phone battery dies.
4 You're driving along when your car runs out of gas.

As long as you can walk to a gas station, you'll be able to buy gas.

PRONUNCIATION

Intonation in conditional sentences

3.4 **A** **Listen to the conditional sentences. Draw arrows to mark rising (↗) or falling (↘) intonation.**

1 Provided you don't run (__), the bull won't chase you (__).
2 Take a flashlight (__) in case it gets dark (__).
3 Unless you find a water source (__), you won't survive (__).

3.4 **B** **Listen again and repeat the sentences.**

SPEAKING

A PREPARE **Read the scenario. Make a list of survival priorities.**

You are on a small plane that has crashed on a river in a jungle. You can swim to the side of the river, but you can only take a few things with you before the plane sinks. As far as you know, you're a long way from the nearest town and may have to spend a few nights in the jungle.

1 Make a shelter
2 …

B PLAN **You have found the items below in the plane. Write notes on how you could use each item to help you achieve your priorities from Exercise A.**

C DISCUSS **Work in groups. Together you must decide on three survival priorities and how you will use the items from Exercise B.**

A: I think we should use the rope to make a shelter.
B: That's fine by me, as long as we can save some of the rope for fishing.

LISTENING

A SPEAK Work in pairs. Look at the pictures and discuss the questions.

1 What fears are shown in the pictures?
2 Do you think these fears are rational (i.e. based on facts, not emotion) or irrational? Why?
3 What other common fears can you think of?

3.5 **B LISTEN FOR GIST Listen to an extract from an audiobook about fear. Put the topics in the order they are discussed.**

___ the influence of memory
___ potential dangers of the modern world
___ the physical effects of fear
___ how we assess a perceived threat
___ the brain's initial response

3.5 **C LISTEN FOR DEFINITIONS, EXAMPLES AND EXPLANATIONS Listen to the extract again. Complete the notes below with no more than three words or a number. Use the information in the box to help you.**

Listening for definitions, examples and explanations

Speakers usually use the following to make their ideas clearer:

Definitions

To explain topic-specific language, speakers usually provide definitions. These are usually clearly signaled by phrases such as *This is defined as …*, *This means …*, but can also be given mid-sentence (e.g. *Claustrophobia – a fear of being in a small or crowded place – is frequently …*).

Examples

To help clarify an idea, speakers use examples. These are signaled by phrases such as *For instance …*, *Such as …*, *An example of this is …*

Explanations

To make something easier to understand, speakers may also give explanations. These can be signaled by phrases such as *In other words …*, *That's to say …*, *Let me explain …*

Natural reactions

The amygdala is the section [1]________ *associated with our emotional responses.*

[2]________ *is the body's natural response to a perceived threat.*

The hippocampus and the prefrontal cortex help us to distinguish between a [3]________ *and a perceived threat.*
Our [4]________ *influence this decision.*

We usually focus on dramatic or emotional events (e.g. although skin cancer causes over [5]________ *deaths a year, people worry more about plane crashes).*

Increased stress and anxiety can have a [6]________ *on our immune system > could lead to physical and mental health issues. Issue of the modern world?*

D SPEAK Work in pairs. Discuss the questions.

1 Do you think the 'fight or flight' response is useful in the modern world? Why/Why not?
2 Why do you think people frequently refuse to change their mind about something even when shown evidence against it?
3 What kinds of things do people fear now that they didn't fear 20 years ago?

VOCABULARY

Phrasal verbs to describe problems

A Match the phrasal verbs (1–7) to their definitions (a–g).

1 go through
2 sort out
3 put up with
4 talk over
5 deal with
6 work out
7 weigh out

a do what is necessary to solve a problem
b accept someone or something unpleasant in a patient way
c accept and control a difficult emotional situation so that you can start to live a normal life again despite it
d experience something difficult or unpleasant
e solve a problem by considering the facts
f discuss a problem or a plan
g consider the good and bad aspects of something in order to reach a decision about it

B **Choose the correct verbs to complete the questions.**

1. Do you think you are good at ***working out / dealing with*** how to solve problems?
2. Do you ***talk over / deal with*** your plans with the people around you?
3. What could you ***put up with / sort out*** more easily – a room full of spiders or snakes?
4. When was the last time you ***weighed out / put up with*** the risks and benefits before making a decision?
5. What scary situation have you recently had to ***go through / weigh out***? What happened?
6. How would you ***sort out / weigh out*** a situation where everyone was panicking?
7. In general, how well do you ***deal with / go through*** risky situations?

C **SPEAK** **Work in pairs. Discuss the questions in Exercise B.**

VOCABULARY

Dependent prepositions: adjectives

Dependent prepositions: adjectives

Some adjectives are usually followed by specific prepositions. These are called 'dependent prepositions' and they are followed by either a noun or *-ing*. For example:

My mother has always been terrified of spiders. NOT ~~*My mother has always been terrified about spiders.*~~

Choose the correct prepositions to complete the sentences.

1. I'm really anxious ***about / to*** speaking in public.
2. I feel a little ashamed ***of / for*** my fear of flying. I know it's not rational.
3. I'm sick ***about / of*** feeling this way – I really need to get some help.
4. I'm envious ***for / of*** people who can stay calm in dangerous situations.
5. They became suddenly aware ***of / from*** the danger around them.
6. I'm not really scared of anything, but I try to be sensitive ***toward / for*** people with a lot of phobias.

SPEAKING HUB

A **PREPARE** **Read the scenarios (1–3). Write notes about what each person is afraid of and how it affects their life.**

1. Emily Ronson is a 26-year-old graphic designer working in Seattle, Washington. She takes the subway to work every day but hates every minute of the 40-minute trip. Being in tight spaces with a lot of people makes her feel incredibly anxious. Sometimes, she feels so overwhelmed that she gets off the train and waits until it's less busy. Sometimes, this makes her late for work. She's ashamed of her fear so she hasn't told anyone about it.
2. Helen Masters is a retired police officer from Brazil. Several times over the past decade, she has had to cancel her vacation because she had a panic attack shortly after boarding the plane and demanded to get off. She knows this is an issue but has decided to live with it. Now she rarely travels out of the country and cannot see her grandchildren because they live in the UK.
3. Tom Hawksby is a 43-year-old accountant at a large computer software company in New York. Recently, the company hasn't been doing well and hundreds of people have lost their jobs. Tom is worried that he'll lose his job, too, and finds it difficult to sleep at night. This is making him tired and angry at work.

B **DISCUSS** **Work in groups. Use your notes from Exercise A to discuss the questions.**

1. Which of the fears do you think are irrational? Which are rational? Why?
2. How well do you think each person copes with their fear?
3. Do you think their fear is a big issue? Why/Why not?
4. What would you do in their position?

C **PRESENT** **Choose one person from your group to present the main points of your discussion to the rest of the class.**

- Discuss priorities in a survival situation
- Talk about fears and offer advice

The great Tepui challenge

COMPREHENSION

A Work in groups. You are going to watch a video of people climbing Amaurai Tepui, a mountain in Venezuela. What do you think are the biggest challenges they will face?

B Watch the video. What makes the climbers think about giving up?

C Watch the video again. Are these sentences true (T) or false (F)? Correct the false sentences.

1 The team starts day five of the climb near the summit of the mountain. T / F
2 Presenter, Steve Backshall, hopes the improved weather indicates the end of the storm season. T / F
3 The team is attempting to become the first to climb this part of the mountain. T / F
4 One indication of the coming storm is the mass movement of birds. T / F
5 The team survives the storm by climbing back down the mountain. T / F
6 Steve thinks it would be a shame to give up having come so far. T / F

D Work in pairs. Read the extracts from the video. What do the words in bold refer to? Watch the video again to check your answers.

1 **It** would be nice after yesterday, wouldn't it?
2 There's a big storm coming and **they** know it.
3 **It** left us clinging to the cliff.
4 We've got to get off **this thing**; someone's going die.
5 … nothing is worth risking **this** for.

E Work in groups. Discuss the questions.

1 What do you think Steve means when he says, 'You could taste the fear'?
2 Would you like to take part in such an extreme challenge? Why/Why not?

AUTHENTIC ENGLISH

A Work in pairs. Read the extract from the video. What do you think *fingers crossed* means?

Steve: What do you reckon? Do you think our luck's changing?
Cameraman: Fingers crossed. It would be nice after yesterday, wouldn't it?

B *Fingers crossed* is actually part of a longer idiom. Which of the following do you think completes it?

a Have your … b Keep your … c Make your …

C Work in groups. Read the information in the box and guess the meaning of the shortened idioms in bold.

Shortened idioms

Some idioms are so common in informal spoken English that speakers don't need to say them in full for listeners to understand them.

I've always been unhappy there but having my pay cut was ***the last straw*** *[that broke the camel's back].*

He called you a liar? Well, ***if the shoe fits*** *[wear it].*

I'm not surprised Max had a party while we were away. You know what they say – ***when the cat's away*** *[the mice will play].*

I was just thinking that, too. ***Great minds*** *[think alike].*

D Work in pairs. Take turns reading the sentences and responding with an appropriate shortened idiom.

1 Why does my boss keep saying I'm lazy?
2 Nobody was doing any work when I got back.
3 Apparently we both bought him the same leaving gift.
4 Well, I worked pretty hard so hopefully I'll pass.
5 So, what made you fire her in the end?

Snake Mountain

SAM MALCOLM AMANDA HARRY EMILY

A Work in pairs. Why do you think people take part in extreme challenges (e.g. climbing mountains, sailing great distances, etc)?

B Watch the video. Write notes about Malcolm's story (e.g. where it happened, who he was with, etc).

C Work in pairs. Summarize Malcolm's story. Use your notes from Exercise B to help you.

SPEAKING SKILL

A Watch the video again and complete the extracts.

Sam: And I bet having all those snakes around doesn't make it any easier.

Malcolm: Eh? Snakes?

Sam: 1 ____________________, if it's called 'Snake Mountain', I assume there are a lot of snakes.

Malcolm: … we needed an adventure before we started trying to make our way in the world. Well, 2 ____________________, we were looking for an excuse to postpone looking for a job.

Malcolm: None of us knew what we were doing! Well, 3 ____________________, Peter was a pretty good climber, but the rest of us, well …

Malcolm: We couldn't see a thing. Well, 4 ____________________, but visibility was down to about a meter.

Malcolm: So we just carried on all the way to the summit. Though, 5 ____________________, I wasn't really thinking straight at the time!

B Work in pairs. What is the function of the phrases you wrote in Exercise A?

C Read the information in the box to check your answers to Exercise B.

> **Backtracking**
>
> Sometimes in conversation we need to correct a mistake in something we've said. This is called backtracking. To do this, we use phrases such as:
>
> *What I mean is … / What I meant was …, That is to say …, What I should say is … / What I should have said was …, That's not entirely true …, When I say … I really mean …*

D Work in pairs. Student A – Talk about your trip to work or school today in great detail. When necessary, rephrase what you said to make your description clearer. Student B – Listen and ask questions, forcing Student A to backtrack. Then swap roles.

SPEAKING HUB

A PREPARE Brainstorm a list of interesting, dangerous or exciting trips or journeys you have been on.

B PLAN Choose a trip or journey from your list in Exercise A. Write notes about the following:

- Where were you and why?
- When did this happen?
- Who were you with?
- What were the key events?
- How did you feel before, during and after?

C SPEAK Work in groups. Take turns telling your stories. Listen and ask questions where appropriate. Reformulate and backtrack if you need to.

A: So I was all alone on the boat and I could see a storm coming. I kept saying to myself, 'Fingers crossed that I don't sink.'

B: Weren't you scared?

A: Well yeah, to be honest, I was terrified. But it was still an amazing moment.

D REFLECT Whose story was the most exciting? Was it the story itself or the way it was told that made it so exciting?

Describe a trip or journey

➤ Turn to page XXVI to learn how to write a short story.

Unit 3 Review

VOCABULARY

A **Choose the correct options (a, b or c) to complete sentences.**

1 All I could hear was water _____ down the rock face.
   a crunching   b trickling   c hissing
2 As he leaned forward, the branch _____, sending him falling toward the ground.
   a snapped   b rumbled   c crunched
3 The old wooden bridge _____ under the weight of all of the cars.
   a snapped   b groaned   c growled
4 Suddenly, a young child walked into the road. Slamming on the brakes, the car _____ to a halt.
   a screeched   b crunched   c slammed
5 The gravel _____ under the car's tires as it slowly pulled away.
   a hissed   b snapped   c crunched
6 In a rage, she stormed out of the room and _____ the door.
   a smashed   b creaked   c slammed

B **Complete the second sentence so it has a similar meaning to the first, using the words in bold.**

1 It was a terrible experience for them to endure.
   go through
   They had to ________________________________.
2 Someone needs to organize the details of the party.
   sort out
   They need to ________________________________.
3 Try not to get so stressed at work.
   stay calm
   Try ________________________________.
4 I can't quit my job until I find a new one.
   put up with
   I'll have to ________________________________.
5 The management team is discussing the issues together before they make a decision.
   talk over
   Before making a decision, ________________________________.
6 The government must do something about the high level of unemployment.
   deal with
   The government ________________________________.
7 What's wrong with my computer?
   work out
   Can you ________________________________.
8 Let's look at the options and decide which one is best.
   weigh out
   To decide ________________________________.

C **Complete the collocations with the adjectives in the box.**

anxious	ashamed	aware	envious	sensitive	sick

1 You should be ________________ of your behavior! It's embarrassing!
2 I'm ________________ of having to clean up after you all the time.
3 I'm feeling a little ________________ about the job interview next week.
4 I think she's ________________ of your results – you're always at the top of the class.
5 Maybe you just need to be more ________________ toward other people's feelings.
6 You need to be more ________________ of how your actions affect the people around you.

GRAMMAR

A **Choose the correct options to complete the sentences.**

1 They ***left / were leaving*** the house and ***walked / were walking*** to the station.
2 I ***felt / was feeling*** pretty nervous until we ***scored / were scoring*** the second goal.
3 I ***hadn't taken / hadn't been taking*** my cell phone, so I ***had / was having*** no way of contacting them.
4 By the time I ***had gotten / got*** to the movie theater the movie ***started / had already started***.
5 ***I'd been waiting / I'd waited*** in line for 40 minutes before someone ***had served / served*** me.
6 I ***packed / was packing*** my suitcase when the phone ***rang / had rung***.
7 I ***was working / worked*** at my desk when a bird ***flew / was flying*** into the window.
8 He was exhausted because he ***had worked / had been working*** all night. He ***hadn't slept / hadn't been sleeping*** for 24 hours.

B **Complete the sentences with *as long as, as soon as, in case, provided (that)* or *unless*. Sometimes more than one option is possible.**

1 Call me ________________ you hear from him!
2 Don't disturb me ________________ it's really urgent.
3 You should bring a snack ________________ you get hungry.
4 ________________ you work hard, you'll get a pay raise this year.
5 I'm going to buy extra food ________________ more people come to the party.
6 ________________ you finish the swimming portion, you need to get right onto your bike.
7 I won't accept a contact request on LinkedIn ________________ I know them already.
8 It looks like we should get there on time ________________ the traffic isn't too bad.

4 THE FUTURE

> The future belongs to those who believe in the beauty of dreams.
>
> Eleanor Roosevelt

A father and daughter programming a VR simulator.

OBJECTIVES

- talk about future plans and goals
- make predictions about the future of work
- evaluate future predictions
- debate a range of transportation proposals
- give your opinion on automation in the workplace
- write a for and against blog post

Work with a partner. Discuss the questions.

1. Read the quote. What do you think Roosevelt means? Do you agree with her? Why/Why not?
2. What technological developments do you think will change the world in the future?
3. Are you generally optimistic or pessimistic about the future of the world? Why?

4.1 My future

- Talk about future plans and goals
- Make predictions about the future of work

G future forms **V** noun + preposition collocations; nouns and verbs with the same spelling
S identifying evidence **P** nouns and verbs with the same spelling

LISTENING

A Look at the pictures (a–e). Rank these life decisions from most to least important.

B SPEAK Work in pairs. Compare your ideas from Exercise A. Explain your reasoning. What do you agree about? What do you disagree about?

4.1 **C LISTEN FOR GIST** Listen to a podcast about turning points in people's lives. Match the speakers to the change they talk about.

1 Lucy a planning how to spend their retirement
2 Hadiyah b packing in preparation for a year of traveling
3 Frank c getting organized for a new arrival

4.1 **D LISTEN FOR DETAIL** Listen to the podcast again. Choose the correct option (a, b or c) to complete the sentences.

1 Lucy is planning to …
   a take a course in Spain
   b drive across Russia
   c work in the UK
2 Which country isn't Lucy going to?
   a Russia
   b China
   c Brazil
3 Hadiyah's husband …
   a thinks they are having a boy.
   b thinks they are having a girl.
   c is happy with a boy or a girl.
4 Who in Hadiyah's family are they thinking of naming the baby after?
   a one of the grandmothers
   b one of the aunts
   c one of her sisters
5 Frank has just bought …
   a a new car.
   b a new RV.
   c a fishing rod.
6 Frank is planning to …
   a go on a cruise.
   b retire in Florida.
   c take a road trip.

4.1 **E LISTEN FOR KEY INFORMATION** Listen again. Use the table to write notes about each speaker

	Lucy	Hadiyah	Frank
What is each speaker excited about?			
What hasn't each speaker decided?			
What new skill does each speaker talk about?			

F IDENTIFY ASSUMPTIONS Work in groups. Read the extracts (1–2). Do you agree with the assumptions each speaker makes? Why/Why not?

1 Everyone there speaks some English, anyway.
2 Everyone wants to retire, don't they?

a whether to have a family

b what to wear

c where to live

d what job to do

GRAMMAR

Future forms

A Listen and complete the extracts with the correct future form of the verbs in parentheses.

4.2

1. I ________________ (*fly*) to Paris because I have a friend there.
2. The classes ________________ (*be*) three days a week from nine to four.
3. Then, I ________________ (*visit*) as many countries as I can.
4. Parents are always really busy, so I ________________ ________________ (*definitely / have*) to get better at managing my time.
5. Do you think you ________________ (*miss*) work?
6. That's a good idea. I ________________ (*add*) it to the list!

B WORK IT OUT Choose the correct tenses to complete the rules.

Future forms

We use the [1]***simple present / present progressive*** for definite future arrangements.

We use [2]***going to / will*** + base form to talk about general intentions.

We use [3] ***going to / will*** + base form for decisions made at the moment of speaking.

We use [4]***simple present / present progressive*** for timetabled events.

We use [5]***will + base form / present progressive*** for making predictions.

We use [6]***will / going to*** + base form for predictions based on something we know.

C Go to the **Grammar Hub** on **page XII**.

D PRACTICE Complete the sentences with the correct form of the verbs in the box.

break come fly go leave miss see text

1. There's no milk left? OK, I ________________ Bea and ask her to pick some up.
2. That chair doesn't look very strong – I think it ________________!
3. We ________________ with JetBlue on the way out, but haven't booked the return flight yet.
4. The next train to Cambridge ________________ at 5:12 pm.
5. She probably ________________ – she doesn't really like parties.
6. After college, I ________________ traveling for a year. Not sure where though.
7. We're still miles away from the airport – we ________________ our flight!
8. I ________________ her on Friday, actually. We have a meeting at 2 pm.

VOCABULARY

Noun + preposition collocations

Noun + preposition collocations

Some nouns and prepositions are commonly used together. For example, we can say *the reason for* but not ~~*the reason of*~~.

Correct the prepositions in each sentence.

1. Congratulations for passing the exam!
2. I'm hoping to take a course for accounting.
3. I need to make more time of my family.
4. We're planning to visit a lot of places of Europe.
5. There's the possibility to changing jobs next summer.
6. I'm a little worried. There's the risk for not getting into college.

SPEAKING

A PREPARE You are going to interview your partner about their plans and goals for the future. Write questions about:

- home
- study
- work
- family
- travel
- achievements

1 What are you going to do after your course finishes?
2 Would you like to go traveling?

B SPEAK Interview your partner. Ask follow-up questions to find out more information.

A: When does your course finish?
B: At the end of July.
A: So, what are you going to do afterward?
B: Hmm … I'm not sure. I'll probably try and find a job in a café or something.

READING

A SPEAK Work in groups. Which jobs do you think will be most affected by robots in the future? Why?

B SCAN Read *The future of work* quickly. Which of your ideas from Exercise A are mentioned?

THE FUTURE OF WORK

Few people would argue that society hasn't [1]**benefited** enormously from technological advancements. However, the future of many jobs may be hanging in the [2]**balance** due to the increased use of robotics in the workplace. According to Osbourne and Frey from Oxford University, almost 50% of jobs worldwide are at risk of being automated over the next 20 years. Taxi drivers could be replaced by driverless cars. In some warehouses, robots already move [3]**produce** around more efficiently than workers. Even the role of teachers could be dramatically affected as more and more of the learning process moves online. There's also a greater risk of change in certain countries where there are a high number of people employed in manufacturing. For example, the World Bank estimates that some countries risk up to 60% of jobs possibly being replaced by robots and automation, simply because technology is usually able to [4]**produce** more than human workers, with better accuracy and attention to detail. Yet many economists argue that despite the risks of increased automation, there are still many opportunities and [5]**benefits** ahead.

Although to many this may feel like a new problem, in reality it is a [6]**challenge** that has existed for years. Since the invention of the printing press, machines have continued to replace humans in the workplace. In fact, people have always worried about technology taking their jobs. During the Industrial Revolution in England, the Luddites – a group of clothes and textile makers – protested against new technology in factories by destroying machinery. They weren't against the technology, but they didn't like the [7]**control** and power it gave to factory owners to make working conditions worse. In the late 1950s, there were also widespread protests across the US in response to the [8]**influence** of automation on the shipping industry.

Although technological advances frequently [9]**challenge** society, overall levels of unemployment have never risen consistently. Periods of increased unemployment are usually temporary and associated with a recession. We don't run out of work – work simply changes and new jobs are created. People were once employed to open doors on trains and take people's tickets. Farmers, factory workers and elevator operators have all lost their jobs due to technological changes. People have simply moved on and found new types of employment.

Automation will no doubt [10]**influence** society greatly as it starts to [11]**control** more and more aspects of our lives. However, arguably, it won't change the total number of jobs in the economy. Studies into the impact of automation on employment focus only on which existing jobs could be replaced. They do not address the subject of which new jobs might be created. While planes and boats may not have a crew on board, they will still need to be operated by someone remotely. As more and more of life moves online, we may find we need fewer traditional police officers and that experts in preventing online crime will become increasingly important. Jobs that we cannot even imagine right now will become vital.

While many of our jobs are no doubt under threat, it is a dramatic exaggeration to present the idea that huge numbers of people will find themselves unemployed because of automation. Humans will always be vital in the workforce, just not necessarily in ways we are used to. Technology may even free up humans to work less and allow them more free time to [12]**balance** the pressures of work, family and other interests.

Glossary

recession (n) period when trade and industry are not successful and there is a lot of unemployment

C IDENTIFY EVIDENCE Read the article again. Underline the evidence used to support the arguments below. Use the information in the box to help you.

Identifying evidence

Good writers use evidence to support the argument or point they're trying to make. This can include references to specific studies, examples and statistics.

1 A large proportion of jobs are at risk from technological developments.
2 Some countries may suffer more than others due to automation.
3 Jobs have always been at risk from technological developments.
4 Many old jobs now no longer exist.
5 New jobs will be created that do not currently exist.

D SPEAK Work in pairs. Discuss the questions.

1 Do you think society needs to worry about automation affecting people's jobs? Why/Why not?
2 How might the increased use of robots and automation benefit society?
3 What skills do you think people need to develop to protect themselves from automation?

VOCABULARY

Nouns and verbs with the same spelling

A Scan the article again. Which of the words in bold (1–12) are nouns? Which are verbs?

B Complete the sentences with the correct form of the words in Exercise A.

1 One of the ______________ of robotics could be more free time for individuals.
2 We need to ______________ the convenience of automation with the need for employment.
3 We should constantly ______________ companies that get away with paying lower taxes.
4 There's no doubt that technology ______________ the way in which all industries work.
5 Some people think that automation gives companies more ______________ over workers.
6 Robots make it quicker and easier for companies ______________ their products.

PRONUNCIATION

Nouns and verbs with the same spelling

4.3 **A** Listen to the pairs of sentences. Are both forms of the words in bold pronounced the same way?

1 a The key **benefit** of increased automation is greater efficiency.
  b Technology should be used to **benefit** humans, not replace them.
2 a I think we'll all need to **upgrade** our skills.
  b This system is an **upgrade** to the previous one.

4.4 **B** Listen to the pairs of sentences. Underline the stressed syllable in each of the words in bold.

1 a An **increase** in automation will have a negative impact on jobs.
  b We need to **increase** the number of automated jobs in education.
2 a Robots are increasingly used to **produce** more and more products.
  b A lot of people are eating local **produce** to reduce their environmental impact.
3 a Many people would **reject** the idea of a machine being a doctor.
  b Products produced by machines usually lead to fewer **rejects** being made.

SPEAKING HUB

A PREPARE Would you be happy for a robot to do any of these jobs? Why/Why not? Write notes.

- a doctor
- a bus driver
- a waiter
- a sales clerk
- a teacher
- an accountant

B DISCUSS Work in groups. Discuss your ideas from Exercise A. Are there any other jobs that you think could or couldn't be automated?

C PRESENT Explain the main points of your discussion to the class. Which jobs do you think could be automated? Which couldn't? Why?

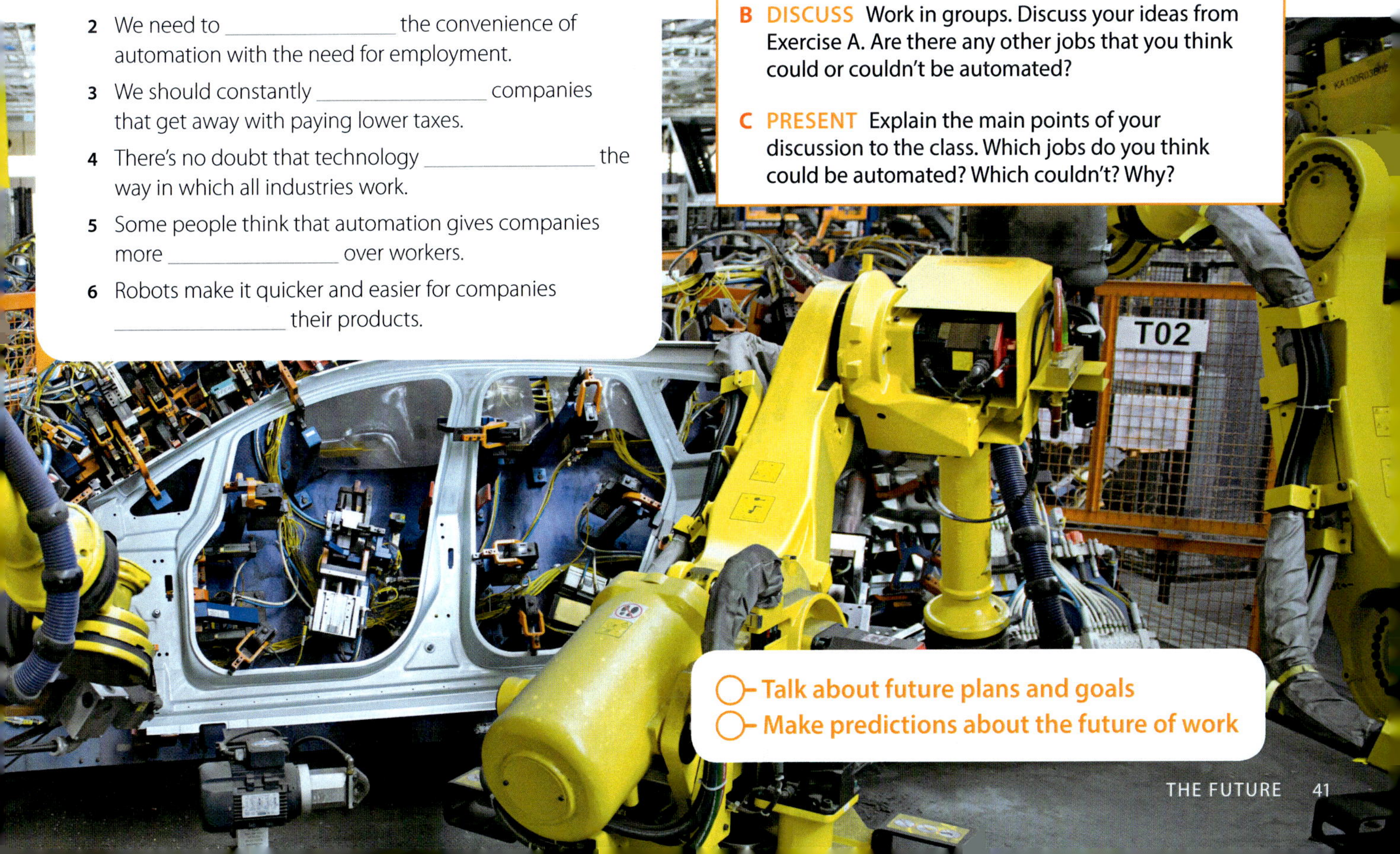

- Talk about future plans and goals
- Make predictions about the future of work

- Evaluate future predictions
- Debate a range of transportation proposals

G – future perfect, future progressive and future perfect progressive
S – identifying agreement and disagreement V – intensifiers P – intonation with intensifiers

READING

A SPEAK Work in groups. Discuss which of the following will become common within the next decade.

- driverless cars
- virtual reality in the classroom
- space tourism
- 3D printing in the home

B PREDICT Work in pairs. Look at the subheadings in *When science fiction becomes science fact*. What predictions do you think each section will make about the future?

C READ FOR GIST Read the article quickly. Which of your ideas from Exercise B are mentioned?

D IDENTIFY OPINION Read the article again. Write Y (Yes) if the statement agrees with the writer's opinion. Write N (No) if it contradicts the writer's opinion. Write NG (Not Given) if it is impossible to say what the writer thinks.

1 The author thinks pollution is the main threat to cities. ___
2 AI and robotics will dominate both our home and work lives. ___
3 Humans and robots will work side by side. ___
4 Social media will affect people's real-life status. ___
5 People will have little contact with each other. ___
6 We need laws to restrict the influence of social media. ___

WHEN SCIENCE FICTION BECOMES SCIENCE FACT

In 1989, the movie *Back to the Future 2* predicted that 26 years into the future, people would make video calls, use wearable technology and tablet computers, and play video games hands-free. While these predictions probably seemed pretty unrealistic at the time, all have come true in some form or another. Even the famous hoverboard could soon become a reality, as car giant Lexus has recently developed a working prototype. So, are predictions made in movies and TV always this accurate? Here we take a look at some of the key predictions made in science fiction over the past 30 years and assess which, if any, are likely to come true.

ENVIRONMENT

Many movies set in the future show changes to our environment. *Blade Runner* is set in the year 2049 and shows a dark future in which pollution levels in the city are shockingly high, and the sun is rarely seen. The natural environment has been almost completely destroyed and industrial cities dominate the landscape. While this movie focuses on the pollution and poor air quality in major cities, in reality the biggest environmental threat to cities is arguably rising sea levels. Recent estimates suggest that if we are unable to dramatically reduce the amount of carbon dioxide released into the atmosphere over the next few decades, [1]sea levels will have risen so much by 2050 that hundreds of millions of people will lose their homes. At present, the city most affected would be Shanghai. Projections show that the majority of the city will disappear under water if global temperatures increase by just three degrees.

TECHNOLOGY

Perhaps the most common types of predictions made in movies center around technology. According to Alex Proyas's movie *I, Robot*, by 2035 robots will have evolved to such a point that they will be able to carry out most human tasks.

[2]By 2035, we will have been living with computers for around 100 years, and while many predictions estimate that robots will be doing almost 50% of jobs worldwide within the next 20 years, a world like Proyas's is still a long way from reality. [3]It is much more likely robots will be working alongside humans, rather than replacing them.

E SPEAK Work in groups. Discuss the questions.

1 Which of the predictions in the article do you think will come true? Why?

2 What else do you think might happen in each of the categories over the next twenty years?

GRAMMAR

Future perfect, future progressive and future perfect progressive

A **Scan the article again. Match the highlighted sentences (1–3) to the things they describe (a–c).**

a an action or situation that will be finished before a specific time in the future ___

b an action or situation that will continue up to a specific time in the future ___

c an action or situation that will be in progress at a specific time in the future ___

COMMUNICATION

Movies are also full of predictions about the future of communication. The communicators in *Star Trek* are incredibly similar to modern cell phones, and the 1927 classic *Metropolis* showed video calls long before the creation of Skype. Our increased reliance on smartphones is taken a step further in the movie *Her*, where the main character has a relationship with a computer operating system that has a female voice.

If it's still popular in 2025, we will have been using Facebook for just over twenty years. The Netflix series *Black Mirror* shows a future where the 'like' feature of Facebook impacts on people's actual lives. The more likes someone gets, the higher their social status is in real life. As a result they can get better cars, houses and jobs. Although this is unlikely to happen, it does draw our attention to the worrying impact of social media on society.

B WORK IT OUT Scan the text again and complete the box with one more example of each tense.

Future perfect, future progressive and future perfect progressive

We use the **future perfect** to talk about something that will finish before a specific point of time in the future.

1 ______________________

We use the **future progressive** to talk about an action or situation that will be in progress at a specific time in the future.

2 ______________________

We use the **future perfect progressive** to talk about an action or situation that will continue up to a specific time in the future.

3 ______________________

C Go to the **Grammar Hub** on **page XII**.

D PRACTICE **Complete the predictions with the future perfect, future progressive or future perfect progressive form of the verbs in parentheses.**

1 I ______________ (*change*) jobs by the end of the year.

2 I ______________ (*live*) in the same place in thirty years.

3 I ______________ (*visit*) five new countries by the end of the decade.

4 By the end of the month, I ______________ (*buy*) a new phone.

5 By the end of the decade, I ______________ (*work*) for the same company for over twenty years.

6 In five years, I ______________ (*still / study*) English.

E SPEAK Work in pairs. Which predictions in Exercise D do you think will become true for you? Why?

SPEAKING

A PREPARE **Read the following predictions from different science fiction movies. Which do you think will become true? Write notes.**

Police will be able to predict the future, preventing serious crimes before they happen. *Minority Report* (2002)

You will be able to pay to have your memory of a relationship that went wrong permanently erased. *Eternal Sunshine of a Spotless Mind* (2004)

Humans will learn how to communicate with aliens. *Arrival* (2016)

The Earth will be so damaged that humans will look for a new planet to call home. *Interstellar* (2014)

The rich will control cities from high-rise towers, while the poor will work machines underground. *Metropolis* (1927).

B SPEAK Work in pairs. Compare your ideas from Exercise A. Explain your reasoning.

1

2
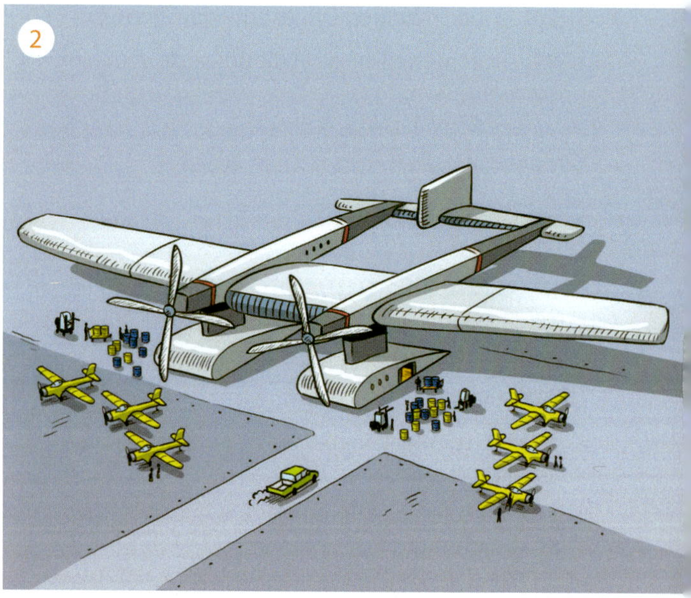

LISTENING

A SPEAK Work in pairs. Look at the pictures (1–3) and discuss the questions.

1 Which of the predictions about future transportation came true?

2 Which didn't come true and why do you think they failed?

3 How do you think transportation will change over the next ten years?

4.5 **B LISTEN FOR GIST Listen to a public debate about the future of transportation. Put the modes of transportation in the order they are discussed.**

___ hypersonic jets ___ driverless cars

___ hyperloop trains ___ flying bikes

4.5 **C IDENTIFY AGREEMENT AND DISAGREEMENT Listen again. Who makes the following points – Mark or Sarah? To what extent to they agree with each other? Use the information in the box to help you.**

Identifying agreement and disagreement

When arguing about a topic, speakers use expressions such as *I completely agree*, *I can't see …*, *Yes, but …*, etc to signal agreement or disagreement. These are typically followed by reasons and examples to counter or support the original point.

Speakers also highlight agreement or disagreement by responding with a single adverb (e.g. *Seriously?*, *Definitely!*, etc).

1 Driverless cars will soon become a common sight on our roads.

2 Driverless cars have better reactions than human drivers.

3 Hyperloops are safer than existing train systems.

4 Hyperloop train systems are unlikely to get the funding they need.

5 We're unlikely to develop flying cars within the next two decades.

6 There may be a market for space tourism in the future.

D SPEAK Work in pairs. Read the driverless car scenario Sarah describes in the discussion. What do you think the car should do? Explain your reasoning.

How can a car make a decision about what to do in a dangerous situation? Should it protect the driver at all costs? What if doing so might mean injuring somebody else? What does it do then? I just think it would be incredibly dangerous to have driverless cars on the road.

VOCABULARY

Intensifiers

A Read the extracts from the discussion. Complete the definitions below with the words in bold.

1 The way we get around is going to be **entirely** transformed.

2 I **firmly** believe there is no chance driverless cars will become popular.

3 It's **undoubtedly** true that driverless cars will have more consistent and quicker reactions than most drivers.

4 But it would **greatly** improve our lives!

5 Hyperloop train systems are **widely** expected to happen.

6 … **especially** things that save significant time, like the Hyperloop train…

7 … it will become **significantly** cheaper over time.

8 You seem **incredibly** focused on speed!

a ______________ completely, or in every way

b ______________ in a way that is relevant or that has an important effect on something

c ______________ used for saying that something is certainly true or is accepted by everyone

d ______________ very much

e ______________ extremely

f ______________ by a lot of people, or in a lot of places

g ______________ strongly

h ______________ used when mentioning conditions that make something more relevant, important or true

B Choose the correct intensifiers to complete the sentences.

1. Many of these inventions seem *undoubtedly* / *incredibly* unlikely to happen.
2. It's *entirely* / *greatly* possible that all cars will be driverless in the future.
3. There are *significantly* / *firmly* more passengers using the system than it was designed for originally.
4. Travel times would be *greatly* / *entirely* improved.
5. You are *undoubtedly* / *especially* right.
6. I *firmly* / *widely* believe that safety is more important than convenience.
7. That is *especially* / *widely* true when it comes to a company making a profit.
8. It is *significantly* / *widely* believed that commercial flights will eventually be powered by solar energy.

C Go to the Vocabulary Hub on page XIX.

D SPEAK Work in pairs. Use intensifiers to give your opinions on the topics below.

- the likelihood of space tourism
- police traveling by hover bikes
- the widespread use of hyperloop trains

Space tourism in our lifetime seems incredibly unlikely.

PRONUNCIATION

Intonation with intensifiers

4.6 **A** Listen to the extract from the debate. What intonation does the speaker use on the intensifiers: rising (↗), falling (↘) or rise-fall (↗↘)? What effect does this have?

They're **undoubtedly** cheaper than building a normal high-speed train and travel times will be **greatly** reduced.

4.7 **B** Listen and repeat the sentences.

1. The city is incredibly congested!
2. The idea is entirely unrealistic. It will never happen.
3. Considering the environmental impact has become increasingly important.
4. Travel times will be greatly reduced.

SPEAKING HUB

A PLAN Read the information cards and write notes about the advantages and disadvantages of each form of transportation.

CITY TRAIN

Completion:	2030
Design:	Spacious and modern. Built-in wi-fi. First-class meeting tables
Cost:	$5 billion
Ticket cost:	$10 day ticket
Speed:	Much faster than road vehicles. Delays less likely

ECO BUS

Completion:	2022
Design:	Eco-friendly using renewable energy
Cost:	$300 million
Ticket cost:	$3 day ticket
Speed:	Faster than cars because it uses a designated bus lane. Delays possible

TROLLEY SYSTEM

Completion:	2025
Design:	A simple subway train. Many roads will need to be redesigned to fit trolleys
Cost:	$2 billion
Ticket cost:	$5 day ticket
Speed:	Relatively slow-moving. Delays possible

B PREPARE Work in three groups. You are going to propose a new transportation system for your city. Group A – City Train, Group B – Eco Bus, Group C – Trolley System. Prepare you arguments.

C DISCUSS Debate the best method as a class. Remember to question the weaknesses in the other methods.

- Evaluate future predictions
- Debate a range of transportation proposals

Café Hub

4.3 The robot revolution

A – *right* **S** – asking for clarification

Flippy the robot

COMPREHENSION

A Work in pairs. You are going to watch a news report about a burger-flipping robot. What do you think the advantages and disadvantages of this kind of technology are?

B Watch the report. Which of your ideas from Exercise A are mentioned?

C Watch again. Complete the sentences with no more than three words from the report.

1. A combination of image recognition and ____________ ____________ tells Flippy which burgers need turning over.
2. The introduction of Flippy may lead to ____________ ____________ in the future.
3. CaliBurger will spend an estimated ____________ ____________ a year on maintenance.
4. Human employees frequently find the working conditions difficult and many leave after ____________ ____________.
5. Flippy isn't fully autonomous yet and regularly ____________ ____________ that a human employee wouldn't.
6. David Zito, the CEO of Miso Robotics, is confident that Flippy ____________ with time.
7. The presenter believes it won't be long before Flippy can both ____________ and serve customers.
8. Roboticists predict that new ____________ ____________ will emerge to replace those lost.

D Work in groups. Do you agree with the following predictions made in the report? Why/Why not?

1. It won't be long before the majority of unskilled jobs are automated.
2. In the future, it will be odd to go to a restaurant that isn't almost fully automated.

AUTHENTIC ENGLISH

A Read the extract from the report. Why do you think the speaker says *right*?

It's not a very fun job, **right**? Er, it's hot, it's greasy, it's dirty, erm, it hurts your wrist, **right**?

B Read the information in the box and check your answers to Exercise A.

> ***right***
>
> In informal spoken English, speakers frequently use *right* in place of a question tag to check information or to ask if someone agrees with them.
>
> *You have tomorrow off,* ***right?***
> (= You have tomorrow off, don't you?)
>
> *You know where you're going,* ***right?***
> (= You know where you're going, don't you?)

C Read the extract in Exercise A again. Which regular question tags could be used instead of *right*?

D Work in pairs. Take turns using prompts (1–6) to make sentences with *right*.

1. You want to check that the movie starts at 9 pm.
2. You think your friend has met Yuki before.
3. You're not sure if a friend can speak Japanese.
4. You think a colleague is going to Seville next week.
5. You think a friend finishes early on Fridays.
6. You want to check if your friend knows how to get to the station.

So, the movie starts at 9 pm, right?

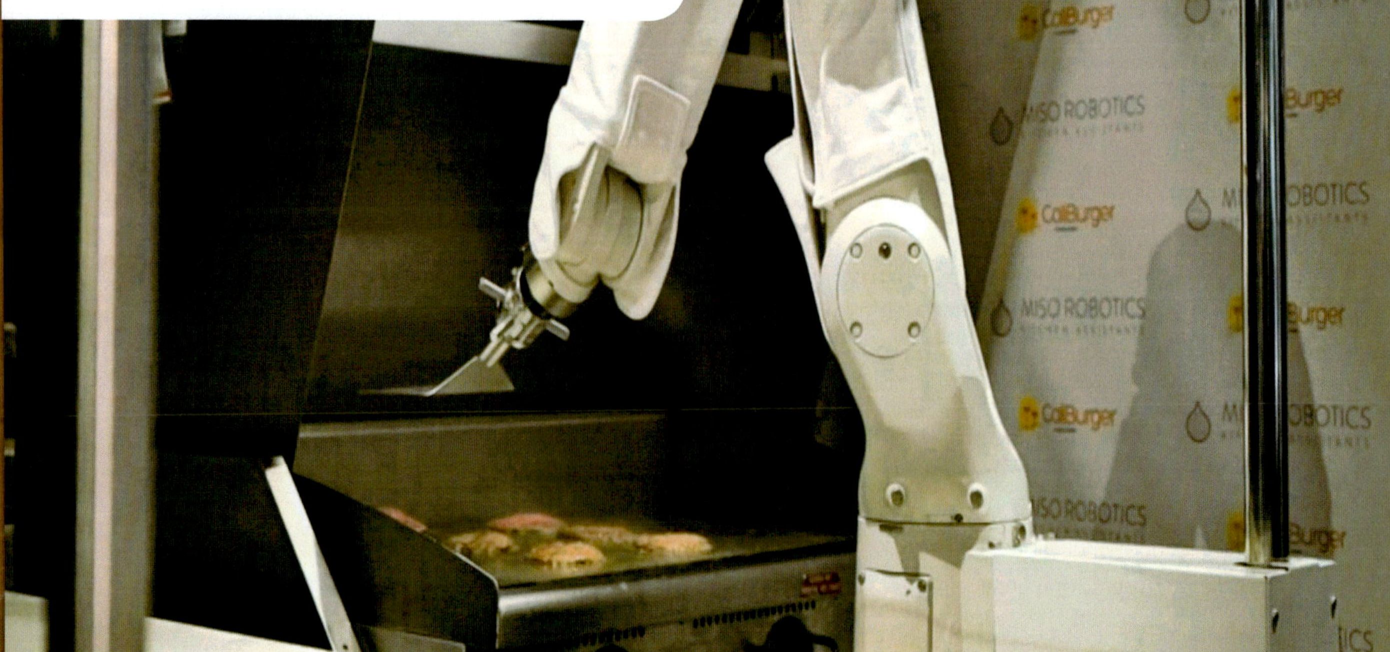

The perfect coffee

A Work in pairs. What's your favorite café? Why do you like it so much?

B Watch the video. Choose the best summary (1–3) of what Sam thinks customers want from an independent café.

1. They want to be served quickly and efficiently.
2. They want to make use of the latest technology.
3. They want to feel like a valued part of a community.

SPEAKING SKILL

A Watch the video again. Complete the box with examples from the conversation.

Asking for clarification

In conversation, we frequently need to check that we have understood something correctly. A common way to do this is to use a signaling phrase followed by an explanation of what we think the speaker meant.

Sam: *I want the people who come to our café to feel that it is their space. So I often allow local clubs to hold meetings here or we host events like book signings or talks.*

Amanda: So you mean that *the café can be a hub for the local community?*

We use a number of other phrases for asking for clarification, some of which are more formal than others:

More formal

1 ______________________

2 ______________________

Less formal

3 ______________________

4 ______________________

B Work in pairs. Tell your partner about your job or a job you would like to have. Listen to your partner and ask for clarification of what they tell you. Then swap roles.

Talk about:

- what skills and knowledge you need
- who you work with
- what you like/dislike about the job
- what your responsibilities are
- what equipment you use

SPEAKING HUB

A PREPARE Work in pairs. You are going to conduct an interview about increased automation in the restaurant industry.

Student A – You are a journalist. Choose which questions to ask from the list below and add some of your own.

Student B – You are the interviewee. Write notes about your responses to the questions below.

- How might the industry benefit from increased automation?
- Which jobs do you think are most at risk from this trend?
- How do you think the public would react?

B SPEAK Conduct the interview. Ask each other for clarification if you need to.

Correct me if I'm wrong, but you seem to be saying that you'd be happy for robots to help prepare, but not serve your food. Is that right?

C DISCUSS As a class, discuss whether increased automation in the workplace is mainly positive or negative.

Give your opinion on automation in the workplace

➤ Turn to page XXVII to learn how to write a for and against blog post.

Unit 4 Review

VOCABULARY

A Choose the correct prepositions to complete the sentences.

1 I want to take a course *in / on / for* accounting next year.
2 There's a risk *with / of / for* the company going out of business before the end of the year.
3 Do you have any knowledge *of / in / on* spreadsheets?
4 Congratulations *about / for / on* the birth of your new baby daughter!
5 There are a lot of historic places of interest *at / in / on* the northern part of the country.
6 Is there any possibility *for / of / about* getting a refund?

B Complete the sentences with words from the box.

balance	benefit	challenge
control	influence	produce

1 We are being expected ________________ far more than is humanly possible!
2 I'm so exhausted all the time. I think I just need a better work–life ________________.
3 Always ________________ yourself to try something new is extremely important.
4 The trend toward digital ________________ the new direction of the company.
5 If this deal goes through, XKOM ________________ 65% of the market.
6 One of the ________________ of exercise is that it lowers your stress levels.

C Choose the correct options (a, b or c) to complete the sentences.

1 He usually exaggerates so I'm not ___ sure I believe him.
a entirely **b** firmly **c** widely
2 They've ___ improved the new model.
a entirely **b** incredibly **c** significantly
3 ___, everyone survived the plane crash.
a Undoubtedly **b** Incredibly **c** Widely
4 The price of tickets may vary ___ between distributors.
a firmly **b** greatly **c** especially
5 I ___ believe that closing the company was the right decision to make.
a firmly **b** widely **c** significantly
6 New England is usually pretty cold, ___ in the winter.
a greatly **b** incredibly **c** especially
7 The population will ___ continue to rise as more people move there for work.
a incredibly **b** undoubtedly **c** firmly
8 It is ___ believed that AI will place many jobs at risk.
a widely **b** especially **c** entirely

GRAMMAR

A Complete the article with *will*, *going to* or the present progressive form of the verbs in parentheses. Sometimes more than one answer is possible.

Four changes to make to your life

At the start of every year, we all make promises to change certain aspects of our life. 'I [1] ________________ (*exercise*) more and 'I [2] ________________ (*eat*) more healthily' we say. But we typically fail to keep our promises. So what simple changes can we make that will make a big difference and be easy to achieve?

1 Get up and go to sleep at the same time. You [3] ________________ (*feel*) a lot more refreshed.

2 Be punctual. It reduces stress. If you start arriving early for things, you [4] ________________ (*find*) that life starts to feel less frantic.

3 Routine is good, but you should also be spontaneous occasionally. When a friend says, 'I [5] ________________ (*go*) the beach this weekend, do you want to come?' Say, 'Great! I [6] ________________ (*come*).'

4 Try to be optimistic. For example, if your company is struggling, don't think 'I [7] ________________ (*lose*) my job.' Be positive and think about the new good job you might get.

Make these simple changes in your life and I am sure you [8] ________________ (*be*) happier in the long run.

B Choose the correct options to complete the sentences.

1 Can we meet later? I *'ll be watching / 'll have watched* the World Cup final then.
2 At the end of this month, I *'ll be working / 'll have been working* at this company for 20 years!
3 Just think – this time next week, we *'ll be lying / 'll have been lying* on a beach in Hawaii.
4 I can't believe she's changing jobs again. She *'ll have had / 'll be having* three different jobs this year!
5 I *won't be finishing / won't have finished* this work by the deadline. I just don't have enough time.
6 *Will you be going / Will you have gone* to Sarah's party on Saturday?
7 In three years, I *'ll have completed / 'll be completing* college and I'll be starting to look for work.
8 This is ridiculous! In ten minutes time I *'ll have been waiting / 'll be waiting* for almost two hours!

5 CHANGE

I cannot say whether things will get better if we change; what I can say is that they must change if they are to get better.

Georg C. Lichtenberg

A traditional roof against a modern skyscraper in Seoul, South Korea.

OBJECTIVES

- summarize a sequence of past events
- evaluate a range of proposals
- talk about changes in your town or city
- evaluate candidates and put together a team
- discuss ways to help the environment
- write a problem solution article

Work with a partner. Discuss the questions.

1 Read the quote. What do you think Lichtenberg means? Do you agree with him? Why/Why not?

2 What are the biggest changes in the world that have happened in your lifetime?

3 What is the most positive change you have ever made?

5.1 Changing environment

- Summarize a sequence of past events
- Evaluate a range of proposals

S – identifying cause and effect
V – green vocabulary
G – the passive voice; causative *have* and *get*
P – glottal stops

READING

A SPEAK Work in pairs. Look at the food chain diagram and discuss the questions.

1 What does the diagram show?
2 In this diagram, the wolf is the top predator. What do you think that means?
3 What would happen if you removed the wolf from this food chain? Why?

B SCAN Read *How wolves change rivers* quickly and check your answers to Exercise A.

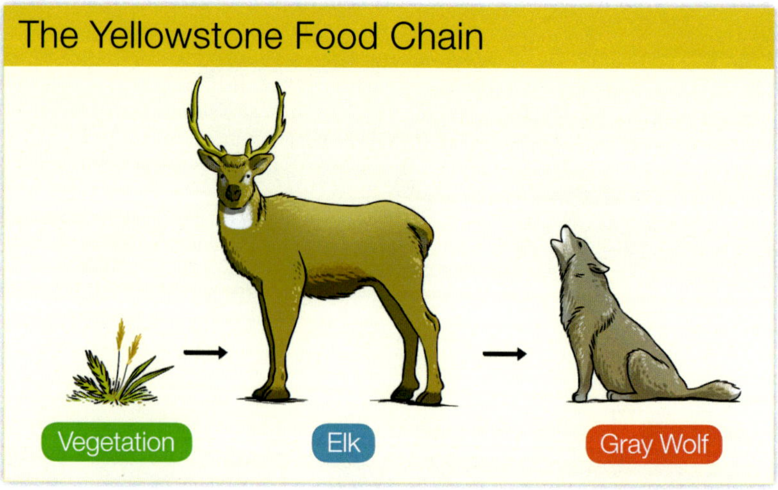

HOW WOLVES CHANGE RIVERS

Wolves are top predators and their beneficial effects on entire ecosystems are gradually being understood.

Wolves are crucial for maintaining a healthy ecosystem – a fact that many people overlooked when they were being hunted and killed in vast numbers across the United States at the start of the 20th century.

Meanwhile, the populations of other animals exploded. The entire ecosystem of the American countryside changed as a result of rapidly expanding populations of elk.

After years of political discussion, conservation biologists finally got their way and the gray wolf, *Canis lupus*, was reintroduced to several areas in the northern Rocky Mountains of the United States. One of those areas was Yellowstone National Park.

Although researchers only reintroduced a total of 41 wolves to the park, their beneficial influences soon became clear, and continue to be seen to this day. Since wolves are top predators that mainly hunt sick or aging elk, their reintroduction had two main effects. First, it slowed the expansion of the elk population, which had exploded without natural predators. Second, it actually improved the overall health of the elk population since only the strongest and fittest survived.

The presence of wolves even changed elk behaviors. For example, they stopped eating in valleys where they could easily be attacked by wolves. Because of this, native plants were able to regrow, increasing biodiversity by providing food and shelter to a growing variety of plants and animals.

Amazingly, the presence of wolves also changed many rivers in the park. After the reintroduction of the wolves, researchers noticed that riverbanks became stronger, the rivers became deeper and small pools formed. Why? Again, the plants that had been eaten by the elk had time to recover, strengthening the riverbanks and in turn, changing the geography of the park itself.

Basically, humans conducted a huge real-life experiment by removing and then reintroducing a top predator from a large area of land. Initially, the changes caused by the lack of wolves were too small to be noticed. But the results of their reintroduction clearly indicate that wolves are essential to restoring and maintaining the ecosystem of the entire region.

This type of relationship is known as a 'trophic cascade'. In Yellowstone National Park, researchers observed the effect when the removal of the top predator started a chain of effects that affected the entire web of life. Similar effects have been identified throughout the natural world, from the Amazon rainforest to the eastern Pacific Ocean.

As more species are reintroduced around the world, no doubt more will be learned about the impact each has not just on ecosystems, but also on the surrounding landscapes.

Glossary

biodiversity (n) the variety of different types of plant and animal life in a particular region
ecosystem (n) all the living things in an area and how they affect each other and the environment
predator (n) an animal that kills and eats other animals

C IDENTIFY CAUSE AND EFFECT Read the article again. Are the sentences true (T) or false (F)? Correct the false sentences. Use the information in the box to help you.

Identifying cause and effect

Texts frequently indicate a cause and effect relationship between different events. These relationships are usually signaled by fixed phrases such as *cause, bring about, lead to, as a result of, the main consequence was*, etc.

1. Wolves started to die out because there were not enough elk to eat. *T / F*
2. Growing elk numbers affected all the other plants and animals. *T / F*
3. Reintroducing wolves meant elk populations grew. *T / F*
4. Reintroducing wolves made elk populations healthier. *T / F*
5. A wider range of plants started to grow again as wolf numbers grew. *T / F*
6. The regrowth of plants meant that rivers became deeper. *T / F*

D SPEAK Work in groups. What animals are in danger of extinction in your country? What is being done about it?

GRAMMAR

The passive voice

A Scan the article again and underline ten examples of the passive voice. The first has been underlined for you.

B SPEAK Work in pairs. Discuss the questions.

1. What tenses are the examples in Exercise A?
2. Which include a modal verb?
3. Which are in the infinitive form?

C WORK IT OUT Choose the correct options to complete the rules.

The passive voice

We form the passive voice with *be* + [1]***simple past / past participle***.

The passive voice can be formed with [2]***all / some*** tenses – only the form of *be* changes.

We use the passive voice when:

- we [3]***know / don't know*** who or what caused an action
- it's [4]***important / not important*** who or what caused an action
- we want to focus on the person or thing that [5]***did the action / received the action***.

D PRACTICE Complete the sentences with the correct passive form of the verbs in parentheses.

1. As the population continues to grow, more and more land ________ (*use*) for farming.
2. Very few fossil fuels ________ (*burn*) before the Industrial Revolution.
3. Thousands of trees ________ (*cut down*) every year before the government changed the law.
4. The future of humans ________ (*could / threaten*) by further increases in temperature.
5. Many species ________ (*affect*) by climate change over the decade.
6. Plastic bags ________ (*ban*) recently in many countries.
7. Global temperatures ________ (*rise*) for over a century.
8. Some people feel that the use of packaging needs ________ (*control*).

E Go to the Grammar Hub on page XIV.

SPEAKING

A PREPARE Go to the Communication Hub on page XXII.

B DISCUSS Work in pairs. What are the main predators in your country? What other animals would be affected if they became extinct?

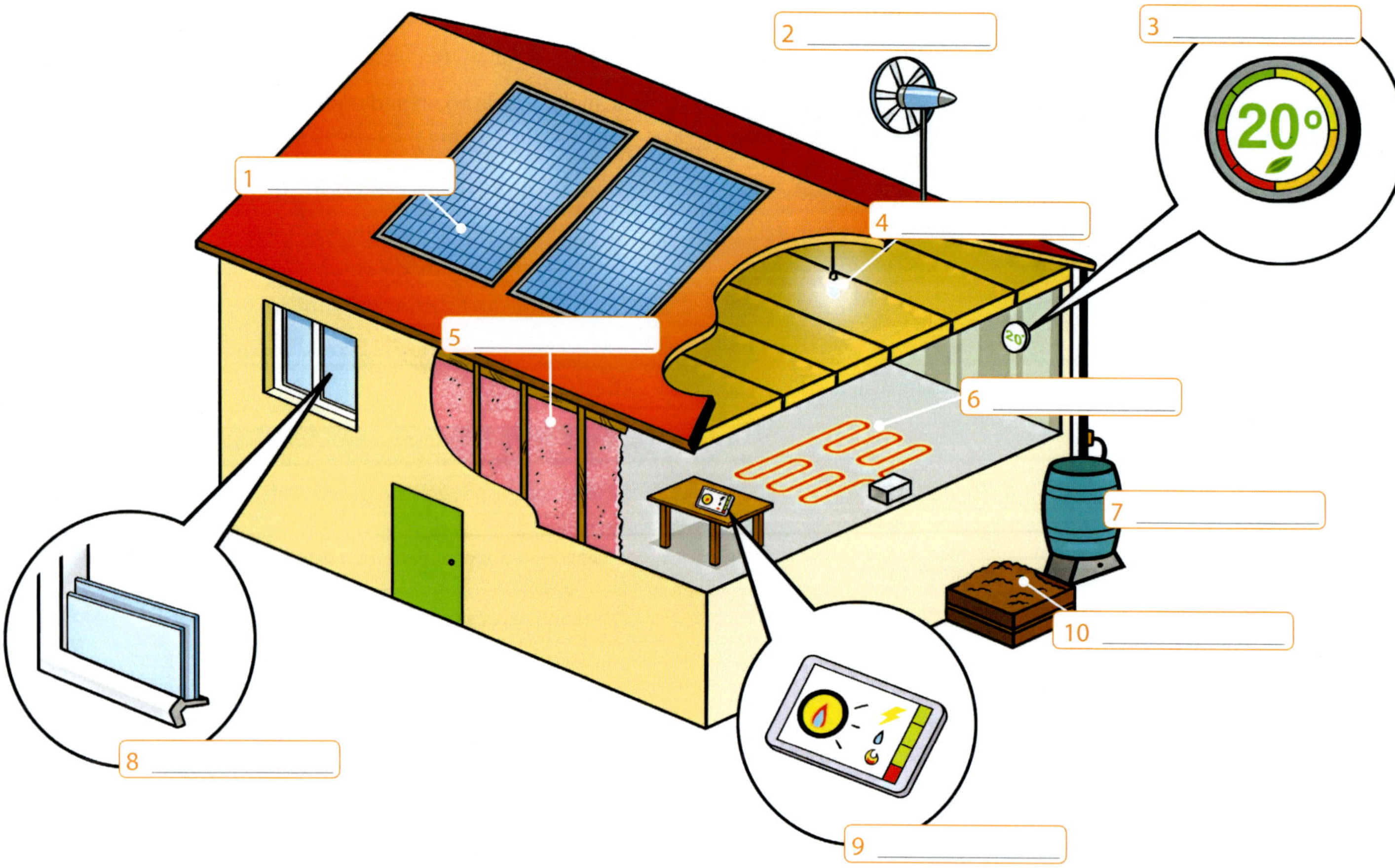

VOCABULARY

Green vocabulary

A Label the picture with words in the box.

compost heap	double glazing	energy-efficient lightbulb
insulation	smart meter	solar panels	thermostat
underfloor heating	rain barrel	wind turbine

B Complete the sentences with words from Exercise A.

1. Turning down your ________ by just one degree can save money and energy.
2. Using ________ to produce energy from the sun can save you money.
3. ________ can be used to extract heat stored in the ground through the floor of the house.
4. ________ last much longer and use less energy than traditional ones.
5. Use a ________ to capture rain which can then be used in the garden and the toilet system.
6. Families frequently throw away a lot of food that could instead have been put in a ________.
7. Using a ________ can produce clean energy on windy days.
8. Installing a ________ helps keep track of energy use and may even save money.
9. Since warm air rises, it is important that you have ________ to keep the heat in.
10. ________ is much better at keeping heat in than traditional windows are.

C SPEAK Work in pairs. Which of these do you have in your home? Which would you install if you had the money?

LISTENING

5.1 **A LISTEN FOR KEY WORDS** Listen to a radio interview about an eco-friendly home. Which of the features in the vocabulary section are not mentioned?

5.1 **B LISTEN FOR DETAIL** Listen again. Complete the sentences with no more than four words from the interview.

1. Harry is making changes because he was surprised by his ________.
2. He made simple changes himself, such as putting ________ in each room and fitting ________.
3. The solar panels make ________ of the energy he needs.
4. The beehive means the roof is a source of ________ as well as energy.
5. The rain barrel now means the ________ uses rainwater.
6. The underfloor heating helps lower Harry's ________.
7. The smart fridge means they ________.
8. The new shower ________ to save water and energy.

GRAMMAR

Causative *have* and *get*

5.2 **A** Listen and complete the extracts from the interview.

1 Ah, I can see you're ________________ solar panels ________________.

2 We're ________________ underfloor heating ________________.

3 We need ________________ the walls better ________________.

B PRACTICE Complete the sentences using the prompts in parentheses. Use the information in the box to help you.

Causative *have* and *get*

We use the causative *have* and *get* (*have / get* + object + past participle) to say that someone does something for us – usually for tasks we can't or don't know how to do ourselves. Compare these sentences:

Camille is installing solar panels on her roof.
(= she is doing it herself.)

Camille is having solar panels installed on her roof.
(= someone is installing them for her.)

1 I ____________________________ (*have / the car / repair*) at the garage last weekend.

2 We're ____________________________ (*get / the house / paint*) right now.

3 We're also ____________________________ (*have / a smart energy meter / fit*) to check how much energy we're using.

4 We ____________________________ (*have / a roof garden / create*) last year to help keep heat in.

5 I'd like ____________________________ (*get / new flooring / install*) in the living room.

C Go to the Grammar Hub on page XIV.

PRONUNCIATION

Glottal stops

5.3 **A** Listen to the extract from the interview. Is the /t/ in the highlighted words pronounced or not pronounced?

We're also getting a smart meter installed. Hopefully, it'll help us keep an eye on how much – or how little – energy we're using!

5.4 **B** Listen and repeat the sentences.

1 It's a great way to save money on your bills.

2 We'd like to start growing our own food.

3 We should save about $100 a year.

4 We need to get quotes for the underfloor heating.

SPEAKING HUB

A PLAN A local school has $30,000 to spend to make the school more environmentally friendly. Write notes about the advantages and disadvantages of each idea.

ORGANIC GARDEN
Cost $500. The food grown could be served in the school cafeteria and save the school $300 a year. It would mean less playground space for the children.

DOUBLE GLAZING
Cost $25,000. This would save the school $2,000 a year in heating bills. The installation would take a long time and some classrooms couldn't be used for a while.

WIND TURBINES
Cost $10,000. There is the potential to save $1,000 per year but the school is not in a very windy location.

SOLAR PANELS
Cost $16,000. There is the potential to save $1,400 per year and the school is in a sunny location.

WATER SAVING TOILETS
Cost $3,000. This solution won't save the school any money, but it will reduce waste water a lot.

ENERGY SAVING BULBS
Cost $300. Saving the school $60 per year. This solution is quick and easy to implement.

B DISCUSS Work in groups. Discuss how to spend the $30,000. Explain your reasoning.

C PRESENT Explain which options you chose in Exercise B and why.

- Summarize a sequence of past events
- Evaluate a range of proposals

5.2 Changing places

- Talk about changes in your town or city
- Evaluate candidates and put together a team

V – describing areas of a city; prefixes
S – listening for rhetorical questions
P – words that lose a syllable
G – *-ing* and infinitive forms

READING

A PREDICT Work in pairs. Look at the pictures of Dubai. What do you think causes a city to grow so quickly? What do you think the effects of such quick growth are?

B SCAN Scan *Rise of the megacities* and check your predictions from Exercise A.

C READ FOR ORGANIZATION Read the article again. Fill in the blanks (1–6) with the sentences (a–f).

a Gyeonggi, on the southern outskirts of the city, has gained more than five million residents in the last 30 years.

b Today, it is a city of over a million but 60 years ago, its population was under 20,000.

c However, in recent years, rapid urbanization has been happening at a rate never seen before.

d Unfortunately, for many people, especially in poorer countries, this has not always been the case.

e At the heart of this rapid expansion in urban populations are the same factors that have been there for centuries.

f So, where and why is this happening at such an astounding rate?

D SPEAK Work in pairs. What are the main advantages and disadvantages of living in a major city?

Rise of the MEGACITIES

Large cities are not a new phenomenon. Attracted by work, better facilities and living standards, there have been cities with a population of over a million people for around 2,000 years. [1]__ This is particularly evident in the Middle East and across Asia, where many cities have swelled to populations in excess of ten million. Places that even just a few decades ago were nothing more than small farming towns or fishing villages now have millions of people living in them. [2]__

Seoul, in South Korea, is a prosperous **urban** area today, but in the 1950s it was a much poorer and smaller place. Once Seoul began to expand, much of the population growth was in the central **commercial** area. This has changed in the last 20 or 30 years, since much of the growth has been in the **suburbs**, where huge **residential** areas have been built on the edge of the city. [3]__ Overpopulation has meant redeveloping traditional **industrial** areas of the city, where vast **housing** projects have expanded the population greatly. Although the growth of Seoul has been extraordinary, it has been a large city for decades. Abu Dhabi, on the other hand, was once not much more than a small village, and has grown immensely in recent times. [4]__ It is not the only city to grow at this rapid rate, so what has led to this rapid expansion?

Population growth in general has come about due to falling death rates and improved life expectancy, but city populations are growing for numerous reasons. [5]__ High levels of unemployment and a lack of resources have always pushed people away from **rural** areas. There is a perception that life will be better in a city, as the future residents are attracted to the prospect of well-paid jobs, greater opportunities to find work, better health care and education. [6]__ All too many cities have illegal **slums** with poor living conditions, little or no electricity and limited access to clean drinking water. Yet this does not seem to deter new residents as both the central area and suburban populations continue to expand.

The trend of urbanization is unlikely to slow down any time soon, with millions of people expected to move to urban areas in the future, no doubt creating more megacities in the process. From Bogota to Chengdu, the march of the megacities shows no signs of stopping across the world.

VOCABULARY

Describing areas of a city

A **Scan the article again. Complete the definitions with the words in bold.**

1 ________________ (n) an area where people live that is outside the city
2 ________________ (adj) relating to industry
3 ________________ (adj) relating to towns and cities, or happening there
4 ________________ (n) a poor area of a town where the houses are in very bad condition
5 ________________ (adj) relating to where people live rather than work
6 ________________ (n) buildings for people to live in
7 ________________ (adj) relating to business
8 ________________ (adj) relating to or in the country

B **Choose the correct options (a, b or c) to complete the sentences.**

1 Over half of the world's population live in ___ areas and this is expected to grow.
a urban **b** commercial **c** slums
2 Depopulation in ___ areas has led to even less work and fewer facilities.
a commercial **b** suburb **c** rural
3 The ___ area is home to some of the largest banks and financial companies in the world.
a industrial **b** commercial **c** residential
4 When people have families, they frequently move to the ___ to have more space.
a suburbs **b** housing **c** residential
5 ___ areas with good transportation connections are usually more expensive to live in.
a Slum **b** Industrial **c** Residential
6 A lack of affordable ___ can lead to people living in poor conditions.
a suburbs **b** housing **c** slums
7 When traditionally ___ areas are in decline, many of the old factories are frequently converted to apartments.
a industrial **b** commercial **c** rural
8 The biggest ___ in the world has over half a million people living in poor quality housing.
a suburb **b** slum **c** urban

C SPEAK **Work in pairs. Use the words in Exercise A to describe your city or a city you know well.**

PRONUNCIATION

Words that lose a syllable

5.5 **A** **How many syllables are there in the underlined words? Write the number next to each sentence. Then listen and check.**

1 There are <u>reasonable</u> transportation connections in the area. ___
2 There has been a <u>considerable</u> rise in the cost of living. ___
3 <u>Traditionally</u>, industrial areas have been converted into housing. ___

5.6 **B** **Cross out the syllables that are not pronounced in the sentences below. Then listen and check.**

1 It's preferable to live in a central area since the shopping is better.
2 Much has changed, especially in terms of the transportation system.
3 My personal preference is to live near the transportation network.

VOCABULARY

Prefixes

Prefixes

Prefixes are added to the beginning of a word to change the meaning. For example, *mega-* is added to the beginning of a word to mean *very big or important* (e.g. *megacity*).

A **Complete the words in bold with a prefix from the box.**

extra- il- over- re- sub- un-

1 The cost of housing has led to some _____**legal** housing areas being built.
2 There have been some _____**ordinary** new buildings constructed in the center of the city.
3 _____**population** has become a problem in my city.
4 They have _____**developed** the old industrial area of the city.
5 The _____**urban** areas around the city have expanded rapidly.
6 Many were _____**happy** about the construction of a large grocery store on the site.

B **Go to the Vocabulary Hub on page XIX.**

SPEAKING

A PREPARE **Write notes about important changes in your town or city over the past ten years. Think about:**

- transportation
- shopping
- the cost of living
- housing

B SPEAK **Work in pairs. Tell your partner about how your town or city has changed.**

C DISCUSS **Work in pairs. Discuss the questions.**

1 Do you think the changes in your city have been mostly positive or negative? Why?
2 What changes would you like to see in the future?

LISTENING

A SPEAK **Work in pairs. Read the FAQs page and discuss the questions.**

1 What is Mars One?
2 Would you qualify to be a Mars One astronaut?
3 Would you like to apply? Why/Why not?
4 What do you think you would find most difficult about being a Mars One astronaut?

5.7 **B LISTEN FOR MAIN IDEA** **Listen to three radio interviews with Mars One candidates. Answer the questions with A (Agatha), T (Tim) or B (Bernie).**

Who …

1 is confident about their physical ability? ___
2 would miss the city atmosphere? ___
3 thinks their attitude and work experience are important? ___
4 is going to have little contact with others to prepare for the mission? ___
5 would miss having a normal life? ___
6 is worried about losing part of their morning routine? ___

5.7 **C LISTEN FOR RHETORICAL QUESTIONS** **Listen again. Check (✓) the questions that are used rhetorically. Use the information in the box to help you.**

Listening for rhetorical questions

A rhetorical question is a question asked for effect, not because the speaker expects an answer. They are usually used to emphasize when the speaker thinks something is obvious, or to express surprise, doubt or agreement.

☐ Isn't that scary?
☐ Surely, being a scientist is the most important thing you bring to the team?
☐ Can you prepare yourself?
☐ Can anyone live without coffee?
☐ Can you take a short break?
☐ Who doesn't enjoy a challenge?
☐ Why would I be scared?

D INFER MEANING **Work in groups. Tim says that 'everyone wants to leave their mark behind'. What do you think he means by this? How do you want to make your mark?**

E SPEAK **Work in small groups. Discuss which candidate you would choose for the mission and why.**

HOME | NEWS | FAQS | MESSAGE BOARD

MISSION TO MARS

FAQS

What is the Mars One project?

The Mars One project was founded in 2011 with the goal of starting a human settlement on Mars.

How will candidates be selected?

Candidates will be selected through online applications, interviews, group challenges and simulations.

How old must candidates be?

The selection process is open to anyone over the age of 18.

What physical requirements are there?

Candidates must be healthy and have a good level of fitness. They must be between 157 and 190 cm tall.

What language(s) must you speak?

The official language of the project is English. However, you do not need to have a good level of English to take part in the selection process. You can apply in English, Spanish, Portuguese, French, German, Russian, Arabic, Mandarin Chinese, Korean, Indonesian or Japanese.

When will it happen and how long will it take?

Six teams of four will be chosen for training. They will train together until the launch in 2024. It takes seven months to get to Mars in an extremely challenging environment.

GRAMMAR

-ing and infinitive forms

5.8 **A** **Complete the extracts with the correct form of the verbs in parentheses. Then listen and check.**

1. For centuries, man has been obsessed with the idea of ________________ (*go*) to Mars.
2. I think it's important ________________ (*advance*) science whenever the opportunity presents itself.
3. ________________ (*be*) a scientist isn't enough.
4. I really appreciate ________________ (*drink*) a good cup of coffee every morning.
5. I'll never forget ________________ (*run*) across the Sahara Desert for seven days.
6. I'm going to Mars ________________ (*be*) a part of history.
7. We have to learn ________________ (*live*) independently of planet Earth.
8. Some people get really stressed when they forget ________________ (*take*) their phone with them.
9. In space, all you can ________________ (*hear*) is endless silence.

B SPEAK **Work in pairs. Look at sentences 5 and 8 in Exercise A. What's the difference in meaning of the word *forget* in each of these sentences?**

C WORK IT OUT **Match the examples in Exercise A to the rules in the box.**

-ing and infinitive forms

We use verb + *-ing*:

a after prepositions ___

b as the subject of a sentence ___

c after some verbs (e.g. *admit, appreciate, avoid, finish, give up, mind, suggest*, etc) ___

We use the infinitive:

d after adjectives ___

e to talk about purpose ___

f after some verbs (e.g. *attempt, decide, expect, learn, manage, need, promise*, etc) ___

We use the base form:

g after modal verbs ___

Some verbs can be followed by either verb + *-ing* or the infinitive, but with a change of meaning (e.g. *forget, remember, try, go on*, etc)

h ___ / ___

D Go to the Grammar Hub on page XIV.

E PRACTICE **Complete the sentences with the correct form of the verbs in the box.**

be do get have like plan produce work

1. ________________ a positive attitude is the key to being a good team player.
2. It's important ________________ everyone you work with.
3. One way of ________________ more effective on a team is to become an active listener.
4. Never promise ________________ more work than you can manage. You will let your team down.
5. Only teams with strong leaders can ________________ good results.
6. Always remember ________________ what you need to discuss in a team meeting, so you don't waste any time.
7. I'm worried about not ________________ along with the other people on the team.
8. We need ________________ together if we want to succeed.

F SPEAK **Work in pairs. Do you agree with the sentences in Exercise E? Why/Why not?**

SPEAKING HUB

A Go to the Communication Hub on page XXI.

B PRESENT Tell the class which candidates you chose, which you rejected and why.

- Talk about changes in your town or city
- Evaluate candidates and put together a team

Café Hub

5.3 Getting into the habit

A – conditional counterarguments S – taking the floor

Reward or penalty?

COMPREHENSION

A Work in pairs. Look at the picture. Do you think cups like these are environmentally friendly? Why/Why not?

Glossary

disposable (adj) designed to be used once, then thrown away

B Watch a news report about an environmentally friendly scheme at a university. Choose the best summary (1 or 2).

1. The university found that a reward scheme had no meaningful effect on student behavior. By adopting a penalty scheme instead, they were able to reduce the number of disposable cups sold every year.
2. The university found that a penalty scheme had no meaningful effect on student behavior. By adopting a reward scheme instead, they were able to reduce the number of disposable cups sold every year.

C Watch the news report again and answer the questions.

1. How did the university originally try to encourage students to start using reusable cups?
2. What was the issue with the original scheme?
3. How did the university address this issue?
4. What else did the university do to encourage use of non-disposable cups?
5. Was the penalty scheme a success? Why/Why not?
6. How has the penalty scheme affected sales of hot drinks?

D Work in groups. Do you agree that you have to use penalties to meaningfully change behavior? Why/Why not?

Glossary

high street **(n) (British)** = main street **(n) (American)**
a scheme **(n) (British)** = a plan or system **(n) (American)**

AUTHENTIC ENGLISH

A 01:33–01:41 Watch the last part of the report again and complete the extract.

Presenter: So this might work on a campus. That doesn't mean it's going to work on the high street, where people have a lot more choice.

Interviewee: ______________________ government were to legislate for it.

B Work in pairs. Read the extract again. Why does the speaker use a conditional? Which word does she stress? Why?

C Read the information in the box to check your answers to Exercise B.

Conditional counterarguments

In discussions, speakers sometimes use conditional structures to make a counterargument. These usually begin with conjunctions and use words, phrases or ideas from the original argument. The stress is usually put on the modal verb to emphasize the contrast between the two ideas.

A: *It's a nice idea, but just doesn't work in practice. Nobody wants to carry around a reusable cup everywhere they go.*
B: *But they might if coffee shops offered bigger discounts.*

D Work in pairs. Take turns reading the arguments (1–3) and responding with a conditional.

1. Sadly, most people like the convenience of disposable water bottles. This isn't going to change anytime soon.
2. Social media isn't dangerous. It's just a fun way to stay in touch with old friends.
3. Electric cars are a great idea, but will never replace gasoline-powered vehicles on our roads.

A green suggestion

SAM MALCOLM AMANDA HARRY EMILY

A Work in groups. Do you think where you work or study does enough to protect the environment? Why/Why not?

B Watch the video and answer the questions.

1 What eco-friendly change does Harry suggest?
2 Why does Amanda support this idea?
3 What is Sam's criticism of the idea?

SPEAKING SKILL

A Read the extract from the conversation. Why do you think Amanda finishes Harry's sentence?

Harry: People respond better to a penalty than a …

Amanda: … reward. It's what we do at my office.

B Read the information in the box and check your answers to Exercise A.

Taking the floor

In discussions, one speaker will regularly interrupt another so they can start speaking. This is called taking the floor. In the video, Sam interrupts Harry by saying [1] ____________________ and Malcolm interrupts Sam by saying [2] ____________________.

To keep the floor, we need to avoid interruption. In the video, Harry stops Sam from interrupting him by saying [3] ____________________.

We can also take the floor by agreeing or disagreeing with what someone has said.

Sam: Yes, well, I think we already do a fair bit to help the environment.

Harry: [4] ____________________ *we could do more?*

Amanda: And it does seem to have changed how people behave.

Harry: [5] ____________________. *People begin to feel that it's normal to have their own cup. It's not something that deserves a special reward.*

Sam: [6] ____________________ *we start penalizing them.*

We can also show agreement or understanding by finishing someone's sentence, like Amanda does to Harry.

C Watch the video again. Complete the box with examples from the conversation.

D Work in groups. Discuss one of the following topics using strategies from the box to take or keep the floor.

- recycling
- wind farms
- solar panels
- electric cars
- plastic packaging
- food waste

SPEAKING HUB

A PREPARE Work in groups. Write a list of five ways you could be more environmentally friendly in the following areas:

- travel and transportation
- recycling
- saving water
- eating smart
- reducing and reusing
- clothing

B PLAN Rank the points in Exercise A in order of importance. Try to reach an agreement in the group.

A: I really think recycling plastics is a top priority. We should all carry refillable water bottles with us.

B: Really? But surely people wouldn't want to carry a water bottle everywhere.

A: But they might if governments made plastic bottles expensive and provided a lot of places where we can refill our bottles.

C PRESENT Present your list to the class. Explain your reasoning.

Discuss ways to help the environment

Turn to page XXVIII to learn how to write a problem solution article.

Unit 5 Review

VOCABULARY

A Complete the definitions with the words in the box.

insulation smart meter solar panel thermostat rain barrel wind turbine

1 ______________ a large container used to collect rain for watering plants
2 ______________ a large machine like a windmill used for producing electricity using the wind
3 ______________ material used to prevent heat, cold, noise, etc from passing through something
4 ______________ an electronic device used to record how much electricity is used
5 ______________ a piece of equipment that uses energy from the sun to create electricity
6 ______________ a piece of equipment that controls the temperature in a building

B Complete the sentences with the words in the box.

housing residential rural slums suburbs urban

1 They are building a new ______________ area near me with over 2,000 new homes.
2 The cost of ______________ has increased by almost 20% in the last year.
3 I don't really like living in the ______________. It's too far from the city and there isn't much to do.
4 In countries such as Germany and England, almost 80% of the population lives in ______________ areas.
5 Because of high unemployment, many people leave ______________ areas and move to cities to look for work.
6 In many ______________, many thousands of people have to share just one toilet.

C Complete the article with the correct form on the words in parentheses.

Simple ways to be more environmentally friendly

Climate change is a threat to all of us. You can help tackle this issue by making some of the following changes:

1 Buy a reusable bottle

Many plastics are used just once and can't be [1]______________ (*recycle*). Many people believe single-use plastics are [2]______________ (*necessary*) and should be banned. To help prevent plastic pollution, take a reusable water bottle with you instead of buying a plastic one.

2 Bike to work

Air pollution is also a major problem, particularly in [3]______________ (*crowded*) cities. Campaigners would like heavily polluting vehicles to be made [4]______________ (*legal*). In the past, a lot of bike paths were [5]______________ (*standard*) but there has been a lot of recent investment in building new bike paths. Riding your bike to work is a great way to help reduce pollution while also getting some exercise!

GRAMMAR

A Complete the sentences with the correct passive form of the verbs in the box.

build film finish hold inform left

1 Parts of *Star Wars: The Last Jedi* ______________ in the salt plains of Bolivia.
2 An emergency meeting ______________ to discuss possible responses.
3 The public ______________ about the potential risk and is advised to avoid the area.
4 The house, which was the family home of the Harrogates, ______________ in 1858.
5 As they pulled into their drive, they noticed that the window ______________ open.
6 The new shopping mall was scheduled to be completed by now but it ______________ until next May.

B Complete the sentences with the correct form of the words in parentheses.

1 **A:** Can you give me a ride tonight?
B: No, sorry. I ______________ (*my car / service*) right now.

2 **A:** ______________ (*you / your shower / fix*)?
B: Not yet. Someone's coming to look at it tomorrow.

3 **A:** Have you seen Emily?
B: Yes, she's ______________ (*nails / paint*).

4 **A:** Why are they eating out so much?
B: They are ______________ (*kitchen / installed*) this week.

5 **A:** Everyone on TV has such white teeth!
B: I know. Actually, I'm thinking about ______________ ______________ (*teeth / whiten*).

C Choose the correct options (a or b) to complete the sentences.

1 Chris has offered ___ me with the project I'm doing about homelessness.
a to help **b** helping

2 Mark has been in touch. Did you remember ___ him an email?
a to send **b** sending

3 I don't want ___ to work today, but I have so much to do.
a to go **b** going

4 Lucy texted. They're trying ___ to the party by eight.
a to get **b** getting

5 Our kids miss ___ in Madrid and wish we could move back.
a to live **b** living

6 These videos on YouTube are great to help you learn how ___ the guitar.
a to play **b** playing

Endmatter Contents

Grammar Hub

1.1 Question forms

Questions with *be, have* and *do*

- We usually use the auxiliary verbs *be*, *have* and *do* to form questions. These come before the main verb.

Question word	Auxiliary	Subject	Main verb	
	Is	he	coming	this weekend?
	Have	you	seen	her?
When	did	they	move	in?

Subject questions

- When the question word (*who*, *what*, etc) is the subject, we don't use an auxiliary.

Question word	Main verb	
What	happened	to you?
How	are	you?

Indirect questions

- Indirect questions begin with phrases such as *Can you tell me …?* After the phrase, we use the same word order as a sentence, not a question.

Do you think it will rain? NOT ~~*Do you think will it rain?*~~

Can you tell me where you live? NOT ~~*Can you tell me where do you live?*~~

Questions ending in a preposition

- When a question word is the object of a preposition, the preposition usually comes at the end of the sentence.

Who did you brother live with?

What did you use it for?

Questions with negative auxiliaries

- When we ask negative *wh-* questions, we use the auxiliary verb, even in subject questions. Negative *wh-* questions can be used to confirm something you believe to be true, to express an opinion in a more formal manner or to focus on a smaller number of answers.

*OK, who **doesn't** want pizza? (= I think most people **will** want pizza)*

1.2 Tense review

Simple present	**He enjoys** parties.
Present progressive	**I'm watching** the news.
Simple past	**He got up** early this morning.
Past progressive	**I was walking** the dog.
Present perfect	**I've lived** here for 12 years.
Past perfect	**I'd seen** the movie several times.

- We use the simple present to talk about general truths or actions that always/usually/never happen as part of our daily routines.
- We use the present progressive for things that are happening now or around now.
- We use the simple past to talk about past states or completed actions in the past.
- We use the past progressive to describe the background to a story or something that was in progress at a particular time in the past. We also use it with the simple past to describe an action that was interrupted.

We were driving home when we had an unexpected phone call.

- We use the present perfect to talk about a state or action that started in the past and is still happening now. We also use it to announce news.
- We use the past perfect to talk about a past action that occurred before another past action. This tense is frequently used with the simple past.
- With the negative and question forms of these tenses, we use an auxiliary verb (*be*, *do* or *have*, depending on the tense).

She doesn't feel well.

It didn't cost a lot.

I haven't finished yet.

Had they been there before?

Be careful!

- Certain time words and expressions, such as *now*, *just*, *already*, *recently*, *every day*, etc, help us to identify which tense we need to use.

*I was traveling across the country **at the time**.*

*I have **just** finished the last series on Netflix.*

*Actually, I saw him at the gym **yesterday**.*

1.1 Question forms

A Correct the mistakes in each question.

1 Does he lives near here?
2 What she has done to her hair?
3 Where you work?
4 Which is team winning?
5 Haven't you already be on vacation?
6 Who with do you live?
7 When he told you that?
8 What was happened next?

B Rewrite the direct questions as indirect questions.

1 Where did you get your information?
Can you tell me ______________________________?
2 Is it going to snow later, do you think?
Do you think ______________________________?
3 What do you think of the new recycling laws?
Can I ask you ______________________________?
4 Where does Alejandro come from?
Do you know ______________________________?
5 Has the mail arrived yet?
Could you see if ______________________________?

C Complete the questions in the interview.

Interviewer: Where [1] ______________________________?
Mia: I'm from Seattle, Washington.
Interviewer: How long [2] ______________________________?
Mia: I've been here for about five years now.
Interviewer: Who [3] ______________________________?
Mia: With friends, but I'm looking to find an apartment of my own.
Interviewer: So when [4] ______________________________?
Mia: I guess I decided to become an actor when I was about five!
Interviewer: What [5] ______________________________?
Mia: I don't have much free time, but when I am free, I like spending time with friends and family.
Interviewer: Do you think [6] ______________________________?
Mia: Oh yes. I think I'll always be an actor. I can't imagine doing anything else!

➤ Go back to page 5.

1.2 Tense review

A Choose the correct options to complete the sentences.

1 I ***am*** / ***was*** watching television when I started to feel sick.
2 Joanna was ashamed because she ***has*** / ***had*** done something wrong.
3 I ***am never feeling*** / ***have never felt*** relaxed around him – I don't know why.
4 We ***were taking*** / ***had taken*** the wrong turn and were now completely lost.
5 I'm pretty sure I ***met*** / ***have met*** you at Jenna's party last year.
6 While I ***was walking*** / ***had walked*** home, I slipped on some ice and broke my ankle.
7 I ***live*** / ***have lived*** here for about a year and a half now.
8 James ***studies*** / ***is studying*** French at Harvard next year.

B Complete the sentences with the correct form of the verb in parentheses.

1 Jochen is an anxious person who ______________________________ (*not like*) doing new things.
2 It wasn't awkward at the party because I ______________________________ (*already meet*) everyone there.
3 The question is: why was Tom there – who ______________________________ (*wait*) for?
4 I have some really exciting news – I ______________________________ (*start*) a new job!
5 We ______________________________ (*work*) on a secret project these days.
6 Tell me about yourself. How long ______________________________ (*work*) for this company?

C Complete the sentences with the correct form of the verbs in the box. Use contractions where possible.

forget	have	know	meet
snow	think	walk	work

1 It ______________________________ heavily and I wasn't wearing a winter coat.
2 She ______________________________ for the company for almost five years now.
3 It's difficult because he ______________________________ many people in the area.
4 We ______________________________ much money back then, but we were happy.
5 I knew I ______________________________ her before, but I couldn't figure out where.
6 I ______________________________ about starting my own company.
7 I ______________________________ down the road in the sunshine when out of nowhere, it suddenly started pouring rain.
8 She only realized she ______________________________ her passport when she got to the airport.

➤ Go back to page 7.

Grammar Hub

2.1 Present perfect and present perfect progressive

	Positive	Negative	Question
Present perfect	**He's improved** his fitness level.	**They haven't finished** their meeting yet.	**Have you lost** weight?
Present perfect progressive	**I've been trying** to give up sugar.	**She hasn't been sleeping** very well.	**Have you been avoiding** me?

- We use the present perfect for finished actions with a present effect, and the present perfect progressive for unfinished actions.

  I've read that book before, actually.
  (= I finished the book.)
  I've been reading a great book recently.
  (= I started it and I'm still reading it.)
- We use the present perfect to emphasize the result of an action, and the present perfect progressive to emphasize the action itself.

  I've cleaned the bathroom.
  (emphasizing the result: the bathroom's now clean)
  I've been cleaning the bathroom all morning.
  (emphasizing the action: the cleaning)
- We use the present perfect to suggest that something is permanent and the present perfect progressive to suggest that something is temporary.

  I've lived here my whole life. (= long-term/permanent)
  I've been living here while I look for a new apartment.
  (= short-term/temporary)
- We use the present perfect to say how often something has happened and the present perfect progressive to say how long something has been happening.

  I've been to the gym every day this week. (= number of times)
  I've been going to the gym for the past two months.
  (= length of time)

Be careful!

- We don't usually use state verbs such as *be*, *have*, *know* and *seem* in the present perfect progressive.

  She's had short hair for several months now.
  NOT ~~She's been having short hair for several months now.~~

2.2 *used to / would / be used to / get used to*

	Positive	Negative	Question
used to	**I used to work** in a hotel.	**He didn't use to get** so stressed.	**Did she use to have** long hair?
would	**They would take** the bus to work.	**She wouldn't have** anything for breakfast.	**Would he usually come** home late?
be used to	**He's used to getting** up early.	**I'm not used to eating** such spicy food.	**Are you used to driving** on the right now?
get used to	**He** soon **got used to wearing** glasses.	**I haven't gotten used to** the cold weather.	**Are you getting used to living** in the country?

- We use *used to* + base form to talk about past habits, repeated actions and states or situations that have changed.

  I used to get up really early on the weekend.
  He didn't use to have a beard.
- We also use *would* + base form to talk about past habits and repeated actions.

  The children would spend hours playing in the yard.
- We use *be used to* + verb + *-ing*/noun to talk about a situation which is now normal or familiar. We use the negative form to talk about a situation which is new or strange.

  I'm used to living on my own.
  I'm not used to the cold weather.
- We use *get used to* + verb + *-ing*/noun to talk about a situation which is becoming more familiar.

  I'm getting used to working in an office.
  I haven't gotten used to the food yet.

Be careful!

- We cannot use *would* to talk about past states.

  They used to live in Panama. NOT ~~They would live in Panama.~~

2.1 Present perfect and present perfect progressive

A Choose the correct options to complete the conversations.

1 **A:** How long have you *known* / *been knowing* Emily?
B: Uh, about five years now, I think.

2 **A:** Did you tell everyone about the change of venue?
B: I think so. Oh no! I've just *realized* / *been realizing* that I forgot to tell Piotr!

3 **A:** How's your essay going?
B: I've *planned* / *been planning* it for the past three hours so I'm almost ready to start writing.

4 **A:** Who'll be there this evening?
B: Just me and my sister. She's *stayed* / *been staying* with me while her apartment is being redecorated.

5 **A:** I saw Toby in town today.
B: Yes, his boss has *given* / *been giving* him a week off from work.

6 **A:** So, what have you been up to?
B: I've been *working* / *worked* on a new book. I should finish it by the end of the year.

B Complete the sentences with the present perfect or present perfect progressive form of the verbs in the box. Add pronouns if necessary.

avoid	be	decide	do	find	know	leave	notice	only go out	think	use	wait

1 They ______________ about moving now that their son ______________ home.

2 Ren ______________ the new shampoo for six months and she ______________ a big improvement in her hair.

3 Lucia ______________ to quit her job because she ______________ it more and more stressful over the last few months.

4 Why ______________ me? ______________ something to upset you?

5 I ______________ Farid for years, but we ______________ for a few weeks!

6 I ______________ for you for hours! Where ______________ all this time?

C Use the prompts to write sentences in the present perfect or present perfect progressive.

1 Kim / not work / here for long, so she / not met / all of her colleagues yet
______________.

2 I think Jamila and Kalid / already / send out / the invitations
______________.

3 I'm afraid I / not clean / the living room yet because I just / not have / time
______________.

4 Jimmy / drive / for hours, so he must / be / exhausted
______________.

5 I / know / about this for a long time
______________.

6 How long / it / be / since you / quit / your job
______________?

7 You / visit / this museum before
______________?

8 We / eat / vegan food for two months now
______________.

➤ Go back to page 17.

2.2 *used to / would / be used to / get used to*

A Choose the correct options to complete the sentences.

1 People *didn't use to* / *wouldn't* be able to look everything up on Google.

2 Sofia is slowly *used* / *getting used* to living back home with her parents.

3 *Did you use to* / *Would you* have a smartphone when you were younger?

4 *I'm still not used* / *I didn't use* to having short hair!

5 The children always *got used* / *used* to spend their allowance on candy.

6 Jakob *got* / *was* used to wearing glasses fairly quickly.

7 *Were you* / *Have you gotten* used to the new software yet?

8 As a child, Milo *would* / *was used to* become demotivated very easily.

B Complete the text messages with the correct form of *used to, be used to* and *get used to*.

How's the new job going? Have you [1] ______________ the commute yet?

Not really. It [2] ______________ take about 20 minutes to get to work. Now it takes over an hour!

I know the feeling! I [3] ______________ having a long drive to work – I've been doing it for a while now – but I still [4] ______________ getting up so early!

It's horrible, isn't it? I [5] ______________ get up at seven thirty. These days, that's when I have to leave the house. And I'm still [6] ______________ getting home so late, either.

➤ Go back to page 19.

Grammar Hub

3.1 Narrative tenses

	Positive	Negative	Question
Simple past	**The rescue team found** Jose and **carried** him to safety.	Unfortunately, **the rescue team didn't see** the survivors.	So what **did you do** next?
Past progressive	At the time, **most of us were trying** to get some sleep.	**I wasn't looking forward to** the trip.	What **were you doing** when the storm hit?
Past perfect	They returned to find that **the tornado had destroyed** their house.	They suddenly realized that **the helicopter hadn't seen** their signal.	**Had you been** in that kind of situation before?
Past perfect progressive	**She'd been swimming** for hours by the time she was rescued.	Although **they hadn't been driving** long, everyone was exhausted.	How long **had you been climbing** for?

- We use the simple past for completed actions that are the main events in a story.

  After some hours alone in the woods, Wei ate his last chocolate bar.

- We use the past progressive (*was/were* + verb + *-ing*) to describe:

  a actions in progress at a particular point in a story.

  He was charging his phone at the time.

  b longer actions or situations that are interrupted by a shorter action.

  They weren't wearing life jackets when the boat capsized. NOT ~~They didn't wear life jackets when the boat capsized.~~

  c the general background of a story.

  The skies were getting dark, the winds were picking up and the passengers were beginning to worry.

- We use the past perfect (*had* + past participle) to describe past actions or situations that happened before one of the main events in the story, or before the story began.

  A lot of insects had bitten Francesco before he decided to use the insect repellent.

- We use the past perfect progressive (*had* + *been* + verb + *-ing*) to describe longer actions or situations that started before one of the main events and have continued up to that point.

  We'd been waiting for hours before we were rescued.

Be careful!

- We usually use the past progressive after *while* and *as*.

  While she was standing by the side of the road, a car with dark windows pulled up.

- We can usually use either the simple past or past perfect after *as soon as* and *by the time*.

  By the time I'd realized what was happening, Jilly had left.

3.2 Alternatives to *if* in conditionals

- We use *unless* to mean *if … not*.

  Generally, bears won't attack you unless they think you're a threat. (= They won't attack you if they don't think you're a threat.)

  Unless this weather improves, we'll be stuck in the camp all day. (= If the weather doesn't improve, we'll be stuck in the camp all day.)

- We use *provided (that)* and *as long as* to mean *only if*.

  They should be back soon provided (that) they don't take a wrong turn. (= They should be back soon, but only if they don't take a wrong turn.)

  As long as you stay on the path, you won't get lost. (= You won't get lost, but only if you stay on the path.)

- We use *in case* to talk about doing something now to prepare for a possible future situation.

  I'll take a waterproof jacket in case it starts raining. (= because it's possible it will start raining)

  She's going to stay in a safe spot in case she encounters a bear. (= because it's possible that she will encounter a bear)

- We use *as soon as* to mean *in the shortest possible time / immediately*.

  I'll call you as soon as I hear anything. (= I'll call you immediately after I hear something.)

Be careful!

- Even though we're talking about the future, we use a present tense after future time clauses.

  We'll leave as soon as the storm clears. NOT ~~We'll leave as soon as the storm will clear.~~

  Elephants won't attack you unless you run toward them. NOT ~~Elephants won't attack you unless you will run toward them.~~

3.1 Narrative tenses

A Choose the correct options (a, b or c) to complete the sentences.

1 Nozomi ___ her bike when it started raining.
a was riding b rode c had ridden

2 We ___ down the side of the mountain when our rope snapped.
a had climbed b were climbing c climbed

3 The ship ___ into a rock, but no one was hurt.
a had crashed b was crashing c crashed

4 I ___ my tent when suddenly I heard a strange noise in the forest behind me.
a packed away b had packed away c was packing away

5 The next day, they saw that the hurricane ___ the house off the ground!
a was lifting b had lifted c lifted

6 When the wave hit the ship, everyone ___ to panic.
a had started b started c was starting

7 The sun ___ and the conditions were perfect for hiking.
a was shining b had shone c shone

8 We ___ for eight hours when the captain told us to prepare for an emergency landing.
a were flying b had been flying c flew

B Complete the story with the correct form of the verbs in the box.

approach carry faint fall fly happen serve take off

Something strange [1] ________ the last time I was on a plane. I [2] ________ to Moscow on a business trip. We [3] ________ from Frankfurt about an hour before, and the cabin crew [4] ________ drinks. Suddenly, one of the cabin crew near me just [5] ________ to the floor. We didn't know if he [6] ________ or had had a heart attack. Other members of the crew rushed to help him, and [7] ________ him to the back of the plane. Just as we [8] ________ Moscow, the captain made an announcement, telling us that the crew member was fine. I was very relieved.

➤ Go back to page 27.

3.2 Alternatives to *if* in conditionals

A Choose the correct options to complete the sentences.

1 They'll survive in the woods ***provided / unless*** they have enough food.

2 ***Unless / Provided*** we leave right now, we'll never make it back to the camp before dark.

3 I'll let you start the fire ***as soon as / as long as*** you know what you're doing!

4 Do Yoon is bringing extra water ***as long as / in case*** we run out.

5 Let's give Margie a call ***as soon as / as long as*** we reach the cabin.

6 ***As long as / Unless*** you have a better suggestion, let's have pizza tonight.

7 I wrote their number on a piece of paper ***in case / unless*** my phone battery dies.

8 We'll go fishing at the river tomorrow ***as long as / in case*** it doesn't rain.

B Are these sentences correct or incorrect? Rewrite the incorrect sentences.

1 We'll call the police as soon as we will get to safety.

2 I'll cancel the trip unless Tara will decide to go with me.

3 You can go to the party provided you're back home by 11 o'clock.

4 Unless the taxi doesn't come soon, we're going to be late.

5 Take some seasickness pills with you in case the ocean will be rough.

6 Will you call me as soon as you arrive at the airport?

7 He'll sleep on the ship as long as the weather won't be too bad.

8 I'll take the risk provided you think it's worth it.

C Match the numbers (1–10) with the letters (a–j) to make conditional sentences.

1 Provided you don't make any sudden movements, ___
2 She won't use her credit card ___
3 You won't get into trouble ___
4 Astrid should give David the money now ___
5 As long as you promise to pay him back, ___
6 I'll come with you as ___
7 Unless we stay late, ___
8 I'm going to take a map with me ___
9 Provided that we stay somewhere cheap, ___
10 I'll buy the tickets ___

a provided you tell the truth.
b I'd love to come with you to Paris.
c in case she doesn't see him later.
d in case we get lost.
e we'll never get all this work done on time.
f he said that he would get the food for the party.
g unless it's an emergency.
h as soon as they're available online.
i you should be perfectly safe.
j long as we make sure we're back home by five.

➤ Go back to page 31.

Grammar Hub

4.1 Future forms

- We use *will* + base form:

  a for decisions made at the moment of speaking (including promises, offers, plans and requests).

  That's a good idea – I'll call him now.
  That looks heavy – I'll carry it for you.

  b to make predictions based on personal opinions or feelings (usually with adverbs like *definitely, certainly, possibly*, etc to show how sure we are).

  Tom will definitely be late – he always is!
  Mom won't like that movie. It's not her sort of thing.

- We use *be going to* + base form:

  a to talk about general intentions and plans made before the moment of speaking.

  I'm going to look for a new job.

  b to make predictions based on present evidence.

  The traffic's not moving – we're going to be late!

- We use the simple present to talk about a timetabled or scheduled event.

  Our flight leaves at 8:30 am on Monday.
  My job interview is tomorrow morning.

- We use the present progressive to talk about future arrangements and fixed plans.

  We're staying in a hostel for the first three nights. (= We've already booked the hostel.)
  I'm meeting Sarah at 7:30 pm outside the restaurant. (= We've already arranged to meet at that time and place.)

4.2 Future perfect, future progressive and future perfect progressive

	Positive	Negative	Question
Future perfect	**The movie will have started** by the time we get there!	**I won't have finished** the report by tomorrow morning.	**Will you have left** by then?
Future progressive	**I'll be seeing** her on Monday, so I could ask her then.	**We won't be using** driverless cars for at least another 50 years.	So, what **will you be doing** this time tomorrow?
Future perfect progressive	In 2041, **we'll have been using** the internet for 50 years.	**I won't have been running** long enough to try a half-marathon in July.	How long **will you have been traveling** by then?

- We use the future perfect (*will* + *have* + past participle) to talk about something that will be finished before a specific time in the future.

  By 2050, we will have greatly improved the air quality in our cities.

- We use the future progressive (*will* + *be* + verb + *-ing*) to talk about an action that will be in progress at a specific time in the future.

  Hopefully, I'll be working in New York by then.

- We use the future perfect progressive (*will* + *have* + *been* + verb + *-ing*) to talk about an action or situation that will continue up to a specific time in the future.

  On July 9th, I'll have been working here for seven years.

- Certain time words and expressions are used with these tenses.

  In 50 years, we'll have stopped using gas-powered vehicles.
  This time next year, we'll be studying in France.
  By 2020, we will have been living together for 20 years.

Be careful!

- Do not confuse these three tenses. The future perfect is used for *completed* actions in the future, while the future progressive is used for actions *in progress* at a certain point in the future. The future perfect progressive refers to how long something will be in progress before a certain point in the future.

  I will have paid for my house by 2025. NOT ~~*I will be paying for my house by 2025.*~~
  I will be living in the US in five years. NOT ~~*I will have lived in the US in five years.*~~
  I will have been living here for 15 years in 2025. NOT ~~*I will be living here for 15 years in 2025.*~~

4.1 Future forms

A Choose the correct options to complete the sentences.

1 I *have / am having* French class every Monday night at seven o'clock.
2 *I'm meeting / I will meet* friends for lunch on Sunday.
3 *We'll probably / We're going to* move this year but I'm not certain.
4 It looks like they *will / are going to* win. They're 4–0 up with only a minute left to play.
5 I think the plane *arrives / will arrive* late.
6 I've had enough of this job! I'm *looking for / going to look for* a new one.

B Complete the post with the correct future form of the verbs in parentheses. Use contractions where possible.

Emily | 20 mins ago

So, big news! I have a place at NYU to study Performing Arts, so [1] __________ (*I / move*) to New York in September! Apparently, I can stay in the residence halls near the main campus, but I've decided [2] __________ (*I / look for*) my own apartment. Wouldn't that be amazing? [3] __________ (*I / definitely / have to*) get a job to pay the rent, but it would be nice to have my own space. I've never lived in another country before, so [4] __________ (*it / be*) difficult to be so far away from my family. But everyone's been so supportive! Anyway, my [5] __________ (*flight / leave*) early on August 28th so if any of you want to meet up before then, just send me a message and [6] __________ (*I / get back*) to you.

C Are these sentences correct or incorrect? Rewrite the incorrect sentences.

1 Having my young nephews to stay in the house next week is being exhausting!
2 The lecture starts at seven tomorrow evening, not eight.
3 I'm afraid that we aren't going on a cruise this year.
4 I'm feeling really tired, so I think I go to bed soon.
5 Are you starting looking for a job anytime soon?
6 We meet Andy and Karim for lunch on May 12th.
7 I probably won't get there until at least ten thirty.
8 I'm helping you do the dishes, if you like.

➤ Go back to page 39.

4.2 Future perfect, future progressive and future perfect progressive

A Choose the correct options (a, b or c) to complete the sentences.

1 It's a nine-hour flight. My plane leaves at 9 am, so at 11 am, I ___.
   a 'll be flying over the Atlantic   b 'll have landed in New York
2 Do you really think you'll ___ at the same company in ten years?
   a have worked   b be working
3 This time next year, he ___ for Real Madrid for ten years.
   a 'll have been playing   b 'll be playing
4 Do you think you ___ English in five years?
   a 'll have studied   b 'll still be studying
5 Is it possible that they ___ the use of fossil fuels by the time our children grow up?
   a 'll be banning   b 'll have banned
6 What will you ___ at three tomorrow? If you're free, let's meet up for coffee.
   a have done   b be doing
7 Next Sunday, I ___ here for two years.
   a 'll have been living   b 'll be living

B Complete the sentences with the future perfect, future progressive or future perfect progressive form of the verb in parentheses.

1 __________ (*you / finish*) your studies by the end of the year?
2 I started learning English over four years ago, so in December, I will __________ (*study*) it for exactly five years.
3 Within the next ten years, robots __________ (*take*) over a lot of tasks.
4 What kind of world do you think we __________ (*live*) in 50 years from now?
5 If the sea level rises, these cities __________ (*completely / disappear*) in 100 years.
6 In June of next year, you __________ (*work*) here for five years.

➤ Go back to page 43.

Grammar Hub

5.1 The passive voice; causative *have* and *get*

The passive voice

Simple present	**Most of the children are taken** to school by bus.
Present progressive	**We aren't being told** the truth about the extent of the damage.
Present perfect	**Has the amount of waste been reduced**?
Simple past	**The deer was killed** by a hunter.
Past progressive	**The forest was being cut down** by construction companies.
Past perfect	**The law hadn't been changed** for years.
will	How **will the park be affected** by the road?
Modals	**The plans can't be changed** now.
The infinitive	**This area** is too polluted **to be used**.

- We use the passive voice (*be* + past participle) when:
  - **a** we don't know who or what caused something to happen, or when this is not important.
    A fire was started in a small area of forest near the park entrance. (= We don't know who started the fire.)
  - **b** we want to focus on the action, not what caused it.
    Huge amounts of CO_2 are being added to the atmosphere every year. (= The focus here is the CO_2 – we aren't really interested in who or what is adding it.)
  - **c** it's obvious from the context who or what caused the action.
    The law has already been changed in many countries. (= It's obvious that it was the government of these countries that changed the law.)

Be careful!

- When we say who performed an action, we use *by*.
  *The research is being carried out **by** the US National Park Service.*

Causative *have* and *get*

Positive	Negative	Question
I'm having solar panels **installed**.	**We haven't had** the windows **replaced** yet.	**Are you getting** a smart meter **fitted**?

- We use causative *have* and *get* (*have/get* + object + past participle) to say that someone does something for us – typically for tasks we can't or don't know how to do ourselves.
  My parents are having a new garage built.
- We can also use causative *have* to describe something unwelcome or negative happening to us.
  I've had my bike stolen twice this month!

5.2 *-ing* and the infinitive

- We use verb + *-ing*:
  - **a** after prepositions.
    *I'm thinking **about moving** to another company.*
  - **b** as the subject or object of a sentence.
    ***Traveling** around South Korea was amazing.*
  - **c** after certain verbs (e.g. *admit, avoid, finish, mind*, etc).
    *I **don't mind living** in the suburbs.*
- We use the infinitive:
  - **a** after adjectives.
    *It can be **difficult to find** your dream job.*
  - **b** to talk about purpose (i.e. what someone wants to achieve).
    I came to New York to improve my level of English. (= This explains why I came here.)
  - **c** after certain verbs (e.g. *agree, attempt, decide, hope, manage, promise*, etc).
    *Has the City Council **agreed to build** more housing?*
- The base form is always used after modal verbs (e.g. *may, might, would*, etc) and after the verbs *let* and *make*.
  *I think I **would make** an excellent candidate for the Mars One program.*

Be careful!

- Some verbs can be followed by either verb + *-ing* or the infinitive, but with a change of meaning (e.g. *forget, go on, regret, remember, stop, try*, etc)
  *I'll never forget **waking up** in Tokyo for the first time. (= I have a memory of this.)*
  *My daughter never forgets **to call** me on my birthday. (= She doesn't forget to do this.)*

5.1 The passive voice

A Rewrite the sentences in the passive voice, omitting the agent where appropriate.

1 Millions of people watch the World Cup final.
The World Cup final ______________________.

2 High CO_2 levels are causing global warming.
Global warming ______________________.

3 We've recently fitted our attic with insulation.
Our attic ______________________.

4 When did they announce the winners of the competition?
When ______________________?

5 The council is going to cut down the tree.
The tree ______________________.

6 A plumber needs to install this kind of shower.
This kind of shower needs ______________________.

B Complete the paragraph with the correct passive form of the verbs in the box.

pick up confirm deliver inform pack print send take

ONLINE SHOPPING
behind the scenes

Someone has just ordered some new clothes online. But what happens behind the scenes before the items can [1] ____________ to their door? Once the credit card payment [2] ____________, an order confirmation email [3] ____________ automatically to the customer, and the people on the packing team [4] ____________ of the order. One of them then picks up the items from the warehouse in order for them to [5] ____________. Next the shipping label [6] ____________, and either the package [7] ____________ by a courier or it [8] ____________ to the post office for its trip to the customer.

➤ Go back to page 51.

Causative *have* and *get*

Put the words in the correct order to make sentences with causative *have* and *get*.

1 getting / I'm / the / locally. / posters / printed
____

2 to / bike / going / get / repaired? / your / When / you / are
____

3 the heating system / at / an electrician. / by / need / get / looked / I / to
____

4 has / her / hair / wife / six weeks. / My / every / cut
____

5 teeth / tomorrow. / having / checked / are / their / The dogs
____

6 new / expensive? / Will / very / having / installed / a / kitchen / be
____

7 having / After / better. / painted, / house / it / much / so / looked / our
____

8 had / their / neighbors / house / night. / into / Our / last / broken
____

➤ Go back to page 53.

5.2 *-ing* and infinitive forms

A Choose the correct options to complete the sentences.

1 We agreed ***to do*** / ***doing*** our project on the topic of megacities.
2 He really appreciates ***to be*** / ***being*** able to travel so much.
3 The council has passed a law ***protect*** / ***to protect*** old buildings.
4 They let us ***walk*** / ***to walk*** around the museum at night.
5 Did you manage ***to book*** / ***booking*** the tickets for the tour?
6 They made her ***completing*** / ***complete*** an online application form.
7 I'm really looking forward to ***having*** / ***have*** a few days off from work.
8 ***Invite*** / ***Inviting*** so many people to dinner really wasn't a good idea.

B Are these sentences correct or incorrect? Rewrite the incorrect sentences.

1 After a poor start, he went on winning the game in the end.
2 I fondly remember to visit Abu Dhabi when I was about your age.
3 I forgot to tell you that I entered that photography competition.
4 We regret informing passengers that the flight to Seoul has been delayed.
5 Stop to talk about your vacations all the time – it's making me jealous!
6 We tried to book tickets for the Coffee Museum in Dubai but it was closed.

➤ Go back to page 57.

Vocabulary Hub

1.1 Feelings

A Label the pictures (1–8) with the adjectives in the box.

awkward	devastated	disgusted	frustrated	furious	overwhelmed	relieved	stunned

1 ______________

2 ______________

3 ______________

4 ______________

5 ______________

6 ______________

7 ______________

8 ______________

B Choose the correct options (a, b or c) to complete the sentences.

1 I was so ___ I had to leave the room. I didn't want a serious argument.
a furious **b** stunned **c** relieved

2 I was ___ when I lost my ring. My grandma had given it to me when I was little.
a disgusted **b** relieved **c** devastated

3 I was ___ by the lack of help. How could people just watch and do nothing?
a furious **b** overwhelmed **c** disgusted

4 To be honest I felt a little ___. We hadn't parted on good terms.
a awkward **b** relieved **c** frustrated

5 I'm so ___ we didn't miss our flight! I don't know what we would have done if we had.
a furious **b** stunned **c** relieved

6 I think my grandpa gets pretty ___ that he can't do everything for himself anymore.
a furious **b** overwhelmed **c** frustrated

➤ Go back to page 3.

1.2 Personality adjectives

A **Match the personality adjectives (1–8) with the definitions (a–h).**

1 I loved his talk. He was so **passionate** about what he was saying. ___
2 You're always so **optimistic**. I wish I could be more positive like you. ___
3 Don't be so **pessimistic**. It might not be so bad. ___
4 She's really **ambitious**. She wants to own her own company in two years. ___
5 Try not to be so **sensitive**. I'm sure he didn't mean to upset you. ___
6 He's really **naïve**. He'll believe anything you tell him. ___
7 She was **determined** to finish the race, even though she was injured. ___
8 You need to be really **flexible** to work here. They are always changing our jobs. ___

a thinking that the worst thing will happen in every situation
b likely to become upset quickly
c lacking experience in life and too ready to trust or believe in others
d showing or expressing strong beliefs, interest or enthusiasm
e able to make changes or deal with a situation that is changing
f being hopeful about the future and expecting that good things will happen
g not willing to let anything prevent you from doing what you have decided to do
h wanting to be successful, rich, famous, etc

B **Complete the job ads with adjectives from Exercise A. Use each adjective only once.**

Salesperson

We are looking for a new salesperson to join our team. We need hard-working people who can reach our high targets. You should be [1] ______________, with big plans for your career. We work long hours, including weekends, so you will need to be [2] ______________ about when you work. Some of our products are challenging to sell so you will need to remain positive and not develop a [3] ______________ attitude.

CHARITY WORKER

Is someone being [4] ______________ and unrealistic when they think they can change the world? We don't think so! We welcome [5] ______________ people who believe that we really can make a difference and that even small things can have a huge impact. We are looking to hire someone who can be [6] ______________ toward people's needs and who is [7] ______________ to help make other people's lives better. If you are [8] ______________ about making the world a better place, then this could be the job for you!

➤ Go back to page 9.

2.1 Health and fitness

Complete the sentences with the words and phrases in the box.

level of fitness	life expectancy	mental health	physical	processed foods	reduce the risk	slow the aging process

1 To remain healthy, adults should do at least 150 minutes of moderate ______________ activity, like bike riding, every week.
2 The average ______________ for women is typically two or three years longer than for men.
3 Some ______________ contain high levels of salt, fat and sugar.
4 Eating a balanced diet and exercising regularly may help ______________.
5 A healthy diet and regular exercise can both significantly ______________ of high blood pressure.
6 Improving your ______________ can help to fight various heart-related diseases.
7 Surprisingly, exercise can also be good for your ______________ because it reduces levels of stress and anxiety.

➤ Go back to page 14.

Vocabulary Hub

3.1 Descriptive verbs

Complete the sentences (1–8) with the verbs in the box.

crackling creaked growling rumbled screeched slamming smashed whirring

1 It was pouring rain and thunder ______________ in the distance.

2 The tires ______________ as she tried to stop the car in time.

3 The floorboards ______________ under his weight as he tried to tiptoe down the stairs.

4 They sat around the ______________ fire, wondering what to do next.

➤ Go back to page 29.

5 He stormed out of the room, ______________ the door behind him.

6 Shining his flashlight through the chain link fence, Todd was greeted by an angry ______________ dog.

7 The figure ______________ the window and reached inside.

8 The fan was ______________ in the corner of the room.

4.2 Intensifiers

Choose the correct options (a, b or c) to complete the sentences.

1 The risks of this kind of technology are ___ greater than any potential benefit.
   a intensely
   b utterly
   c considerably
2 All of the medical professionals that we spoke to said that the idea robots could perform complex surgery was ___ ridiculous.
   a disastrously
   b extremely
   c utterly
3 To be honest, the results were ___ unexpected. I thought we'd need to run several more tests.
   a considerably
   b totally
   c painfully
4 Seeing a computer program that I designed beat a human competitor is ___ satisfying.
   a intensely
   b totally
   c disastrously
5 If we don't put the proper safety measures in place, the results could be ___ bad.
   a disastrously
   b utterly
   c intensely
6 I am ___ sorry to announce that Maria Sanchez will be retiring from the field of robotics.
   a utterly
   b totally
   c extremely

➤ Go back to page 45.

5.2 Prefixes

Choose the correct prefix to complete the sentences.

1 Levels of pollution were so high they needed to ***decontaminate* / *uncontaminate*** the river.
2 They were ***disqualified* / *unqualified*** from the race for cheating.
3 In order to improve travel times, they decided to ***upgrade* / *downgrade*** the subway system.
4 The solution was ***unpossible* / *impossible*** to put into place.
5 The company ***misled* / *disled*** the community about the development.
6 People don't use the train because they feel it is ***overpriced* / *underpriced***.
7 The cost of building new road networks was significantly ***underestimated* / *overestimated***.
8 The excellent infrastructure has allowed the city to ***overperform* / *outperform*** many similarly sized cities.

➤ Go back to page 55.

Communication Hub

3.1 Groups

A PREPARE Work in pairs. Use the pictures (a–g) to tell a story.

B PLAN Join another pair. Together work out the details of your story. Use narrative tenses to help describe the sequence of events.

➤ Go back to page 27.

1.2 Student A

Read the text and write notes about:

- who the person is and why they're famous
- any challenges they faced and how they overcame them
- any other interesting/relevant information

Emily Blunt

Emily Blunt was born in London in 1983. As a young girl, she felt confident and had a lot to say but unfortunately, she struggled because of a stutter. The stutter made it very difficult for Emily to say anything and between the ages of 12 and 13, she was badly bullied by other children. Strangely, whenever she spoke in a different accent or a funny voice, she lost the stutter and was able to communicate. Spotting her talent for different voices and for making people laugh, one of her teachers encouraged her to take part in the school play. But how could someone who struggled to speak stand up in front of the whole school and perform? Emily did the play in one of her funny voices and caught the acting bug. She has since gone on to win a BAFTA and a Golden Globe for her acting and has starred in many successful movies such as *Sicario*, *The Girl on the Train* and *A Quiet Place*.

Glossary

stutter (n) to have difficulty saying something because you can't stop yourself from repeating the first sound of some words several times

➤ Go back to page 7.

5.2 Groups

A PLAN You're going to select three candidates to join the Mars One mission. Read the profiles and write notes on who you would like to select and why.

ADRIAN JENKINS

Leadership Has led teams of dozens of men in dangerous situations.

Personality traits Very determined and strong-minded. Always believes he is right. Not willing to listen to others.

Certifications An MBA.

Unique skills Worked as paramedic. Is an expert in emergency situations.

LINA WANG

Leadership No leadership experience.

Personality traits Quickly forms strong relationships with others. A very creative problem-solver.

Certifications Currently completing a PhD in Physics.

Unique Skills Is recognized as one of the most talented scientists in the world for her age. Three products she has designed have won international awards.

ANA RAMOS

Leadership Has led small teams of marine biologists.

Personality traits Excellent attention to detail. Very organized and well prepared.

Certifications A PhD in Marine Biology.

Unique Skills Experience at spending time in small spaces. Has been on many long research trips to isolated places.

NICOS ALEXOPOULOS

Leadership Has led teams of surgeons for over ten years.

Personality traits Hard-working, with a never-give-up attitude. A perfectionist.

Certifications Certified doctor.

Unique Skills Has worked in many hospitals including many years with Doctors Without Borders in very difficult environments.

VIKTOR POPOV

Leadership No leadership experience.

Personality traits Prefers to spend time on his own. Finds relationships with others difficult.

Certifications Engineering degree.

Unique Skills An experienced explorer. Has done survival training in the jungle and the desert.

GRACE ADEBAYO

Leadership Leads team of volunteers to help build schools and medical facilities in rural areas.

Personality traits Kind, caring and open-minded.

Certifications A degree in Agriculture.

Unique Skills Experienced at growing food in difficult climates.

B DISCUSS Work in groups. Compare your choices in Exercise A. Agree on two candidates to join the Mars One mission.

➤ Go back to page 57.

Communication Hub

5.1 Pairs

A Work in pairs. Read the scenario and predict the cause and effect relationships between the pictures (1–10).

A chemical was sprayed to kill the mosquitoes.

In the early 1950s, an outbreak of malaria threatened the survival of the Dayak people of Borneo. Not knowing how to control the spread of the disease, the islanders turned to the outside world for help.

B Work with another pair. Compare you ideas from Exercise A.

➤ Go back to page 51.

1.2 Student B

Read the text and write notes about:

- who the person is and why they're famous
- any challenges they faced and how they overcame them
- any other interesting/relevant information

Jean-Dominique Bauby

Jean-Dominique Bauby was born in France in 1952. He was an actor and author. He also edited the famous fashion magazine *Elle*. In December 1995, at the age of just 43, he suffered a massive stroke. When he finally woke up, he discovered he had been asleep for 20 days. Most of his body had been paralyzed by the stroke and he had lost his speech. Despite his physical problems, he started writing the book *The Diving Bell and the Butterfly*. He did this by blinking his left eye while someone was reading the alphabet very slowly. He wrote and edited the book completely in his head while dictating one letter at a time. Unfortunately, two days after the book was published, he died. The book went on to be made into a movie, which was nominated for four Oscars and won two Golden Globe Awards.

Glossary

stroke (n) a sudden change in the blood supply to the brain

➤ Go back to page 7.

Write a formal letter asking for information

W structuring formal letters

A Read the letter and answer the questions.

1 What is the purpose of the letter?
2 Who will read it?
3 Why does the writer use a formal register?

B Match the parts of the letter (1–5) with their function (a–e).

a expected response
b reason for writing
c sign-off
d salutation or greeting
e information required

To: French language club
From: John

1Dear Sir / Madam,

2I am writing to inquire about the French language club you organize to find out whether the club is suitable for me or not.

3First, I was wondering if you could tell me how many members there are. Also, could you tell me when you meet and how often? I want to make sure it's possible for me to attend regularly. Could you also tell me how much it costs? Is there a fee to join and then a weekly fee to pay? Lastly, would it be possible to tell me the approximate level of the group members and whether we have any formal lessons as well?

4I would be grateful if you could let me know by email before the next meeting. Hopefully, I will be able to join before then. Thanks in advance for your help.

5Kind regards,
John

C Complete the box with sentences from the letter.

Structuring formal letters

Saying why you're writing
I am writing to apply for …
1 ______

Organizing information
Could you let me know …?
2 ______

Asking for a response
If you could …
3 ______

Sign-off
Yours truly …
4 ______

WRITING

A PREPARE Read the task below and write notes about who you are writing to, what you need to know and what action you expect them to take.

You are interested in joining the hiking club in your area. Write a letter of inquiry and find out:

- how many members there are in the club
- how often they organize walks and where they go
- ask whether there are any fees involved in joining
- what specialist equipment you need.

B PLAN Organize your notes into an appropriate structure for a letter of inquiry.

C WRITE Write your letter of inquiry. Use your plan to help you.

D EDIT Work in pairs. Edit your partner's essay. Check:

- spelling and punctuation
- all information in the task has been covered
- an appropriate structure/tone has been used

Write an article giving advice

W– Using different structures to give advice

A Work in pairs. You are going to read an article titled *Clear the mess and clear your mind*. What advice do you think the author might give?

B Read the article quickly. Which of your ideas from Exercise A does the author mention?

Clear the mess and clear your mind

What better way to start the new year than getting rid of some clutter? Doing so will not only make your house feel more organized, but could also lower your stress levels. Hopefully, the following tips should help you get started!

Throw things away

We keep far more things than we really need to and many of these can be thrown away or given to someone else to use.

- Do you really need or like all of your clothes? Why not go through your closet and see if there's anything you can donate to charity?
- If you don't watch it, listen to it or read it, sell it on eBay. You'll make a little bit of money and have more space!
- Don't forget to look in the garage. Most people use these areas to store things they just don't need or want.
- Don't keep broken things that you know you'll never fix.

Stay motivated

Decluttering can be hugely satisfying, but only if you can stay motivated. Use these basic rules to help you:

- Make sure you don't spend too long decluttering. If you are tired, take a break. It's much harder to make good decisions when you can't think properly!
- Don't leave a task incomplete. If you don't finish what you started, you're likely to become demotivated.

Good habits

Clutter can quickly build up again, so it's important to develop good habits for the future. Use these basic rules to help you:

- Avoid putting things into a pile. Putting them back where they belong will help keep things neat.
- Remember to never buy something on impulse. You can always buy it later if you really want it.

C Read the article again. Complete the table with examples from the text.

Using different structures to give advice
if + simple present + imperative
1 ______________________
2 ______________________
negative imperative
3 ______________________
4 ______________________
5 ______________________
positive imperative
6 ______________________
7 ______________________

D Rewrite the sentences using the words in bold.

1 Drinking coffee after 9 pm is not a good idea.
Avoid ______________________.

2 Why not try putting $20 into a savings account every week?
Try to ______________________.

3 If you don't use your gym membership, cancel it.
It's a good idea to ______________________.

4 Maybe you could turn your phone off in the evenings.
Try ______________________.

5 Try to exercise at least three times a week.
Don't forget to ______________________.

6 Recording the food you eat every day is a good idea.
Remember to ______________________.

WRITING

A PREPARE Work in pairs. Brainstorm advice you could give about one of these topics:

- reducing stress
- improving your diet
- getting in shape

B PLAN Organize your notes from Exercise A into a plan for an article. Think about the clearest way to present your ideas, using headings where appropriate.

C WRITE Write your advice article. Use your plan to help you.

D EDIT Work in pairs. Edit your partner's essay. Check:

- spelling and punctuation
- use of expressions to give advice
- appropriacy of the ideas (e.g. Is the advice clear? Is it good advice?)

You can write…

W using adverbs to add detail to a story

A Work in pairs. What is the worst vacation experience you have ever had?

B Read the story and answer the questions. Underline the parts of the text that gives you the answers.

1 What did they regret?
2 Did anyone fall into the sea?
3 Where did they have to sleep?

Vacation from HELL

Two years ago, my wife and I took a summer vacation in Sicily, Italy. The town we were staying in was beautiful, but there wasn't a lot to do. So, a few days into our stay, we decided to book a boat trip to the volcanic Aeolian islands. I'd just bought a new camera, so I was really looking forward to trying it out in such an amazing place. However, the night before we were due to leave, a terrible storm hit the south coast of Italy, so we assumed our trip would be canceled. The next morning, as we were strolling down to the harbor, the sea looked **incredibly** rough as the waves smashed against the rocks. **Surprisingly**, the trip went ahead anyway. We boarded the boat and waited **nervously** for it to leave. The waves were getting pretty violent and I thought about getting off several times but decided to wait and see if things would be better at sea. It was a decision that I was soon to regret as the boat rumbled out of the harbor.

At first, everything was **strangely** calm, and we wondered why we had been so nervous in the first place. But then the wind started to howl all around us. We rocked backward and forward as huge waves slammed **violently** against the boat, soaking us to the skin. Terrifyingly, benches were thrown from one side of the boat to the other and people all around us were sliding across the deck. **Fortunately**, no one fell over the side.

Finally, we reached the islands. We **rapidly** left the boat and sat shaking on the harbor wall. The staff assured us that the boat would return in three hours, but we were too terrified to go through that again. Strolling around the island, we tried **desperately** to find a hotel for the night so that we could return the next morning on the larger and safer car ferry. However, it was the peak of the summer and all of the hotels were booked up so we had no choice but to spend the night on the beach. An exciting day out had swiftly turned into the trip from hell!

C Read the story again and put the events in the order they happened.

___ arranged a boat trip
___ nervously boarded the boat
___ searched desperately for a hotel
___ a terrible storm erupted
___ waves smashed across the boat
___ slept on the sandy beach
___ walked to the harbor expecting the trip to be canceled
___ benches were thrown side to side and people slid across the deck

D SCAN Complete the box with the highlighted adverbs in the text.

Using adverbs to give detail to a story

We use adverbs of manner (e.g. *slowly*, ____________, ____________, ____________, ____________) to talk about how something happens.

We use adverbs of stance (e.g. *strangely*, ____________, ____________, ____________, ____________) to describe how we feel about something.

E Rewrite the sentences using the adverbs in bold.

1 It was incredible how dangerous the roads were on the island.
incredibly
The roads ____________________.

2 We were nervous as we waited for the rescue team to come.
nervously
We waited ____________________.

3 I was surprised the rescue team took such a long time to arrive.
surprisingly
The rescue team ____________________.

4 It didn't take long for the fire to spread through the building.
rapidly
The fire ____________________.

WRITING

A PREPARE You are going to write a short story about a nightmare trip or vacation. Write notes about:

- the location
- the people involved
- how you felt
- the key events
- contextual details (e.g. the weather, landscape, etc)

B PLAN Organize your notes from Exercise A into a plan for a short story.

C WRITE Write your short story. Use your plan to help you.

D EDIT Work in pairs. Edit your partner's story. Check:

- spelling and punctuation
- use of adverbs
- use of narrative tenses

4 Writing

Write a for and against blog post

W – structuring a for and against blog post

A Read the introduction to the blog post. What issue is the writer going to discuss?

B Work in pairs. Brainstorm ideas for and against the issue.

C Scan the blog post. Which of your ideas from Exercise B are mentioned?

About Blog Contact Search

In order to deal with congestion in cities, some people think that private vehicles should be banned from city centers. Others, however, feel that this is an unrealistic solution and that alternatives would work more effectively. This post will consider both perspectives.

[1]One of the arguments in favor of banning cars is that they are simply unnecessary if public transportation is effective. The needs of individuals can arguably be met by heavy investment in public transportation and the replacement of roads with bike paths. A good example of a city that has taken this idea to heart is Oslo, which plans to ban all cars from the city center by 2019 – approximately six years before a nationwide city ban comes into effect. Oslo is planning to replace almost 50 kilometers of road with bike lanes by the time the city goes car-free.

[2]On the one hand, banning cars seems like a simple way to address congestion in city centers. Yet, on the other hand, serious investment is required to make this feasible. One issue is that extensive public transportation networks would be required to replace cars in city centers. Many networks are seriously outdated or limited in their coverage. Furthermore, many countries simply do not have the financial means to build and extend their networks on such a scale.

[3]I believe that banning cars from city centers is only feasible in cities that already have an effective public transportation system. For everywhere else, cars are simply the most efficient way to get around.

[4]To conclude, while many cities are making steps toward banning cars from city centers, doing so requires heavy investment which many countries may not be able to afford. Realistically, we are a long way from car-free city centers.

D Match the paragraphs (1–4) to their functions (a–d).

a Arguments for ___ **c** Conclusion ___
b Personal opinion ___ **d** Arguments against ___

E Complete the box with phrases from the blog.

Structuring a for and against blog post

Introduction
Many people think that …
1 ______

To give arguments for and against
Some people argue that …
Others think …
2 ______
3 ______
4 ______

To give examples / more information
For example …
5 ______

To give your opinion
I am convinced that …
6 ______

Conclusion
In conclusion, …
7 ______

WRITING

A PREPARE Read the blog topic and write notes of arguments for and against.

Building more bicycle lanes is the best way to address pollution in city centers.

B PLAN Organize your notes from Exercise A into a plan for a for and against blog post.

C WRITE Write your blog post. Use your notes to help you.

D EDIT Work in pairs. Edit your partner's blog. Check:

- spelling and punctuation
- use of phrases to structure their argument
- strength of ideas

5 Writing

Write a problem solution article

W – describing problems and solutions

A Read the introduction to the problem/solution article. What is the main focus of the article?

> **Overcrowding in cities is among the principal dangers facing society today. This article will first look at some of the problems this causes and then suggest a number of possible solutions.**

B Work in pairs. Brainstorm possible problems and solutions for this topic.

C Scan the blog post. Which of your ideas from Exercise B are mentioned?

The main issue facing cities today is overcrowding, and the result is added pressure on public facilities. Schools, hospitals and roads are pushed to the breaking point as the city struggles to keep up with the rapid population increase. A good example of this is the pressure placed on hospitals and doctors, who are expected to deal with growing numbers of patients despite no increase in staff. One way to tackle the increased pressure on public facilities is to regulate building. When building new housing, rules should be put in place to ensure that enough new facilities are constructed at the same time. For instance, for every 1,000 new apartments, an elementary school and a doctor's office should be built by the construction firm.

One of the other foremost problems that occurs as a consequence of overcrowding is the increased levels of traffic. As a result, air pollution increases and traffic slows down. For example, in Mexico City, traffic has slowed to an average of around 10 kmph. One solution might be to build more bike lanes around city centers. This will allow commuters to navigate the city more quickly and will lower the CO_2 emissions. One example where this has been done successfully is Copenhagen in Denmark, where hundreds of meters of bike paths have been built.

In order to tackle the problems of overcrowding, cities should focus not only on building more housing but also on providing the infrastructure needed to support the growing population.

D Read the first paragraph again. Put the following in order to show the paragraph structure.

___ state the solution
_1_ state the problem
___ explain how this will solve the problem
___ show the results of the problem
___ give an example of the solution
___ give an example of the problem

E Complete the skills box with phrases from the article.

Describing problems and solutions

Introduction
X is one of the biggest issues we face …
1 ________________

Problems and results
The biggest threat to …
The foremost problem …
2 ________________
3 ________________

Examples and results
The result is …
4 ________________
A good example of this is …

Solutions and explanations
One way to tackle the issue of X is to …
5 ________________
This will allow …

WRITING

A PREPARE Work in pairs. Brainstorm problems and solutions in response to the following:

> **What are some of the difficulties of living and working in a megacity?**

B PLAN Organize your ideas from Exercise A into a plan for an article.

C WRITE Write your article. Use your plan to help you.

D EDIT Work in pairs. Edit your partner's article. Check:

- spelling and punctuation
- structure and organization
- strength of ideas

Irregular Verbs

Base form	Simple past	Past participle
be	was/were	been
become	became	become
begin	began	begun
break	broke	broken
bring	brought	brought
build	built	built
buy	bought	bought
can	could	(been able to)
catch	caught	caught
choose	chose	chosen
come	came	come
cost	cost	cost
cut	cut	cut
do	did	done
drink	drank	drunk
eat	ate	eaten
fall	fell	fallen
feel	felt	felt
find	found	found
forget	forgot	forgotten
get	got	got
give	gave	given
go	went	gone/been
grow	grew	grown
have	had	had
hear	heard	heard
hit	hit	hit
hold	held	held
hurt	hurt	hurt
keep	kept	kept
know	knew	known
leave	left	left
lend	lent	lent

Base form	Simple past	Past participle
let	let	let
lose	lost	lost
make	made	made
mean	meant	meant
meet	met	met
must	had to	(had to)
pay	paid	paid
put	put	put
read	read	read
ride	rode	ridden
run	ran	run
say	said	said
see	saw	seen
sell	sold	sold
set	set	set
shut	shut	shut
sing	sang	sung
sit	sat	sat
sleep	slept	slept
speak	spoke	spoken
spell	spelled	spelled
spend	spent	spent
stand	stood	stood
steal	stole	stolen
take	took	taken
teach	taught	taught
tell	told	told
think	thought	thought
throw	threw	thrown
understand	understood	understood
wear	wore	worn
win	won	won
write	wrote	written

PHONETIC SYMBOLS											
Single vowels			Diphthongs			Consonants					
/ɪ/	fish	/fɪʃ/	/uw/	new	/nuw/	/p/	pen	/pen/	/s/	snake	/sneɪk/
/iː/	bean	/biːn/	/eɪ/	face	/feɪs/	/b/	bag	/bæg/	/z/	zoo	/zuː/
/ʊ/	foot	/fʊt/	/ɔɪ/	boy	/bɔɪ/	/t/	tea	/tiː/	/ʃ/	shop	/ʃɒp/
/uː/	shoe	/ʃuː/	/oʊ/	nose	/noʊz/	/d/	dog	/dɒg/	/ʒ/	television	/'telɪvɪʒən/
/e/	egg	/eg/	/ju/	use	/juz/	/ʧ/	chip	/ʧɪp/	/m/	map	/mæp/
/ə/	mother	/'mʌðər/	/aɪ/	eye	/aɪ/	/ʤ/	jazz	/ʤæz/	/n/	name	/neɪm/
/ɜː/	word	/wɜːrd/	/aʊ/	mouth	/maʊθ/	/k/	cake	/keɪk/	/ŋ/	ring	/rɪŋ/
/ɔː/	talk	/tɔːk/				/g/	girl	/gɜːrl/	/h/	house	/haʊs/
/æ/	back	/bæk/				/f/	film	/fɪlm/	/l/	leg	/leg/
/ʌ/	bus	/bʌs/				/v/	verb	/vɜːrb/	/r/	road	/roʊd/
/ɑː/	arm	/ɑːrm/				/θ/	thing	/θɪŋ/	/w/	want	/wɒnt/
/ɒ/	top	/tɒp/				/ð/	these	/ðiːz/	/j/	yes	/jes/

Audio scripts

UNIT 1

Lesson 1.1 Listening, Exercise B

1.1 **Mk = Mark S = Sarah F = Fyodor A = Alana**
Mn = Martin Y = Yumi

Conversation 1

Mk: Hello. I haven't seen you here before.

S: Uh, no, I've just joined actually. This is my first Get Together.

Mk: Oh, well, you chose a good group. Everyone here's pretty friendly and we all have a similar level of ability, which helps.

S: That's a relief. I've been learning for about a year or so now. How about you? Have you been playing long?

Mk: Uh, yeah a little bit longer … for about two and a half years. I think I'm alright but I'm no expert.

S: Yeah, me neither. Do you ever perform at all?

Mk: Me? Ha ha! No, no. I'm definitely not good enough for that. I'm just doing this for fun really. How about you?

S: Yeah, same really. It just seemed like a fun thing to do. Anyway, who's leading the group tonight?

Mk: Uh, Lucy, I think. She's actually a professional musician, so we're in good hands.

S: Well I certainly need all the help I can get!

Conversation 2

F: Excuse me, could you tell me where the changing rooms are?

A: Sure. I'm going there now if you want to come with me. I'm Alana by the way. You're new to the Get Together, aren't you?

F: Uh, yeah I am. I've just moved to the area. I was a member of the running Get Together before I moved here.

A: Where were you living before?

F: I was living in Chicago but I got a new job, so I moved to New York. I'm living in Rochester right now, but I might actually move.

A: Oh, really? How come?

F: Well I like Rochester but my apartment is a really long way from the train station and I don't really get along with my roommates.

A: Fair enough. Why don't you like them?

F: Well, one of them works night shifts so he always comes home really late and the other just spends all his time in his room. Maybe I should just look for a place on my own.

A: Maybe, although living with roommates can be pretty fun if you can find the right people.

F: I suppose so. Who do you live with?

A: A couple of friends I've known since college. They can definitely be annoying sometimes, but I wouldn't want to live with anyone else.

F: Sounds fun. Anyway, have you been running long?

A: Uh, no, not long really. I just wanted to, you know, get more into sports and I loved running in college, so I thought I'd give it a try.

F: I see. Are you planning to enter any races this summer or is it a little too soon?

A: Well, I was actually thinking of signing up for the 10K at the end of September.

F: The one in Richmond, Virginia? You definitely should. Ten kilometers sounds like a long way, but it's actually not too bad. I just put in a lot of time training and was completely fine on the day.

A: OK, good to know. Maybe we could do it together?

F: Ha ha! Maybe. I'm doing a half marathon the week before though, so I might not have the energy for another race!

Conversation 3

Mn: Excuse me, could you tell me where I sign in for the book club Get Together?

Y: Uh, yeah, right here actually. I'm running the group tonight. Can I take your name, please?

Mn: It's Martin Pajak.

Y: Oh, yes. I remember your name from your emails. Could I ask you to fill out this form when you get a chance? No rush to return it. Have you had time to finish the book yet?

Mn: Uh, just about! I really like Haruki Murakami.

Y: Oh, really? Me too. Which is your favorite Murakami novel?

Mn: Um, probably *Norwegian Wood*, but I also loved *After Dark*.

Y: *Norwegian Wood* was the first Murakami book that I ever read. I thought it was amazing.

Mn: Oh, well if you like Murakami, you'd probably like Banana Yoshimoto. Especially her first novel, *Kitchen*.

Lesson 1.2 Listening, Exercise B

1.5 **P = Presenter R = Richard**

P: Now we all know that friends are important, but according to our next guest, the type of friends we choose can have a dramatic impact on how successful we are. Here to explain why, is the psychologist Richard Bonnel. Richard, welcome to the show.

R: Thanks for having me.

P: So Richard, we all have hundreds of friends these days …

R: Well, we all know hundreds of people on Facebook, Twitter and other social media sites but how many are actually our friends is debatable. Realistically, research tells us that we can't maintain a friendship group of more than 50 people and, you know, in fact it's probably much smaller if we consider just the people we regularly communicate with.

P: So what type of friends are important to have in your life?

R: Well, our research shows that very successful people surround themselves with six different types of friends. Not six friends but six types. We all need a loyal best friend. Someone who will support us no matter what happens. Someone who knows everything about you. They know all of your secrets but they still love you anyway.

P: I definitely have one of those. There's no way I'd ever let them on this show. They have far too many stories about me!

R: You probably don't need to worry. You can trust them to keep any embarrassing secrets private! Well, they might let one or two things out just for fun … The next type is really important to make your life more interesting. This person is an open-minded adventurer. They always force us into new and different situations. They challenge us. They push us to try new things. They are easy-going and open to new ideas, cultures and activities. None of these things stress them out. Basically, they break us out of our normal routine.

P: I actually think I'm that friend to a lot of people. I'm always taking people to new places and making them do new things.

R: I don't doubt it. These people, they're usually great with people, self-confident and like the attention of others.

P: Are you saying I'm arrogant?

R: No, these people aren't arrogant. They just have a lot of self-belief. Other people probably love it because they are much more cautious than you. You add a little spice to their life! Another type of friend that people need, is one they probably don't always like or want. That's someone who is really honest even when it upsets you.

P: How is that useful?

R: Well, this person will tell you when your hair looks awful or your clothes look terrible. They'll tell you when you're being self-centered and should think about others more. Or they'll tell you you are being stubborn and need to be more flexible. It's tough to hear, but it's usually true.

P: I do have a friend like that. She's very down-to-earth. She just does everything in this very sensible, practical way. I guess she is a helpful person to have around!

R: Right, exactly. Equally, it's important to not just surround ourselves with like-minded people. We should have some friends who are the complete opposite of us.

P: Why would you want to do that? Surely you'd just argue?

R: Maybe, but it opens your mind to different ways of seeing the world. It makes you a more accepting person.

P: True. So, are there any other types of people we should surround ourselves with?

R: Well, the last two are not really types of people but friends we should try to make because of our circumstances. We all move around much more these days and typically have no idea who our neighbors are, but they are important to know. Dependable neighbors can help in difficult situations and make you feel happier about where you live.

P: That is so true. I'm really happy where I live now and it's mainly because of the people living near me.

R: How about work? Are you happy at work?

P: Well, I think I'm pretty lucky. I actually love my job.

R: It's vital that you do. Successful people always work with people they like. Most people spend at least 50% of their waking hours at work. On top of that, people commute to work, work overtime, and think about work. It can take over your life. Imagine feeling isolated at work. No one to talk to. Having no witty people to have a laugh with would make work very boring. A depressing thought, isn't it?

P: When you put it like that, I think I might need to find a new job!

UNIT 2

Lesson 2.1 Listening, Exercise C

2.1 **P = Presenter**

P: OK, let's move onto our next topic. Now, according to a recent survey conducted by The Institute for Social Research, the public, in general, is terrible at sticking to their New Year's resolutions. Apparently, 43% of people surveyed broke their resolution within the first month and 86% lasted less than a year.

To test the accuracy of these results, we sent reporter Emily Hussan out onto the city streets to see just how many of you have managed to successfully give something up for the New Year.

Lesson 2.1 Listening, Exercise D

2.2 **P = Presenter S1 = Speaker 1 S2 = Speaker 2 S3 = Speaker 3 S4 = Speaker 4 S5 = Speaker 5**

Speaker 1

P: Sorry, excuse me. We're interviewing people about whether they've managed to stick to their New Year's resolutions. Did you make any this year?

S1: Yeah, I did actually. Well, the whole family did really. My family and I felt that, well, we really didn't spend enough time together. You know, I found we hardly ever spoke to each other. We, uh, just sat around using our various devices in our own little worlds. We've been living without smartphones and tablets for a couple of months now. I bought everyone really old-fashioned phones that you could only call and text on.

P: How did your children feel about that?

S1: Oh, well, the children went crazy! They were really mad at us!

P: Was it worth it?

S1: Definitely! It was really hard to cope with at first, but since then our lives have, well, changed for the better. We've been spending more time together as a family. And, um, I think we have a better relationship. And you know what? We are all sleeping better as a result of giving up technology.

Speaker 2

P: So, did you try to give anything up for the New Year?

S2: Yeah, I've actually given up coffee.

P: Oh, really? Why?

S2: Well, at the end of last year, I was really stressed at work and it had started to affect my sleep. I was only getting about two or three hours every night and this put me in a bad mood the next day. I thought about exercising more, but I've never really been a gym kind of person. Then I thought, 'Maybe I drink too much coffee.' I used to drink, like, four or five cups a day, but I cut this down to two, then stopped entirely to try and help me sleep better.

P: Good job! And did it work?

S2: Absolutely! I've been living without coffee for months now and get at least seven hours sleep every night. You should try it!

Speaker 3

P: Did you make any resolutions back in January?

S3: Well, I always knew that I didn't have a great diet but didn't realize just how bad sugar is for you. Obviously it can affect your weight, but it can also lead to heart disease, diabetes … even some forms of cancer. Anyway, I read this article that said you should only have a maximum of six teaspoons a day, and I was having way more than that.

P: What, like cakes and chocolate and stuff?

S3: Well yeah, but there's also a lot of sugar in things you wouldn't expect like yogurt, bread …

P: Bread?

S3: Yep! Most processed foods have added sugar. Anyway, I've managed to lose a little weight since cutting down and it's really made me think about my diet in general. I've only had three chocolate bars this month!

Speaker 4

P: So have you made any changes since the New Year?

S4: Not by choice! My car's in the garage right now, so I've been riding my bike to work for the past two weeks.

P: No … sorry, I meant resolutions.

S4: Oh, I see. Yes, well this is going to sound weird, but I've stopped using shampoo.

P: Um, really?

S4: Ha ha! Yep. I've only washed my hair twice this month. Pretty disgusting, huh?

P: It doesn't sound great to be honest.

S4: Well, my hair was pretty greasy at first and I'm sure I didn't smell too great either, but after a few weeks my body seemed to adjust.

P: So why did you decide to give it up? To help the environment?

S4: Uh, no. A lot of people say shampoo contains harmful chemicals, but I don't really think that's true. I actually gave it up because of a friend. She said that my hair was in really bad condition and suggested I try washing it less. I haven't used shampoo since December and my hair feels great. And I've saved a lot of money!

Speaker 5

P: Did you try to give anything up for the New Year?

S5: No, not really. I haven't given anything up for a long time.

P: When did you last give something up?

S5: Um, I'm not sure really. Well actually, I've been vegan for five years now. I wanted to reduce my carbon footprint, which I've managed to do.

P: Oh, really? How's that possible?

S5: Well, it takes so much more water to produce meat.

P: Really? Why?

S5: Well, obviously the animals we eat need to drink water and a surprisingly large amount of water is used to grow their food.

P: Oh, right. How do you feel personally?

S5: I feel healthier. I've lost weight and have more energy.

Lesson 2.2 Listening, Exercise B
2.5 **I = Interviewer F = Frank K = Katie**

I: Many of us have dreamed of escaping the rat race and getting away from our stressful lives, but few of us have ever actually taken the plunge. Well, on today's show we have one family who has done just that. Joining us from their beachfront home is Frank Gerrard and his daughter Katie. Thanks for joining us today. It looks beautiful there! Can you hear me OK?

F: Yes, I can hear you.

I: Now, you've made a dramatic change to your life. What were you doing before?

F: I had a terrible job! I used to work long hours and it was stressful. I was exhausted and overworked. I used to dream of living a quieter and more peaceful life … You know, getting back to nature and that sort of thing. So, I quit my job, sold the family home and we moved here.

I: Wow! That's really a dramatic change! How's it all been going?

F: It's been amazing! We have a small plot of land next to our house and we grow a lot of our own food. I go fishing and hunting every day.

I: Is there a local store?

F: There is, but we hardly ever go. I want to grow or catch everything.

I: So was the change easy for you?

F: Actually, it was a lot harder getting used to the new lifestyle than I thought it would be. When I worked in an office, I was so physically tired all the time because I just sat at my desk all day writing emails. I never really got up and walked around until it was time to go home, and even then I just walked to the station and sat on a train for half an hour. Now I have so many more physical tasks to do to produce the food we need. I'm used to getting up at six o'clock every day now and working hard until it gets dark. Financially, it has also been much harder but we're getting used to it.

I: Would you make the same decision again?

F: For me, definitely! I wouldn't change a thing. As for my family, well I'm not so sure. They miss New York a lot and actually, I'm so busy all the time that we don't really spend that much more time together. We also have way less money now – not that there's much to spend it on!

I: Well this seems like a good point to bring in your daughter. Katie, how did you feel about the decision?

K: I understand why Dad did it. Back in New York, he'd complain about his job constantly. He hated it. Mom just wanted him to be happier. But, well I think it was a stupid idea. He's just having a midlife crisis! Why would anyone want to move here?

I: So, you're not happy there then?

K: No. I used to see my friends all the time in New York. We'd go shopping or hang out in the park. What is there to do here? Walk up another mountain? The internet is terrible too. When I was bored in New York, I used to watch Netflix on my phone or listen to something on Spotify. That kind of thing is just out of the question now because our internet connection is so bad. We also don't seem to have any money now, which is weird – shouldn't we be better off?

I: OK, and what's school like there?

K: It's the worst thing ever! I'm homeschooled now. There's a small school on the island, but my parents want me to take US exams, so Mom is teaching us. I never ever leave the house!

I: Do you think you'll grow to love it?

K: No! I'm really stressed actually. What job can I do here? Where will I go to college? I'm getting used to being isolated from everyone, but I need to think about my future. In New York, I would always think about the exciting jobs and opportunities I could have in the future. I don't want a life like this – all day gathering food. It's boring!

I: Are there any positives about the move?

K: Seriously? No. Well, to be fair, I do enjoy swimming and sunbathing every day, but generally no, I'm bored a lot of the time. I guess I'm not used to it yet.

F: Well, our youngest loves it here. New York isn't great for young children. I was always too worried to let him play outside alone. Now he's out there all day! He would hate to move back to New York. It isn't great for teenagers though, so it might change as he gets older.

K: It definitely will. He's going to be so bored!

I: Well, thank you both for joining us.

UNIT 3

Lesson 3.1 Listening, Exercise C
3.1 **I = Interviewer P = Paul H = Hayley L = Lee**

I: OK, welcome back to the show. Tonight we're talking about extreme sports. Why do so many people take part in such dangerous activities? Where's the fun in putting yourself at such risk? Maybe our next caller can help answer some of these burning questions. Paul, what dangerous sport do you do and why?

P: I'm into climbing. Especially free climbing.

I: When did you first get into climbing?

P: When I was four years old, my dad took me walking in the foothills of the Alps. I can still remember the snow crunching under our feet as we walked together. We always had a lot of fun, but I didn't really get into climbing until I was 17. I remember standing in front of a really steep rock face and thinking, 'Can I do this?'.

I: When did you move onto free climbing?

P: Probably about ten years later. By that point I'd become a pretty good climber and wanted a new challenge. I love the excitement, fear and challenge of it. My father thought it was a great idea because he'd been a good climber too, but my mother was terrified.

I: Have you ever had any accidents?

P: Well, I've had a lot of terrifying moments. Once, I was high up the side of a mountain in Argentina, when the wind started to pick up. It was too dangerous to climb down, so I just had to hold on and wait. In some places, there are also these tiny wooden bridges attached to the side of the mountain to help you get from one ledge to another. Sometimes the wood groans under your weight, which can be a little scary, but so far none have ever actually broken!

I: OK, so what's the most dangerous thing that's ever happened to you?

P: Well, a few years ago I was in South Africa with a few of my friends and we'd almost finished the first part of an all-day climb. I was just pulling myself up when I saw a huge snake right in front of me. I am terrified of snakes, so I just froze as it started to hiss and arch backwards. I waited for another few minutes, not moving, and then it just seemed to get bored and slithered back into a crack in the rock. It was the most terrifying moment ever and it had nothing to do with climbing!

I: Thanks for calling in, Paul. Hope you don't meet any more snakes on your climbs.

I: We have our second caller, Hayley, with us now. Hayley, what dangerous sport are you into?

H: Potholing!

I: What, climbing through caves and things?

H: Yeah, that's right. It's a lot of fun, actually.

I: Hmm …, not sure I'd enjoy it. Anyway, how long have you been potholing for?

H: I first got into potholing in college. There was a climbing and caving society that I joined. I had done a lot of climbing but I'd never done any potholing before. It was amazing!

I: How does it compare to climbing?

H: With climbing, you can see a lot of the route in front of you. Potholing is so dark, and the spaces can be really small, so it's difficult to plan your next move. Usually, you start at the entrance to a cave and simply walk in, but within a few hundred meters you have crawled on your belly, swum underwater, and squeezed your body through tiny gaps. The challenges are just so much more varied.

I: And is it a dangerous sport?

H: It's more dangerous than it sounds. You can suffer from a lack of oxygen or too much carbon dioxide. You can get trapped. You can drown when there's a sudden storm. You can even fall to your death climbing. There are literally hundreds of ways you can die!

I: Sounds scary! What was your most terrifying experience?

H: Once, I got lost when I was deep underground in Mexico. It can be silent for just a few minutes and all you can hear is water trickling around you. It's actually very worrying because you have no maps and no way of communicating with people outside and getting help. Luckily, we managed to get back out the way we had come. By then we had been lost underground for several hours. It was terrifying and took me weeks to get over it!

I: Thank you, Hayley. I have to say, potholing sounds terrifying! So now on to our last caller, Lee. Good evening, Lee.

L: Good evening!

I: So, Lee, what extreme sport are you into?

L: I'm a free runner.

I: OK, so when did you first get into it?

L: It started when I was a child. I used to do gymnastics when I was young, so I was always into climbing and jumping. Then a friend at school showed me a video of a group of people free running and I thought, 'Why not give it a try?'

I: What do you enjoy most about free running?

L: Well, it makes you look at cities in different ways compared to other people. People usually don't even look up when they walk around a city. They focus on everything at eye level – stores, people, cars. You actually really appreciate the architecture more from up high. Every city is a new physical challenge. I get excited and my adrenalin starts pumping!

I: How dangerous is free running?

L: It can be very dangerous. You need to be very aware of your own ability and try not to push yourself too hard. Unfortunately, because it is competitive, people are always pushing themselves to do more and more dangerous things. I have broken a lot of bones. Once, when I jumped between two buildings, I slipped and fell 20 meters. Luckily, I didn't break anything. This other time though, I fell just a couple of meters and I broke my ankle. I can still hear my ankle snap as I landed. It was so painful!

I: Oh, wow! That sounds horrible. Anyway, thanks for joining us, Lee. OK, listeners – we're just going to a short commercial break before we take our next caller.

Lesson 3.2 Listening, Exercise B

3.5 **N = Narrator**

Chapter 2 – Phobias and rational fears

Suddenly, you see something in the corner of your eye. Your palms start sweating, your heart beats faster and your muscles become tense. A tiny spider is crawling across the bathroom wall …

Why is it that many of us fear things that are, relatively speaking, completely harmless, yet don't think twice about real, everyday risks such as driving to work or heart disease?

The ability to calculate risk is essential to the survival of any species. Indeed, one of the most primitive human instincts is to assess our environment for potential threats. This heightened awareness of our surroundings is controlled by a section of the brain called the amygdala. It is responsible for our fear, anger, sadness, and our levels of aggression. It determines how we should react to the things we see before us. Is that a tiger waiting in the bushes or just a trick of the light? Should we run away or stay and fight? This response – commonly referred to as 'fight or flight' – is what makes our heart beat faster and our palms start to sweat. This is actually an essential human instinct, but it's worth noting that for some, the response seems to be overly sensitive. They perceive threats where most people wouldn't and are generally far more anxious as a result. A little like an overly sensitive car alarm that goes off every time somebody walks by.

So it is the amygdala that triggers our initial reaction to a perceived threat. But how do we determine whether the threat is real or not? For this, we rely on the hippocampus and the prefrontal cortex. They compare contextual information with our memories and experience, and decide whether we should be afraid or not. This is useful, because it allows us to decide, for example, to run away when we see a snake in the jungle but remain calm when we see one in a zoo. Essentially, the decision-making part of our brain can tell the emotional part to relax when there is no real threat.

The fact that we rely on our knowledge and experience to determine our emotional response is key to understanding our fears. If, for example, you had a terrifying experience with a dog when you were younger, this is highly likely to influence your reaction to them now. Similarly, if your only knowledge of an airline company is that one of their planes crashed recently, you might well be too afraid to fly with them, even if their overall safety record is very good. Although we are capable of remembering facts or statistics, humans tend to focus on the emotional and the dramatic. For example, according to a cancer research study, skin cancer leads to around two and a half thousand deaths every year. Statistically, this is definitely something worth worrying about. In comparison, there are very few plane crashes every year. Yet when we go on vacation, many of us worry more about the plane crashing than whether or not we remembered to pack our sunscreen.

While our brains are constructed to help us identify, assess and react to potential threats, the heighted levels of anxiety this may cause can actually have a hugely negative effect on our bodies. For example, high levels of stress have a negative impact on the immune system, potentially leading to an increased risk of depression, heart disease and diabetes. And unfortunately, it seems that modern society is designed to increase stress and anxiety. We've become accustomed to 24-hour news coverage, instant access to information and a constant flow of messages, yet it could well be that instead of improving our lives, these all have a negative impact on our physical and mental health. If this is true, how we adapt to our increasingly connected world will be fundamental to our continued survival as a species.

UNIT 4

Lesson 4.1 Listening, Exercise C

4.1 **P = Presenter L = Lucy H = Hadiyah F = Frank**

P: Lenox is a small town in Massachusetts, in the US. Like many other towns in this area, not a lot has changed here over the years, but for these three residents, life is about to change forever.

Lucy Warner has just graduated from high school and is going to start studying for a law degree at Harvard in the fall of next year. However, since she's never left Lenox, she wants to take a year off to go traveling. When I spoke to her, she was busy packing her bags.

L: Can you pass me that bag? The red one behind you …

P: Sure. First of all, congratulations on graduating!

L: Thanks!

P: So, when do you leave?

L: Next Sunday!

P: Wow! So soon.

L: I know! Scary!

P: So, anything specific planned?

L: Well, um, I'm flying to Paris because I have a friend there. Then I'm taking the train to Spain, where I'm staying for a couple of months.

P: Oh right. Why so long in Spain?

L: I want to improve my Spanish. I speak a little, but it's well, just tourist Spanish really. I'm starting a month-long course in Spanish in September. The classes are three days a week from nine to four.

P: That sounds great.

L: Yeah, I don't know. It's just a little fun really. I don't really need another language – everyone there speaks some English anyway!

P: Sounds cool though. Any other exciting plans?

L: I'm really excited about taking the Trans-Siberian Express across Russia into Asia. I think it'll be amazing, a once in a lifetime experience. After that I'll probably spend a lot of time in China. Then, I'm going to visit as many countries as I can.

P: All without flying?

L: Well I'm definitely flying to Australia! I want to work there for a few months and then I might go to the United Kingdom. I don't know if I'll have enough money, though.

P: Another person from Lenox about to have a massive life change is Hadiyah Khan. Hadiyah is expecting her first baby. When I spoke to her, she was busy decorating the nursery. So, big changes ahead for you.

H: Yeah, I'm a little worried about it all actually!

P: Yeah, I think that's only natural. When's the baby due?

H: At the end of May, although apparently first babies are always late! A lot of our time is going to be spent getting things ready for the baby.

P: Do you know if it's a boy or a girl?

H: We don't – we wanted to keep it a surprise. My husband thinks it's going to be a girl, though.

P: Oh really? Why?

H: Everyone in our family has had girls!

P: Have you chosen any names yet?

H: No, we can't decide. There's the possibility of naming her Farrah after my grandma or Nabila after my husband's grandma. If it's a boy, who knows?

P: So, how do you feel?

H: I'm so excited! I've always dreamed of having children. I can't wait for everyone to meet our new baby. I know it's going to be exhausting, though. My sister has two children and I can see it isn't easy. But, you know, it'll be a lot of fun too. I'm honestly just really excited! One thing I am worried about though is getting everything done. Parents are always really busy, so I'm definitely going to have to get better at managing my time.

P: At another stage of their life is Frank Schmitt. Having worked in the local bank for the last 30 years, Frank is now finally retiring. When I caught up with Frank, he was busy buying fishing equipment.

F: What do you think of this fishing rod?

P: Um, I have no idea – I don't know much about fishing to be honest!

F: Me neither. It's just something I finally have time to do.

P: That's right, you're retiring soon.

F: I am, I am, and I can't wait!

P: Do you think you'll miss work?

F: I suppose there's the risk of getting bored, but I doubt it. Everyone wants to retire, don't they? I'll probably just spend the first few months at home relaxing but then we're planning a big vacation.

P: A cruise?

F: No, but another typical senior citizen trip! We bought a huge RV and we're going to travel to different places in the US for a year.

P: Great! Where are you going to go?

F: We haven't planned it exactly. I'm excited to see some of the famous landmarks – the Statue of Liberty, for example. I've been to New York several times, but I've never seen the Statue of Liberty! We're going to start in New York and head down to Florida. After that I'm not sure. I'm looking forward to being more spontaneous!

P: I loved Seattle. You should go there.

F: Really? That's a good idea. I'll add it to the list!

4.5 Lesson 4.2 Listening, Exercise B
P = Presenter M = Mark S = Sarah

P: Good morning, everyone. Welcome to today's debate. Transportation is changing rapidly around the world. More and more cars are becoming electric. Drones are being used for deliveries. So, of all the future predictions about transportation and travel, which are most likely to come true? Here to discuss this with me today are Sarah Atkinson, technology blogger and editor at *The Neo Futurist*, and Mark Edwards, transportation correspondent for *The Evening Express*. So, first, let's talk about driverless cars – do you think we will see these on our roads any time soon?

M: Definitely! The way we get around is going to be entirely transformed. It's not a matter of *if*, but *when* this happens. These are incredibly exciting times!

P: Sarah, what do you think?

S: Sorry, but that is absolutely ridiculous. I firmly believe there is no chance driverless cars will become popular. How can a car make a decision about what to do in a dangerous situation? Should it protect the driver at all costs? What if doing so might mean injuring somebody else? What does it do then? I just think it would be incredibly dangerous to have driverless cars on the road.

M: People's reactions and decision-making are absolutely terrible! It's undoubtedly true that driverless cars will have more consistent and quicker reactions than most drivers.

S: Maybe, but it's still slightly concerning. Driverless cars frequently crash during testing. A driverless bus crashed in its first *hour* of tests in Las Vegas! It's a dangerous development and we simply don't need it.

M: But it would greatly improve our lives! We could work in the car on the way to work. We could have a second car that took the kids to school. You could jump in and out of driverless taxis just paying with your card.

S: The level of associated risk is crazy! Imagine if the car taking your kids to school had an accident. It's a terrifying idea, but fortunately I think it's highly unlikely to happen any time soon.

P: OK, so what about the Hyperloop? Elon Musk's vision of future trains? A pod travels through a tunnel with no friction or air resistance, making it a very fast and efficient way of traveling.

M: Well, I for one think they're an incredibly safe alternative to our current train systems. They could also cut trip times down by 80 to 90%. Imagine that. A four-hour train ride could be completed in less than an hour!

S: Yes, they are very safe, but it won't happen. A Hyperloop train has to be in a fixed tunnel using air pressure and magnets to move the train. The big problem is that they are likely to run just between a few points that are miles apart and go past all of the other big places in between. They will literally go straight past millions of passengers. Governments simply won't spend the money and companies won't either because it will be hard to make a profit.

M: Nonsense! Hyperloop train systems are widely expected to happen. Countries all around the world are investing time and money into their own Hyperloop systems. They're undoubtedly cheaper than building a normal high-speed train and travel times will be greatly reduced. Dubai to Abu Dhabi, normally a two-hour drive, would take just 12 minutes on a Hyperloop train! Why wouldn't cities invest in it?

P: I can imagine some of these developments happening – especially things that save significant time, like the Hyperloop train, and things that free up personal time, like driverless cars. I can imagine companies investing in and developing these ideas because they could make a lot of money, but what about something more futuristic, like the flying cars we see in movies?

M: This always seems like something purely from science fiction, but I don't think flying cars are actually that unrealistic. The technology isn't that far off …

S: Oh, come on. I think you're exaggerating there! We're at least 25 years away from anything like a flying car.

M: Hmm, I don't think so. Dubai police already have self-driving cars and robot police officers. Now they're adding a flying bike to their force. It will greatly improve response times in cities with serious traffic problems.

S: The laws and the health and safety issues here would be frightening!

M: Yes, but society has dealt with major changes before. Imagine what it was like on the early passenger planes taking people on vacation.

That must have been surprising to society and a lot of rules and laws must have been needed, but society coped and moved on.

P: Actually, that brings me to my next point. What about the travel industry? How do you see that changing?

M: Well, I think we're likely to see hypersonic jets and space tourism in the not too distant future.

S: Space tourism? I can't see that really taking off – if you'll excuse the pun! There may be a small market for it, but only among the super rich.

M: Well, we'll see about that. But when it comes to hypersonic jets, I have no doubt that the technology is improving all the time and it's very likely it will become significantly cheaper over time. That means it would be affordable for most people. The Sabre jet developed in the UK could get you from Britain to Australia in four hours. That's almost 20 hours quicker!

S: You seem incredibly focused on speed! I'd be much more interested in a solar plane that was better for the environment. Even if it took me an extra day to get somewhere! In general people think more about the environment today. It's a bigger concern than speed.

M: That could happen as well. I absolutely love the idea of getting places quicker, though. Who wants to sit on a plane for two days? I somewhat agree with your opinion on space travel, though. It's an experience rather than a vacation.

P: Thank you both. Now let's move on to the Q&A section of the debate. Does anyone have any questions on driverless …

UNIT 5

Lesson 5.1 Listening, Exercise A
5.1 **P = Presenter E = Emily H = Harry**

P: We continue this month's focus on going green with a look at eco-friendly homes. Emily Montague reports from a green housing renovation project in Los Angeles.

E: So, Harry, you've decided to make your home much more eco-friendly. What prompted the change?

H: Well, I used to live in a small apartment and I moved into this house a year ago. I was shocked when I got my first energy bill. Three months here cost almost as much as I spent in a whole year in my apartment! I realize that it's a much bigger place, but I just couldn't believe how much more the bill was.

E: So how did you get started?

H: Well, I did some of the easy things myself first. I put energy-efficient lightbulbs in every room and put new attic insulation in, but I wanted to make a lot more changes. If you come out into the backyard, I'll show you what we're working on now.

E: Ah, I can see you're having solar panels installed.

H: We are. By having these, we can produce about 50% of our own energy every year. In the summer, we'll produce more than we need and then we can sell it back to the energy companies. There's something else that's interesting about this roof though …

E: Oh, really? What's that?

H: The company also transformed the roof into a small garden. They put in wild flowers that attract bees. We've had a bee hive put in at the end of the garden and now we produce our own honey. This will make our roof an energy source and a food source!

E: Amazing! Oh, and what's that over there?

H: That's a rain barrel, but it's not just for the garden. We've had our toilet system changed. Our toilet now flushes with rainwater. Any extra water comes down here to this rain barrel for the garden. We save a lot of water this way. These windows are new as well.

E: Aren't they just double-glazing?

H: They are, but they are much more modern and energy efficient. They have a type of glass fitted that reflects energy back into the house. They also have a different type of gas in between instead of air. This helps to further reduce heat loss.

E: I can hear a lot of work going on as well. What else are you having done?

H: You see this box here? It takes heat from the ground into the house. Come into the living room … We're getting underfloor heating fitted. It reduces our energy bills and it looks a lot better than radiators! And, here's the kitchen.

E: Wow! That is one modern looking fridge!

H: I was fed up with throwing out so much food, so I bought this fridge. We order our food online and the fridge knows what we have in it. It then recommends food to cook! It's amazing really and we waste less food.

E: I can hear people working upstairs. What are you having done up there?

H: Come up. We're having a new energy efficient shower installed. It limits how long you can shower for and how much water is used. It obviously saves energy and stops water wastage, but it also saves time.

E: How so?

H: It turns off automatically once you've used a certain amount of water. It means some people can't spend all morning in the shower!

E: Not sure I'm too fond of that idea! Any other plans?

H: Yes, we need to get the walls better insulated. I want to use a natural product though, so we're just waiting for it to be delivered. We're also getting a smart meter installed. Hopefully, it'll help us keep an eye on how much – or how little – energy we're using!

E: Thank you, Harry, for showing us around your home. I have to say, it looks amazing!

5.2 Listening, Exercise B
5.7 **I = Interviewer A = Agatha T = Tim B = Bernie**

I: For centuries, man has been obsessed with the idea of going to Mars. Indeed, for a long time, our little red neighbor was the focus of almost all science fiction but now for some it might become a reality. We spoke to three of the Mars One candidates hoping to take part in the first manned mission to Mars. I caught up with one of the candidates, Agatha Nowak, in the library of her university. Agatha, nice to meet you. Why do you want to sign up?

A: Well, partly this will be a break, you know, a break from the usual day-to-day stuff. Like cleaning, shopping, studying … Also though, I'm a PhD student and I think it's important to advance science whenever the opportunity presents itself. To me, the Mars One project is exactly this kind of opportunity. The technological advancements made after the moon landings were amazing and I think this project could have the same effect.

I: But this is a one-way ticket. You'll never come back to Earth! Isn't that scary?

A: It is, but I'm also really excited.

I: So, why do you think you would be a good candidate?

A: I'm a really positive person with a lot of energy. I work really well as part of a team and get along with everyone. That's going to be key.

I: Surely, being a scientist is the most important thing you bring to the team?

A: I don't know. Maybe. Being a scientist isn't enough, you need to be able to live in a small space with other people for a very long time! We can't, you know, just pack up and leave if we're not happy.

I: True! How are you preparing yourself for it?

A: Can you prepare yourself? I don't know. One guy I know is eating just dried and canned food to get used to the lack of fresh things. I'm not sure that's a great idea. We need as many nutrients as possible before we go!

I: What are you expecting when you first land on Mars?

A: A lot of hard work! We'll have limited food. We'll have to eat dried and rehydrated food at first. Once we establish a community, I think we'll have to attempt to grow our own food, which is going to be challenging. And we also need to build somewhere to live. I've watched people try to build a shelter in the wild on TV and they really struggle. Imagine trying to do it in a spacesuit!

I: What are you going to miss most?

A: I really appreciate drinking a good cup of coffee every morning. Can anyone live without coffee? I read about the coffee machine on the International Space Station, so I'm hoping we get one!

I: Another candidate hoping to join the mission is Tim Davis. Tim loves to challenge himself and is hoping this will prove the ultimate challenge.

I: Can you take a short break?

T: Sure.

I: How far will you run later?

T: Just a short 30K run. Nothing too hard.

I: That sounds pretty far to me!

T: Not really. I've run a lot of marathons and a few ultramarathons. I'll never forget running across the Sahara Desert for seven days. I've always tried to challenge myself physically. I've climbed the tallest mountains in three continents of the world.

I: You like a challenge then?

T: Who doesn't enjoy a challenge? There aren't many left for me on this planet, so why not go to another one?

I: Are you worried or scared at all?

T: Why would I be scared? There's risk in everything we do, and people are just bad at assessing it. Some people worry about flying but you're much more likely to die driving to the airport.

I: True. So, you seem very driven.

T: I am. Everyone wants to leave their mark behind, don't they? Most people choose to have children as their legacy. This will be mine. I'm going to Mars to be a part of history. I'm excited, not scared.

I: What are you going to miss?

T: Well, probably just the simple things in everyday life. I'll miss my friends and family a lot. I'll definitely miss fresh food and just being able to pop into a store to buy something whenever I want.

I: Are you ready?

T: As ready as I'll ever be. I'm not worried about the physical aspect, but emotionally I think it's going to be tough.

I: The last candidate I spoke to is 50-year-old Bernie Johnson. Bernie is an environmentalist from the south. When I caught up with him, Bernie was doing a little last-minute shopping.

B: … yeah, maybe. Can you pass me a bag?

I: Sure, here you go. So, why do you want to sign up anyway? It's such a long way.

B: It's vital for the future of humans! We have to learn to live independently of planet Earth. The world is not going to end anytime soon, but we have made a real mess of things.

I: Why do you think we've been so terrible?

B: Well, you know, we've made a mess of Earth! We've used a lot of natural resources, driven species to extinction and chopped down most of the forests of the world!

I: So, what are you doing to prepare yourself for the mission?

B: I'm trying to live a more isolated life. Some people get really stressed when they forget to take their phone with them. I'm turning off my phone, and permanently disconnecting the internet. For my vacation this year I'm not going away anywhere … I'm staying at home for a month.

I: Is that why you're buying a lot of canned and dried foods?

B: That's right. I'm going to spend a month not talking to anyone except my wife. I'm buying enough food to last for four weeks and we aren't going to leave the living room.

I: Is your wife happy with that?

B: Well, she'd rather be going to Greece or somewhere nice, but, you know, she supports me. It's going to be difficult to live just inside one room, but I think it will be great preparation. I have promised her an amazing vacation next year to make up for it!

I: And how does she feel about you going to Mars?

B: Actually, she seems pretty happy about it …

I: Fair enough. So, if you did get selected, what would you miss about Earth?

B: Well, my wife, obviously. But in general, I think I'll miss being connected to other people. Our world is so small now, really. When you feel lonely you can pick up your phone to connect with a lot of people in seconds.

I: True. Anything else? Like food or something else?

B: Um, I don't know. Actually, yes. Strangely, I think I'll miss everyday noises. I'm used to living in a big city and there are so many sights and sounds to keep you stimulated. In space, all you can hear is endless silence. That could be very disturbing!

Macmillan Education
4 Crinan Street
London N1 9XW

A division of Macmillan Education Limited

Companies and representatives throughout the world

American Language Hub Level 4A Student's Book ISBN 978-1-380-04740-3
American Language Hub Level 4A Student's Book with Student's App
ISBN 978-1-380-04734-2

Text, design and illustration © Macmillan Education Limited 2020
Written by Louis Rogers

The author has asserted their right to be identified as the author of this work in accordance with the Copyright, Designs and Patents Act 1988.

The right of Ben Goldstein to be identified as the author of the Speaking pages in this work has been asserted by him in accordance with the Copyright, Designs and Patents Act 1988.

First published 2020

All rights reserved. No part of this publication may be reproduced, stored in a retrieval system, or transmitted in any form or by any means, electronic, mechanical, photocopying, recording, or otherwise, without the prior written permission of the publishers.

Designed by emc design ltd
Illustrated by Daniel Limón (Beehive illustration) pp 44, 45, 50, 52, XVI, XVIII, XX, XXII
Cover design by Restless
Cover photograph by plainpicture/Westend61/Uwe Umstätter
Picture research by Emily Taylor

Authentic video footage supplied by BBC Studios Distribution Limited
Café Hub videos produced by Sharp Focus

The authors and publishers would like to thank the following for permission to reproduce their photographs:

Alamy/Art Directors p54(cm), Everett Collection Inc p43, Kertu Saarits pp54–55; **BBC Studios Distribution Limited** p46; **Corbis** p31(knife); **Getty Images** pp15(3), 16(d), AFP p10, Ajr images pXXI(tr), Aluxum p29(6), Cecilie Arcurs pXXI(tl), Atsushi p20(cr), Aurora Open p31(bl), Ezra Bailey p32(b), Thomas Barwick p15(6), Leland Bobbe pXXI(br), Dan Brandenburg p3, Niels Busch pXXIV, Peter Cade p4(tr), Caiaimage pp14, 38(c), Cultura RF pp41, 53, Peter Dazeley pp39, 58–59, Digital Vision pp15(2), E+ pp16(a), 32(tr), 38(b), Flashpop p8, Jamie Garbutt pXXI(bl), Geber86 p19(tr), Alexander W Helin p49, Hero Images p37, Hulton Archive Creative p40(tr), iStockphoto pp4(tl), 16(f), 18–19, 20(t), 31(phone, fishing kit), Jupiterimages p33(bm), Ulla Lohmann p25, Jacob Lund Photography pXXIII, Dave Kotinsky p7, John Lamb pp10–11(background), Mikolette p32(tr), Morsa Images pp46–47(background), XXI(cr), Aleksandar Nakic p38(a), National Geographic Creative p28(3), National Geographic Magazines p28(4), National Geographic RF p34, Rick Neves p28(2), Lauri Patterson p16(b), PeopleImages p33(bl), Peter Mason Photography p15(4), Ian Ross Pettigrew p20(cl), Martin Poole p58(tr), Real444 pp6–7(background), RooM RF pp13, Asahi Shimbun p27(tr), Marco Siori/EyeEm p31(lighter), SolStock p5(tl,b), Alexander Spatari p22(br), Steve Cole images p17, Michael Stewart p6(tr), Stocktrek Images pp56–57(b), Svariophoto p16(e), Karwai Tang p6(tl), Tetra images pXXVI, Towfiqu Photography p16(c), Urbancow pXXVII, Klaus Vedfelt p1, VisualCommunications p28(1), Dennis Wagner/EyeEm p51, AJ Watt pXXI(cl), Wilpunt p15(5), Dong Wenjie p33(br), Martin Zwick pp34–35(background); **Photodisc** pp22–23, 29(5), 42–43(background), 56(tr); **Reuters Images**/Joe Brock p27(bl); **Rex Features**/Shutterstock/Paul Cooper pXXII; **Shutterstock**/Pressmaster p38(d); **Thinkstock** p31(rope)

Commissioned photographs by Sharp Focus pp11, 23, 35, 47, 59

Printed and bound in Mexico
Compañía Editorial Ultra, S.A. de C.V.

2021 2020

4 3 2 1

The author and publishers are grateful for permission to reprint the following copyright material: Extract from 'How Wolves Change Rivers – video' by GrrlScientist. Originally published in The Guardian, 03/04/2014. © 2018 Guardian News and Media Limited or its affiliated companies. All rights reserved. Reprinted with permission of The Guardian, pp50–51.

These materials may contain links for third party websites. We have no control over, and are not responsible for, the contents of such third party websites. Please use care when accessing them.

The inclusion of any specific companies, commercial products, trade names or otherwise does not constitute or imply its endorsement or recommendation by Macmillan Education Limited.

American Language Hub

LEVEL 4A
Workbook

with Key + access to Audio

macmillan education

Macmillan Education
4 Crinan Street
London N1 9XW
A division of Macmillan Education Limited

Companies and representatives throughout the world

American Language Hub Level 4A Workbook with Key ISBN 978-1-380-04743-4
American Language Hub Level 4A Workbook with Key + access to Audio
ISBN 978-1-380-04737-3

Text, design and illustration © Macmillan Education Limited 2020
Written by Signature Manuscripts

Signature Manuscripts has asserted their right to be identified as the author of this work in accordance with the Copyright, Designs and Patents Act 1988.

First published 2020

All rights reserved. No part of this publication may be reproduced, stored in a retrieval system, or transmitted in any form or by any means, electronic, mechanical, photocopying, recording, or otherwise, without the prior written permission of the publishers.

Original design by emc design ltd
Page make-up by SPi Global
Cover design based on original design by Restless
Cover photograph by plainpicture/Westend61/Uwe Umstätter
Picture research by Emily Taylor

The author and publishers would like to thank the following for permission to reproduce their photographs:
Alamy/Peter Alvey p33(8), Alamy/Robert Cinega p19(ml), Alamy/Clynt Garnham Environmental p33(3), Alamy/Ian Dagnall p8(br), Alamy/Arno Masse p30(2), Alamy/Tom Pfeiffer p19(br); **Getty Images**/Danilo Andjus p31, Getty Images/AzmanL p12, Getty Images/Bettmann p8(bl), Getty Images/Claudia Burlotti p7(tm), Getty Images/David Chen/EyeEm p20, Getty Images/Robert Cinega p19(tr), Getty Images/Bart Coenders p33(5), Getty Images/Ashley Cooper p28, Getty Images/Nick David p14, Getty Images/Nick Dolding p27, Getty Images/Andrew Errington p24, Getty Images/Filmfoto p33(7), Getty Images/Flashpop p7(tl), Getty Images/Sepp Friedhuber p36, Getty Images/J Galione p30(3), Getty Images/Linda Goodhue Photography p25, Getty Images/Johnny Greig p30(1), Getty Images/Mario Guti p33(1), Getty Images/Dimitrios Kambouris p8(tr), Getty Images/Kristina Kohanova/EyeEm p7(tr), Getty Images/Peetatham Kongkapech p22, Getty Images/Darryl Leniuk p19(bl), Getty Images/Maskot p29, Getty Images/Dieter Meyrl p21, Getty Images/Morsa Images p18, Getty Images/Min p15, Getty Images/Mint Images p32, Getty Images/Vladimir_N p33(2), Getty Images/PeopleImages pp4, 32(man), GettyImages/Praetorianphoto p5, Getty Images/Martin Prescott p33(6), Getty Images/Georgy Rozov/EyeEm p34, Getty Images/Simonkr p19(window), Getty Images/Skynesher p16, Getty Images/Starcevic p38, Getty Images/StefanSchuetz.com p26, Getty Images/Hendrik Sulaiman/EyeEm p33(4), Getty Images/Watsamon Tri-yasakda p32(woman), Getty Images/Vitranc p6, Getty Images/Sharon Vos-Arnold p13, Getty Images/Westend61 pp10, 11, 17, Getty Images/Jian Yi Song/EyeEm p19(mr); **StockstudioX** p35; **Superstock** p8(tl).

Additional sources: Tolentino, M. 2014, *Smart Home market to boom in 2020: New trends in smart elevators + smoke detectors*, SiliconANGLE, p29; Kasimis, C. 2010, *'Demographic trends in rural Europe and international migration to rural areas,'* Agriregionieuropa, vol. 6, no. 21, p37.

These materials may contain links for third party websites. We have no control over, and are not responsible for, the contents of such third party websites. Please use care when accessing them.

The inclusion of any specific companies, commercial products, trade names or otherwise does not constitute or imply its endorsement or recommendation by Macmillan Education Limited.

Printed and bound in Mexico
by Compañía Editorial Ultra, S.A. de C.V.

2021 2020
04 03 02 01

Contents

VOCABULARY
Feelings

A Choose the correct options (a, b or c) to complete the sentences.

1 Work is really stressful right now. I just feel so ___ all the time.
a relieved b awkward c tense

2 How can you eat like that? I'm ___ just watching you.
a thrilled b disgusted c overwhelmed

3 I was ___ to discover that he had stolen money from me.
a horrified b thrilled c tense

4 We were all ___ to hear that Jim had gotten back safely.
a relieved b disgusted c furious

5 My daughter was so ___ when she passed all her exams.
a horrified b devastated c thrilled

6 Sometimes I just feel so ___ by the amount of work I have to do.
a overwhelmed b relieved c awkward

7 I think we all felt really ___ that there was nothing we could do to help.
a impressed b frustrated c disgusted

8 If I lose my job because of this, I will be ___ with you!
a relieved b stunned c furious

9 The Patriots were ___ by the Steelers' last-minute touchdown.
a thrilled b overwhelmed c stunned

10 Actually, I was really ___ by his level of commitment.
a impressed b furious c relieved

B Complete the text with the adjectives in the box.

frustrated impressed relieved stunned tense thrilled

It had been a difficult year at work and Jake (who never won anything) was [1] ___ when he found out that he had won an international vacation in a competition. When he arrived, he loved everything about the place – the hotel, the countryside and the beach, which was only five minutes' walk away. He was particularly [2] ___ by the food at a local restaurant and used to go there every evening to try out different dishes.

One evening, as he was eating, Jake thought the staff seemed a little [3] ___. They were polite to him, but they didn't seem as relaxed as usual, and one of the waiters looked really angry. Jake didn't pay much attention – after all, nobody is bright and cheerful all the time – but a little while later, he thought he heard raised voices in the kitchen. Soon after, there was yelling, but more alarmingly, a lot of smoke coming from the kitchen. Jake was [4] ___ because he couldn't understand what they were saying, but the message soon became clear – the restaurant was on fire and they had to get out fast! While the staff battled in vain to put out the fire, Jake and the other customers looked on from a safe distance, most of them too [5] ___ to even speak.

The following day, they learned that one of the waiters had thrown a pan of hot oil across the kitchen, and that was what had caused the fire. Everyone was shocked when they saw the damage – there was nothing left of the restaurant – but they were all [6] ___ to hear that there were no injuries.

GRAMMAR
Question forms

A Reorder the words to make questions.

1 where / could / nearest / is / the / you / me / tell / bank
______?

2 is / your / name / I / ask / what / can
______?

3 are / what / about / you / thinking
______?

4 there / you / happened / what / when / got
______?

5 meal / the / you / like / didn't / about / what
______?

6 today / is / the / class / taking / who
______?

7 know / you / do / lives / he / where
______?

8 that / you / repeating / mind / would
______?

B Rewrite the direct questions as indirect questions.

1 When is the test?
Could you tell me when ______?

2 What is your name?
Do you mind telling ______?

3 How old are you?
Can I ask you ______?

4 Where do we have to go?
Do you know ______?

5 Where do I sign my name, please?
Excuse me. Could you tell me ______?

6 Please sit down over there.
Would you mind ______?

7 What is your address?
Can I ask you ______?

8 What time is it?
Do you know ______?

C Complete the questions with the correct form of the words in parentheses.

1 You must be joking! Why ______ (*you / not tell*) me this before?

2 What ______ (*you / talk / about*)? I finished it last week!

3 Can you tell me what ______ (*happen / yesterday*)?

4 ______ (*you / know*) the manager personally?

5 So, you said your vacation wasn't great – what ______ (*you / not / like*) about it?

6 You're not from here, are you? Where ______ (*you / grow up*)?

7 Who ______ (*you / talk / to*) outside earlier?

8 ______ (*who / you / go*) to Brussels with tomorrow?

PRONUNCIATION
Intonation in *yes/no* and *wh-* questions

1.1 **A** Circle the arrows to predict which intonation will be used in each question. Then listen and check.

1 Do you need any help with your bags? [↗] / [↘]
2 What time would you like to meet? [↗] / [↘]
3 Do you want anything else to eat? [↗] / [↘]
4 What seems to be the problem? [↗] / [↘]
5 How long have you been living at your current address? [↗] / [↘]
6 Are you ready to go? [↗] / [↘]
7 Have you asked her about it? [↗] / [↘]
8 How much do I owe you? [↗] / [↘]

1.1 **B** Listen again and repeat.

GRAMMAR
Tense review

A **Choose the correct options to complete the sentences.**

1 What ***were you doing*** / ***did you do*** between three and five o'clock yesterday?

2 I made sure ***I'd*** / ***I've*** done all the housework before I left this morning.

3 Apparently, ***he works*** / ***he's working*** this Saturday so he can't come.

4 Sorry, I can't stop – I ***have to*** / ***had to*** pick the kids up in half an hour.

5 I met her while I ***was traveling*** / ***had traveled*** around South-East Asia.

6 You aren't going to believe this – ***I've*** / ***I'd*** passed all my exams! Isn't that great?

7 Conditions were terrible – it was freezing cold and it ***rained*** / ***was raining*** heavily.

8 I ***grew*** / ***have grown*** up in France, but strangely I've never been to Paris.

B **Complete the sentences with the correct form of the verbs in the box. Use contractions where possible.**

close finish leave live see sell out

1 This is ridiculous – I can't believe he ________ ________ the report yet!

2 I ________ just ________ the house when the phone rang.

3 Apparently, all of the tickets ________ by the time she got there.

4 We'd better hurry up – the store ________ at 4 pm on Sundays.

5 Actually, I ________ him on Friday – you should come along.

6 I ________ in New York for eight years, but never went to the Empire State Building.

C **Complete the interview with the correct form of the verbs in parentheses. Use contractions where possible.**

Interviewer: So would you say you [1] ________ (*face*) a lot of challenges in your life up until now? What was your childhood like, for example?

Joe: Well, actually – something pretty crazy happened to me while I was growing up. My parents came to get me from school one day and told me that our house [2] ________ (*burn*) down – there was nothing left of it. I was nine years old. That was quite a challenge.

Interviewer: Wow! That must have been awful. It [3] ________ (*sound*) like a devastating experience, especially for someone so young.

Joe: Yes but, in a funny way, I think I was young enough to get over it – it would be much worse to go through that now.

Interviewer: I see. Apart from that one extreme event, was your childhood a happy one?

Joe: Let me think … Yes, I [4] ________ (*have*) a happy childhood. Things got a little difficult later, though. I [5] ________ (*not be*) very happy in college, so I left. That was really tough because I [6] ________ (*look*) for a job for at least six months before I found one. But I think I [7] ________ (*go*) through my biggest challenge right now, actually. It isn't easy getting started in my profession – especially when you're a foreigner.

Interviewer: No, I guess it isn't. I [8] ________ (*not think*) about that. Good point.

VOCABULARY
Personality adjectives; Noun suffixes

A Match the beginnings of the sentences (1–8) to the endings (a–h). Use the adjectives in bold to help you.

1 Elias is so **stubborn**! He can … ____
2 The manager is pretty **optimistic** about the target. He thinks … ____
3 Don't be so **self-centered**. You should … ____
4 He is talented, but he's **arrogant** too. He … ____
5 She's incredibly **witty** actually. After five minutes with her, I … ____
6 I worry about Kelly being so **naïve**. I'm afraid … ____
7 I think I'm an **open-minded** person – I'm always ready … ____
8 Freya is very **down-to-earth**. You'd never know … ____

a is always telling people how great he is.
b people will hurt her feelings.
c that she was rich.
d never admit when he's wrong.
e think about others for a change.
f to hear different viewpoints.
g the team should reach it by July.
h can't stop laughing.

B Complete the sentences with the noun form of the adjectives in the box.

arrogant confident determined different loyal optimistic responsible stubborn

1 I wish I had had the ____________ to speak up when I see something like that.
2 His ____________ when he was talking about his success was very annoying.
3 The team's ____________ paid off in the end when they got the victory they needed.
4 When everything started to go wrong, Carl began to lose some of his natural ____________.
5 It is the company's goal to encourage brand ____________ so that you keep buying their products.
6 I'm sorry, but the break-in is your fault. It was your ____________ to make sure the office was locked up.
7 Can you tell the ____________ between these two photos? They both look the same to me.
8 His ____________ prevented him from apologizing and saving his job.

PRONUNCIATION
Connected speech: final consonant and initial vowel

1.2 **A Listen and draw (‿) to show the connected speech.**

1 You can't always get what you want in life.
2 Alex isn't an easy person to get to know.
3 Actually, he's not at all like his brother.
4 Marco will support us whatever we end up doing.
5 Everyone at work has been really understanding about it.

1.3 **B Read the sentences. Draw (‿) to join the words where one word ends with a consonant and the next begins with a vowel. Then listen and check.**

1 How far is it to your house – will it take long to walk?
2 My job is much better now that I work from home on Wednesdays.
3 He was generally thought of as lazy and disruptive.
4 I think I've done the best I can on this project.
5 I think it's important to talk to people we don't agree with.

1.3 **C Listen again and repeat.**

READING

A PREDICT Look at the title of the article and the pictures. What do you think these four famous people had in common?

B SCAN Read *Through thick and thin* quickly to check your answers to Exercise A.

C SKIM FOR MAIN IDEAS Read the article again. Choose the correct sub-headings (a–f) to complete the article. There are two extra headings you do not need to use.

- **a** Don't let failure stop you
- **b** Inspiration can strike when you least expect it
- **c** Physical strength can be beneficial
- **d** Discipline and training is key
- **e** Bravery will help you achieve
- **f** Be prepared to take new paths

D READ FOR DETAIL Read the article again and answer the questions. Underline the parts of the text that give you the answers.

1. What effect did Demosthenes's initial failure have on him?
2. What methods did he use to improve his speech?
3. How successful was Spielberg's first movie?
4. What was his first big break?
5. What was Lincoln's first occupation?
6. Which occupation led him to a career?
7. Why did Frida Kahlo change the way she dressed as a child?
8. Did she always want to be an artist?

E REFLECT Think about the answers to these questions.

1. Which of the stories do you find the most inspiring? Why?
2. Apart from the four lessons highlighted in the article, what other things do you think are key to success?

Through **Thick** and **Thin**

When life gets too much for us, reading about people who have struggled against the hard circumstances of their birth and upbringing can put things into perspective. Here are four lessons from inspiring figures who never gave up:

1 ______________________________

If you had a stammer, you probably wouldn't choose public speaking as a profession. Demosthenes – an ancient Greek politician – managed to overcome his speaking difficulties to become the greatest orator of his time. His first attempt at public speaking was a disaster, but criticism just made him more determined. He shut himself away, read a lot and practiced speaking day and night. It is said that he would fill his mouth with small stones and practice speaking with a knife held between his teeth to get rid of his stammer and improve the strength of his voice. All his hard work paid off: he went on to become one of the leading political figures in Athens.

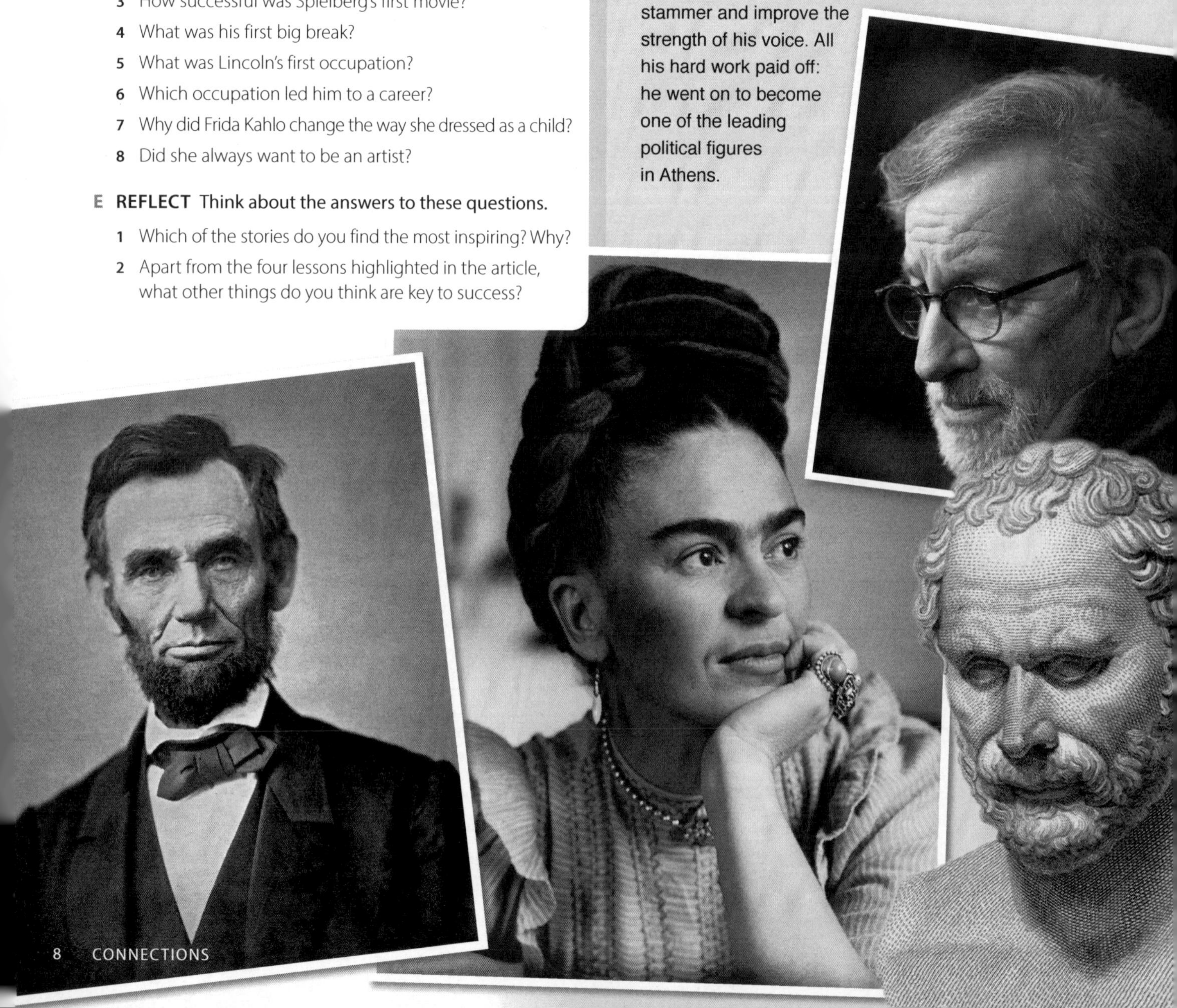

2 ______________________________

Steven Spielberg may not have been born into poverty or suffered a physical disability, but his path to success wasn't easy. The grandson of Ukrainian immigrants, Steven was bullied as a child, and his parents' divorce while he was in high school was a further blow. He dreamed of being a movie-maker, but his first commercial movie made a profit of only $1, and his first TV show was considered so bad that it had to be re-shot by someone else. A year later, he was given a second chance, and this time, there were calls for him to be fired. He admitted that if he hadn't then been given the chance to direct the movie *Duel*, he might have given up. Then came *Jaws* and the rest is movie history.

3 ______________________________

Abraham Lincoln was born in 1809 to poor and probably illiterate parents. His mother died when he was nine years old and Lincoln was immediately put to work on the family farm. He had little formal education, but it is said that he would walk for miles just to borrow books. For a few years, he was a manual laborer and was said to be good at using an axe. Life was tough, but these years strengthened him. He then moved to the town of New Salem, where he tried a variety of jobs – store manager, postmaster, general store owner – mostly unsuccessfully. It was when he decided to become a lawyer and later to go into politics that he finally found his life's work.

4 ______________________________

The challenges faced by the world-famous artist Frida Kahlo started from an early age. When she was just six years old, she caught polio which left her right leg shorter and much thinner than the left – something she wore long skirts to disguise. Perhaps because of her illness, Kahlo dreamed of becoming a doctor, but her ambitions were cut short when, at the age of 18, she was involved in a serious traffic accident. Kahlo's injuries kept her in bed for months and left her in serious pain for the rest of her life. However, it was during her recovery that Kahlo found her true calling – painting. Although she was unable to get out of bed, she could see her reflection in a mirror opposite where she slept and, as a result, many of her paintings were self-portraits – a style for which she became famous.

Glossary

illiterate (adj) somebody who is not able to read or write

orator (n) somebody who makes formal speeches in public or is good at public speaking

polio (n) a serious disease that causes loss of control or feeling in your muscles

stammer (n) a speech difficulty where words or sounds are repeated

LISTENING

A You are going to listen to a lifestyle podcast recorded on a US college campus about a social issue in the UK. Make a list of the top five social issues (e.g. housing, lack of jobs, etc) facing your country.

1.4 **B** **LISTEN FOR GIST** Listen to an extract from the podcast and choose the best title (1, 2 or 3).

1 The effects of social isolation and loneliness on an aging population

2 Government introduces new strategy to tackle loneliness in British society

3 Top tips to help you tackle social isolation in your own community

1.5 **C** **LISTEN FOR MAIN IDEAS** Listen to the full podcast. Put the following topics in the order they are discussed.

___ The decision came about because of recent research.

___ The new minister will develop a strategy based on input from many groups.

___ British government appoints a minister for loneliness.

___ Give practical help to those in need.

___ Try to develop new relationships with your neighbors and classmates.

___ Young people are lonelier than older people.

1.5 **D** **LISTEN FOR DETAIL** Listen to the podcast again. Choose the correct options (a, b or c) to complete the sentences.

1 The idea of a minister for loneliness …
  - **a** is the British Prime Minister's most unusual idea.
  - **b** is unique to the UK.
  - **c** will definitely solve the problem.

2 According to the Cigna survey, the loneliest people in the US are …
  - **a** 16 years old and under.
  - **b** between the ages of 18 and 22.
  - **c** 75 and over.

3 The minister for loneliness will …
  - **a** talk to people who feel lonely.
  - **b** help charities which deal with loneliness.
  - **c** work with different organizations to solve the problem.

4 The first step to helping others is to …
  - **a** use social media to reach out to people.
  - **b** take time to get to know people around you.
  - **c** start a conversation with a stranger.

5 Older people appreciate practical help because …
  - **a** most of them can't drive.
  - **b** they find practical matters boring.
  - **c** it gives them a chance to communicate with others.

E **REFLECT** Think about the answers to these questions.

1 Do you think the appointment of a 'minister for loneliness' is a good idea? Why/Why not?

2 What other ways can you think of to bring people together and tackle the problem of loneliness?

WRITING

A Skim the letter and answer the questions.

1 What is the purpose of the letter?
2 Who is the letter for?
3 Why does the writer begin with *Dear Sir/Madam*?

B STRUCTURING FORMAL LETTERS Read the letter again. Put the functions in the order they appear.

___ request for information
___ sign-off
___ request for a response
___ purpose of the letter
___ salutation or greeting

To: roboticsclub@email.com
From: ajkhatri@mail.com

Dear Sir/Madam,

[1]I want to know a little more info about joining your robotics club. I was looking for a club to join and the projects on your website looked the most interesting. However, I have a few questions I would like to ask before I sign up.

[2]So first things first, how often do you get together and where? I was also wondering if the venue is fully equipped or whether I should bring any of my own tools or parts to the meetings. [3]I also want to know how much I have to pay to be a member and how often. Lastly, are your members all certified in robotics, [4]or do you let anybody join? I am studying electronics in college but am very interested in robotics and subscribe to several magazines on the subject.

[5]Let me know by the end of the week, OK – either by email or telephone. Thank you in advance for your help.

Sincerely,

Arjan Khatri

C Replace the sentences (1–5) with their more formal equivalents (a–e).

a or do you accept people with related skills?
b I am writing to inquire about membership in your robotics club.
c I would be grateful if you could let me know before your next meeting.
d Could you also tell me if there is a membership fee and if it is a one-time or weekly/monthly payment?
e I would like to know how often the club meets, and where.

WRITING PRACTICE

A PREPARE Read the task below and write notes about who you are writing to, what you need to know and what action you expect them to take.

You are interested in joining the local sailing club. Write a letter of inquiry and find out:

- when and how often they meet
- how much previous experience is necessary
- how the club ensures your safety
- what equipment you need.

B PLAN Organize your notes from Exercise A into a plan for a letter of inquiry.

C WRITE Write your letter of inquiry in 150–250 words. Use your plan to help you.

D EDIT Edit your letter. Check:

- spelling and punctuation
- all of the information in the task has been covered
- an appropriate structure/tone has been used.

VOCABULARY
Health and fitness

A Complete the article with the nouns in the box.

anxiety calories cholesterol depression obesity stress

Staying healthy as a student

BY EMILY FISCHER | OCT 15

When you are under a lot of [1] ______________ – for example, when you have a lot of studying to do – you need to make sure that you look after yourself both mentally and physically.
Mentally, you could find yourself suffering from [2] ______________, worrying about even the simplest of things. If left untreated, this could lead to [3] ______________. Many sufferers are so unhappy that they find it difficult to lead a normal life and it can be incredibly difficult to overcome.
Physically, a lot of people tend to overeat, consuming far more [4] ______________ than they can burn off. If this continues, it can lead to [5] ______________, which has its own set of complications. Stress and overeating can both cause an increase of [6] ______________ in the blood, which in turn can cause problems, particularly for the heart.

B Choose the correct options to complete the sentences.

1 *Mental* / *Physical* health issues, such as anxiety and depression, can have serious consequences on your quality of life.
2 Not all *calorie* / *processed* foods are unhealthy, but many of them have added chemicals, salt or sugar which you might want to avoid.
3 The average *life* / *age* expectancy for women in the US is around 78.7 years, while for men it is a little less.
4 Giving up smoking greatly *levels* / *reduces* the risk of serious illness and, in fact, some health benefits can be measured almost immediately.
5 Keeping fit and healthy helps to slow the *aging* / *disease* process, as well as helps you feel younger.
6 This workout is designed for people with an average *lack* / *level* of fitness.
7 A little bit of stress helps us get things done, but if you *benefit* / *suffer* from constant anxiety, it can make it difficult to lead a normal life.
8 I'm actually taking my vacation a little earlier this year as I know I'll be *under* / *in* a lot of pressure over the summer.

GRAMMAR
Present perfect and present perfect progressive

A Choose the correct options to complete the sentences.

1 I've *read* / *been reading* that book you gave me. I've only finished the first few chapters, but it's pretty good.
2 I've *been staying* / *stayed* with Jo all week because they're doing some work on my apartment.
3 I've *been losing* / *lost* five kilos already, but I want to lose at least five more.
4 Where on Earth have you been? I've *called* / *been calling* you all day!
5 Paris? Yes, I've *been* / *been going* there many times. What do you want to know?
6 I've *tried* / *been trying* to finish this project for well over a week now.
7 We've *been spending* / *spent* every summer in Portugal since we got married there 20 years ago.
8 We've *done* / *been doing* this for hours. Maybe we should take a break?
9 I'm really tired actually. I *haven't slept* / *haven't been sleeping* very well recently.
10 He *has written* / *has been writing* six best-selling novels in the past decade.

B Complete the sentences with the present perfect or present perfect progressive form of the verbs in parentheses. Use contractions where possible.

1 ______________________ (*I / finish*) everything I needed to do for today. Can I go home now?
2 Your hands are black! What ______________________ (*you / do*) this morning?
3 I need to be careful with my diet. I think ______________________ (*I / put on*) a little weight since the summer.
4 One good thing I've managed to do for my health is that ______________________ (*I / give up*) smoking.
5 ______________________ (*We / work*) on this all week without a break. I'll be glad when we finish it.
6 I wasn't happy with the service that company provided so ______________________ (*I / stop*) using them.
7 ______________________ (*Mía / bike*) to work while her car is being fixed.
8 Apparently, ______________________ (*he / already / go*) to the gym three times this week!

C Complete the sentences with the present perfect or present perfect progressive form of the verbs in the box.

break call clean finish go (x2) stay wait

1 I can't play on Saturday because I ______________________ my leg!
2 I ______________________ David all morning, but he isn't answering his phone.
3 I ______________________ writing the report yet.
4 We ______________________ to the gym for over a year now.
5 Apparently, he ______________________ the downstairs bathroom, but not the one upstairs.
6 We ______________________ for you since six o'clock!
7 Phil ______________________ to Hungary three times.
8 For the last week, I ______________________ at Tim's place.

PRONUNCIATION
Connected speech: present perfect progressive

2.1 **A** Listen and circle the sentences you hear (a or b).

1 a I'm trying to reach him.
  b I've been trying to reach him.
2 a He's drinking too much coffee.
  b He's been drinking too much coffee.
3 a I've been looking at places to stay on the island.
  b I'm looking at places to stay on the island.
4 a They've been talking about buying a new car.
  b They're talking about buying a new car.
5 a We've been spending more time together as a family.
  b We're spending more time together as a family.

2.2 **B** Listen and complete the sentences.

1 ______________________ living in France for four years now.
2 ______________________ working part time in a café.
3 ______________________ eating a lot less junk food recently.
4 ______________________ spending more time with her family.
5 ______________________ talking about returning to the US.

2.2 **C** Listen again and repeat.

2.2 Lifestyles

GRAMMAR

used to, would, get used to, be used to

A Are these sentences correct or incorrect? Rewrite the incorrect sentences.

1 I'm still not used to living out in the country.
2 He didn't used to have such long hair.
3 We would to sit out on the balcony and talk all night.
4 I found it really difficult to get use to wearing contact lenses at first.
5 You'll have to be used to working longer hours now that you have your new job.
6 Being the youngest in my family, I soon used to being told what to do.
7 I've lived here for 12 years now and I'm still not used to driving on the right!
8 What would you do in the summer when you were a child?
9 I think I'm slowly getting use to such a long commute.
10 I'd always play soccer for hours after school in the park.

B Complete the conversation with the correct forms of *used to, would, get used to* or *be used to.*

Natasha: Is this you in the photo?
Dimitri: Yes. It's a little embarrassing.
Natasha: You [1] ____________ be so sweet!
Dimitri: Thank you. Wait a minute. Are you saying that I'm not sweet anymore?
Natasha: Well, it was a long time ago – I'm sure I'm not the first person to point it out to you! You must [2] ____________ it by now!
Dimitri: One thing I can't [3] ____________ is the fact that I don't feel any older. I mean, I look at photographs of me and I think, 'I don't look like that, do I?'
Natasha: Oh, I [4] ____________ that years ago. Now, I just don't let anyone take my photo!
Dimitri: You know, when I was younger, I [5] ____________ often wonder what I would look like when I grew up. I sometimes [6] ____________ imagine I would look like my dad. I guess I do as I get older.
Natasha: I know, right? People [7] ____________ say that I looked like my mom – but they do now! It's hard [8] ____________ growing older. Oh well – we can't change the aging process I guess.

PRONUNCIATION

Catenation: *used to*

A (2.3) Listen to the sentences. Which sound is omitted in *used to* – /d/ or /t/?

1 He used to be a professional soccer player.
2 I'm slowly getting used to life in Japan.
3 You must be used to the food here by now!

B (2.4) Listen and repeat the sentences.

1 I can't get used to doing everything on my own.
2 I'm not used to having to cook for myself.
3 My mom used to take care of things like that.
4 We always used to eat delicious food at family gatherings.
5 She's used to getting everything her own way.
6 Have you gotten used to driving on the right yet?

VOCABULARY

Adverbs of stance; Adverb + adjective collocations

A Choose the correct adverbs to complete the sentences.

1 *Naturally* / *Simply*, we all want to find a solution as soon as possible.

2 Five years ago, there were plenty of jobs. *Merely* / *Sadly*, this is no longer the case.

3 Social media has *undoubtedly* / *apparently* affected the way we communicate with each other.

4 I didn't do a lot at my old job. I was *naturally* / *merely* there to make the coffee and answer the phone.

5 She is a very unpleasant person and, *undoubtedly* / *frankly*, I don't want her on my team.

6 *Merely* / *Admittedly*, I made a mistake, but we're all human, aren't we?

7 Do you remember Sharon? Well, *frankly* / *apparently*, she's now married and living in New Zealand!

8 I'm sorry, but what's being reported in the press *merely* / *simply* isn't true.

B Replace the phrases in italics with adverbs from Exercise A.

1 *I accept that* I don't do as much to help the environment as I probably should.

2 *To be completely honest*, I don't like her attitude.

3 The money they're offering is *just* to keep us quiet.

4 *Of course*, we will let you know if anything changes.

5 He's just bought a Ferrari, *from what people say*.

6 *Although I wish it wasn't necessary*, I have to leave my job.

C Complete the email with the adjectives in the box.

concerned disappointed easy likely ridiculous

TO ALL DEPARTMENT MEMBERS

From Chang

In my mind, the proposal to ban personal use of the internet in the office is absolutely [1] ________________, and I'm bitterly [2] ________________ with the management's decision. Naturally, I'm deeply [3] ________________ about the invasion of privacy that this might cause, but, frankly, it is ridiculously [4] ________________ for a manager to see if an employee is spending hours on social media and, in such cases, to take disciplinary action. There is no need for such drastic measures and I think it is highly [5] ________________ that the staff will react very badly to the new rule.

READING

A PREDICT You are going to read an article about self-help books. What do you think makes them effective? What are some of the potential issues?

B SCAN Read *How helpful is self-help?* quickly. Which of your ideas from Exercise A are discussed?

C READ FOR GIST Read the article again. Choose the best summary (1, 2 or 3) of the writer's argument.

1 People rely too heavily on self-help books these days.
2 Self-help books may offer some useful advice, but only you can drive real change.
3 The majority of self-help books contain very practical and useful advice.

D IDENTIFY ASSUMPTIONS Read the article again. Underline parts of the text that match the assumptions (1–5).

1 Taking someone's advice is more difficult than giving it to others.
2 Hearing about the similar experiences of others can be helpful.
3 A lot of self-help books are factually inaccurate.
4 Your current situation can affect what you can achieve.
5 People don't need self-help books when the country is doing well.

E REFLECT Think about the answers to these questions.

1 Do you believe that self-help books can actually bring about change in people's lives? Why/Why not?
2 In the conclusion, the writer claims that more people turn to self-help when the economy is bad. Why do think this happens?

How helpful is self-help?

The self-help industry is still booming, offering support for everything from giving up caffeine to managing depression. But is it doing more harm than good? | ***By Daniel Edwards***

When I was younger, change seemed much easier. If you wanted to get in shape, you went for a run. If you didn't like your job, you got another one. It's just common sense, isn't it? Well, to a point, yes: do something outside your comfort zone often enough and you'll soon get used to the discomfort. You may even become good at it. But as we all know, advice is always easier to give than to follow, and change can be scary.

Enter the quick fix – the self-help book. Over the past 20 years, self-help content has exploded, with books, blogs, vlogs, podcasts, all dedicated to giving advice. But whether the huge popularity of the industry proves it is effective is difficult to say. Can we really prove a cause and effect relationship between the book and the reader's happiness? Perhaps they started one title, found it didn't work and tried another. Perhaps other parts of their life – like their job or relationship – just got better. It's impossible to say for certain what led to their happiness.

However, good self-help books do give a clear picture of a problem and how to deal with it. At least you learn something, even if you don't follow the advice given, and it might make you more sympathetic to people with a similar issue. They can also be a source of comfort when facing life-changing experiences such as a death in the family or a divorce. I think we can all agree that knowing how others have coped in similar situations can give you the strength to keep going. Also, they are undoubtedly cheaper than paying for a therapist or other professional help.

While some self-help content does provide good advice, many are, without a doubt, full of unscientific nonsense. I can see how a title like 'Think Yourself Famous' might be attractive, but in reality, we can't just get what we want simply by thinking about it. Another problem is that many of them don't consider social and economic circumstances. If you have the time and the money, a nice home and a loving family, then it becomes that much easier to make positive changes in your life. Whether the idea that it takes 10,000 hours of practice to master something is true or not, at least it makes you realize that some time and effort are required.

The boom of the self-help industry is driven by people's desire for quick solutions to difficult problems. It's also pretty interesting that we only seem to turn to self-help when the economy is bad. However, one thing is clear – whatever inspires you to make a change, only you can make it happen. Which, if you think about it, isn't all that different to how things used to be.

LISTENING

A **You are going to listen to an interview about making lifestyle changes. Which of the following techniques do you think would help? Why?**

- Log your progress in a written diary or online blog.
- Involve a friend or family member in your plans.
- Reward yourself with a special treat when you reach your goal.

2.5 **B** **LISTEN FOR GIST Listen to the interview. Put the techniques in the order they are mentioned.**

___ Use social media to log your progress.

___ Set realistic goals.

___ Ask friends and family for support.

___ Focus on one change at a time.

___ Make a detailed plan of action.

2.5 **C** **LISTEN FOR REASONS Listen to the interview again. Choose the correct options (a, b or c) to complete the sentences.**

1 People often fail to achieve their goals because they aren't …
   a detailed enough.
   b motivating enough.
   c challenging enough.

2 Many people struggle with fitness goals because they …
   a try to make too many changes at once.
   b don't set achievable targets.
   c can't fit them into their schedules.

3 Gudrun's kind of list helps her clients to …
   a prioritize their goals.
   b track their overall progress.
   c clearly define their goals.

4 Many people avoid support networks because they …
   a don't know how to explain their issues.
   b don't want to be judged by friends and family.
   c don't want to admit they have a problem.

5 Writing about your goals on Facebook will …
   a help you stay motivated.
   b mean you're less likely to fail.
   c earn you more likes and comments.

6 One of Gudrun's clients tracked his daily progress to …
   a share with his family.
   b encourage others to do the same.
   c help him stick to his goal.

D **REFLECT Think about the answers to these questions.**

1 Which of the methods discussed in the interview do you think would work best for you? Why?

2 What other methods can you think of that might affect lasting change?

WRITING

A Think about your habits when working or studying. How do you avoid getting distracted? Make a list of five techniques you use.

B Read *How to stop putting things off*. Were any of your techniques from Exercise A mentioned?

How to stop putting things off

The poet Edward Young called procrastination 'the thief of time' because it is the one thing you can never get back. Whatever excuses you find for putting off tasks, it always leads to worry and stress. We all do this at one time or another, depending on the difficulty of the task. But [1] ___ let it become a habit. Here are some tips to help you!

What's the problem?

Emotions are often the cause of procrastination. If it is fear or boredom that's stopping you from getting started, follow these rules:

- Take time to think about your real reason for putting off the task. Is there really a problem? Or is that just an excuse?
- If negative emotions are the issue, [2] ___ replace them with a can-do attitude. Do some physical activity. Believe me, it works!

Getting started

Once you've identified the problem, take the following steps to get started:

- [3] ___ break a big task down into smaller stages that are easier to manage.
- Put it in writing! A written plan of action will give you confidence to see the task through.

Keep going

Now you've begun, follow these simple rules to keep working:

- [4] ___ there are no distractions. Turn your phone off, or put it into airplane mode so you can't check your emails or go on social media.
- [5] ___ any negative thinking now that you got started.
- [6] ___ congratulate or even reward yourself when you complete each part of the task.

Job done

Congratulations! You got your work done. It feels good, doesn't it? I'm sure you feel more confident and you'll no doubt sleep much better tonight.

C GIVING ADVICE Read the article again. Complete the sentences (1–6) with the words and phrases (a–f).

a Avoid
b It's a good idea to
c whatever you do, don't
d Remember to
e Make sure
f try to

D Rewrite the advice using the words in bold.

1 Making a plan before you start is always helpful.
Try to ______________________.

2 Doing some physical exercise will help a lot.
It's a good idea ______________________.

3 Try not to use your cell phone after 10 pm.
Avoid ______________________.

4 Breaking tasks down into stages is very important.
Make sure you ______________________.

5 Remember to reward yourself.
Whatever you do, don't ______________________.

WRITING PRACTICE

A PREPARE You are going to write an article giving advice about public speaking. Use the following questions to write some notes:

1 Would you be nervous if you had to give a speech? How would you control your nerves?
2 What kind of preparation do you think is needed before making a speech?
3 What advice would you give to someone who has to speak in public for the first time?

B PLAN Organize your notes from Exercise A into a plan for an article.

C WRITE Write your article in 150–250 words. Use your plan to help you.

D EDIT Edit your article. Check:

- spelling and punctuation
- use of expressions to give advice
- appropriateness of ideas (e.g. Is the advice clear? Is it good advice?).

Glossary

procrastination (n) delaying something that must be done, usually because it is boring or unpleasant

GRAMMAR
Narrative tenses

A Choose the correct options to complete the sentences.

1 I didn't want to stay for lunch because I *already ate / had already eaten*.

2 Sorry, I couldn't talk earlier because I *tried / was trying* to put my daughter down for a nap.

3 Fearing for his life, he got up, *packed / had packed* his bags and took the first train out of town.

4 The house was a mess when my parents showed up because we *had been decorating / decorated*.

5 Although I *wasn't studying / hadn't studied* very much, I still passed the test.

6 I arrived on time, *was knocking / knocked* on the office door and waited for a reply.

7 Conditions were terrible. It *was pouring / poured* rain and visibility was less than a meter.

8 We *had walked / had been walking* in silence for hours when Dylan suddenly screamed out in terror.

B Complete the sentences with the correct narrative form of the verbs in parentheses.

1 Sadly, by the time we made it to the airport, our flight ____________ (*already / leave*).

2 I saw her get into a taxi just as I ____________ (*leaving*) the party.

3 I had just finished work and ____________ (*look forward*) to a nice quiet evening at home.

4 Looking in horror at his watch, he threw on his coat and ____________ (*rush*) out of the house.

5 I was certain that I ____________ (*lock*) the car, so I wasn't worried about anyone stealing it.

6 She said she was worried about me and thought I ____________ (*work*) too hard recently.

7 Suddenly, Harry ____________ (*remember*) he had left his phone in the office.

8 I ____________ (*get*) ready for bed when I heard a noise downstairs.

C Find and correct eight mistakes with narrative tenses in the story.

When Andrew was walking to work that morning, he had a funny feeling that someone followed him. Although he turned around several times to look, he wasn't seeing anyone. But still, the feeling of being followed continued until the moment he had been arriving at the office. After a routine day, Andrew started to walk home and suddenly remembered how he felt eight hours earlier, because now he felt the same way again – he was sure he was not alone. He decided to vary his route a little. He went to the park and sat in the most open, exposed place he could find. Surely now he would notice if someone watched him. But, after waiting for about 20 minutes, he saw nothing unusual so he went on. When he got home, he was having one last anxious look around. No one was there. Entering the house and collapsing into his favorite armchair, Andrew wondered to himself … did he work too hard for the last few weeks? Was he imagining things? Could there really have been someone following him? While he was sitting there trying to work it all out, his phone had rung and made him jump. His questions were about to be answered.

VOCABULARY
Descriptive verbs

A Complete the sentences with the verbs in the box. Use the pictures to help you.

crackling creaked crunched growled rumbled smashed

1

2

3

4

5

6

1 The firefighter ________ the window and reached inside.
2 The tiger ________ and looked as though it was going to attack.
3 The bridge ________ under my weight as if it was going to collapse.
4 We sat listening to the wood ________ on the camp fire.
5 The crisp snow ________ under our feet as we made our way up the mountain.
6 The volcano ________ into life, firing ash and lava into the sky.

B Choose the correct options (a, b or c) to complete the sentences.

1 All we could hear was the sound of water ___ somewhere in the darkness.
a crunching **b** trickling **c** hissing

2 As Giles reached forward, the branch ___ under him and he fell to the ground.
a snapped **b** rumbled **c** crunched

3 The old ship ___ as it was tossed around by the waves.
a snapped **b** groaned **c** growled

4 The car ___ to a halt, narrowly missing the bus coming the other way.
a screeched **b** crunched **c** trickled

5 From the ___ in the long grass beside him, it was clear there was a snake nearby.
a hissing **b** snapping **c** crunching

6 Angry at the decision, I left the room, ___ the door behind me.
a groaning **b** creaking **c** slamming

7 The chair ___ under his weight as he tried to put the suitcase back on the top shelf in the closet.
a slammed **b** crunched **c** creaked

8 They sat staring at each other, the silence broken only by the occasional truck ___ past the window.
a groaning **b** rumbling **c** creaking

PRONUNCIATION
Dramatic storytelling techniques

3.1 **A** Read the story aloud using pauses, stress and changes in speed to sound dramatic. Then listen and compare your reading with the recording.

The snow lay thick on the ground outside, but inside, I was nice and warm and comfortable sitting by the fire. I was just thinking how relaxing this all was when I realized that I was going to have to go outside for more wood. Annoyed to be leaving the cozy fireside, I pulled my boots and coat on, stepped outside and slammed the door behind me. Outside, the wind was whistling through the trees which were creaking under the weight of the snow. It was cold but peaceful out there. I stopped for a moment and looked at the scene in the brilliant moonlight. Suddenly, I heard the distinct crunch, crunch, crunch of footsteps in the snow. I was not alone …

B Practice reading the story aloud. Try to read it in the same way as the speaker in Exercise A.

GRAMMAR
Alternatives to *if* in conditionals

A Complete the flyer with the words in the box.

as long as | as soon as | in case | provided | unless

IMPORTANT ADVICE CONCERNING BEARS

There are many different types of bears and the best way to stay out of trouble is to find out about which ones you might encounter where you are. Here are some guidelines [1] ______________ you find yourself face to face with one.

- Don't ever surprise a bear. They don't like surprises and are likely to attack you out of fear. For this reason, you should talk, sing or generally make loud noises to announce your presence in the area, [2] ______________ you see a bear that hasn't seen you; in that case, don't make a noise – just slowly move away or wait for it to leave.
- Always carry bear spray. This is your best defense if a bear attacks. [3] ______________ you see a bear coming toward you, spray the area in front of you. This should stop it from coming any closer.
- Know the difference between bears. If you meet a black bear (and you are sure it *is* a black bear), it probably won't attack you [4] ______________ you make a lot of noise. But remember – this will only work with black bears. Other types of bears will probably attack if you do this.
- [5] ______________ you take these basic precautions, you should be able to survive a bear attack.

B Rewrite the sentences using the words in bold.

1 We'll miss our flight if we don't hurry up!
unless
We'll miss ______________.

2 You can borrow the money but only if you pay me back next week.
provided
You can borrow ______________.

3 Bring a change of clothes – it might get cold later.
case
Bring a change of clothes ______________.

4 I'll be asleep, so only call me if there's a problem.
unless
I'll be asleep, so ______________.

5 I promise to let you know when I arrive.
soon
I promise I'll ______________.

6 If you follow these instructions, there won't be a problem.
long
There won't be a problem ______________.

PRONUNCIATION
Intonation in conditional sentences

3.2 **A** Listen to the conditional sentences. Draw arrows to mark rising (↗) or falling (↘) intonation.

1 As soon as you get there, ___ send me a message ___.
2 You'll be OK, ___ provided you stay calm ___.
3 You won't survive ___ unless you stay hydrated ___.
4 As long as the wood is dry, ___ you should be able to start a fire ___.
5 Take a sleeping bag ___ in case you need to stay overnight ___.

3.3 **B** Listen and repeat the sentences.

1 Try to find a safe place for shelter as soon as possible.
2 Provided you don't make any sudden moves, the bear probably won't attack.
3 Unless you know it's safe, don't drink the water.
4 You'll survive as long as you remember your training.
5 Remember to take a map in case you get lost.

VOCABULARY

Phrasal verbs to describe problems; Dependent prepositions: adjectives

A Choose the correct options to complete the sentences.

1 I would rather *put up with* / *talk over* the possible solutions before we take action.

2 Once you've *weighed up* / *figured out* what to do, the hard part is over.

3 Look, there's a problem and someone needs to *weigh it out* / *straighten it out*.

4 The team *went through* / *figured out* a terrifying experience and was lucky to be alive.

5 In my opinion, we need to *weigh out* / *put up* the risks before we set off.

6 I can *put up with* / *straighten out* cold weather, but I hate it when it snows.

7 Why don't you let someone else *talk it over* / *deal with it* for a change?

B Complete the sentences with the correct form of the verbs in the box.

deal with figure out go through put up with straighten it out talk it over weigh out

1 A dispute started and I had to ________________ before it turned into a fight.

2 We ________________ the difficult conditions because we knew it was only for one night.

3 I know that I can ________________ just about any survival situation.

4 We need to ________________ the advantages and disadvantages before we make a decision.

5 I can't ________________ how we're going to cross the river.

6 The team ________________ and decided to return to the camp.

7 I don't want to have to ________________ anything like that ever again.

C Are these sentences correct or incorrect? Rewrite the incorrect sentences.

1 I'm sick about listening to him telling us how brilliant he is.

2 The company has stated that it is dissatisfied with the results.

3 It's very important to be sensitive of the feelings of others.

4 I usually get anxious about flying a week before I'm due to travel.

5 We were enthusiastic about the walk in the woods – until we heard about the bears!

6 Aren't you envious for Marco? He gets to travel all around the world!

7 To be honest, she should be absolutely ashamed of her behavior last week.

8 It seemed that the man wasn't aware from anyone following him.

9 I'm just so sick from him telling me what to do all the time!

10 According to this, the group got lost somewhere in the French Alps.

READING

A PREDICT You are going to read an article about a man who was lost in the jungle for three weeks. Write a list of the kinds of dangers you think he might have had to face.

B READ FOR GIST Read *Lost and in danger* quickly. Which of your ideas from Exercise A were mentioned?

C FOLLOW THE SEQUENCE OF A NARRATIVE Read again and complete the article with the sentences (a–i). There is one extra sentence you do not need to use.

- **a** Yossi, holding onto a piece of the raft, was washed over the edge.
- **b** At this point, they needed a plan that would eventually get them back to civilization.
- **c** But days and nights passed and Yossi realized he was completely alone, with little hope of rescue.
- **d** They had to kill monkeys for food, which Marcus wouldn't eat.
- **e** It took him two days to find the strength and courage to continue.
- **f** Yossi had been saving up to go to the Amazon for some time.
- **g** What he didn't know was that Kevin had persuaded a man with a boat to help him look for his friend.
- **h** But things were about to go disastrously wrong.
- **i** Then he had a bit of luck.

D READ FOR DETAIL Read the article again and answer the questions. Underline the parts of the texts that give you the answers.

1. Where did the group begin their trek?
2. What soon became clear as they trekked along the river?
3. Why did the group eventually split up?
4. How did Yossi lose his supplies?
5. How did Yossi survive the attack of a predator?
6. What bit of luck saved Yossi's life?

E REFLECT Think about the answers to these questions.

1. What do you think motivates people to explore the unknown?
2. What qualities does a person need to survive in a situation such as Yossi's?

LOST and in DANGER

Imagine being lost and alone in the Bolivian jungle. You're exhausted and have no supplies. This is exactly the situation the Israeli author Yossi Ghinsberg found himself in when he went missing for nearly three weeks back in 1981.

1 ___ Discovering a lost tribe was the motivation for the trip, but as it turned out, there weren't really any left. Still determined to explore the jungle, he hitchhiked to Colombia, where he met fellow traveler, Marcus Stamm. They became friends and decided to travel to Bolivia together, where two more men, Karl Ruprechter and Kevin Gale, joined the group. They set off along the Tuichi River, but it wasn't long before they realized that they didn't have enough supplies and that the local villages couldn't provide all they needed. 2 ___ He became weak from hunger and the group decided to turn back.

3 ___ The group agreed to build a raft and sail down the Tuichi River. Once they were on their way, Karl, who had suggested the plan in the first place, decided that he didn't want to continue because the river passed over dangerous rocks and waterfalls. He also told them he couldn't swim. This led to suspicion and distrust in the group, and they decided to separate and make their own way back. Karl and Marcus went on foot, while Yossi and Kevin continued down the river on the raft.

4 ___ In fast-moving water approaching a large waterfall, they lost control of the raft, which began to break into pieces. Kevin managed to swim to the riverbank. 5 ___ Miraculously, he survived the fall, but pulled along by the force of the water and smashing against rocks on the way, Yossi thought he was going to drown. He eventually made it to the shore, but now he had nothing; all the supplies had been lost with the raft. Glad to be alive, but terrified at his situation, he decided the first thing to do was to find Kevin.

6 ___ He found his backpack, which had been washed to the riverbank. Now he set off to find Kevin, thinking this would take just a few hours. 7 ___ Over the 19 days he was alone, he was constantly bitten by insects and on one occasion woke up to find a jaguar staring at him, ready to attack. He improvised, using a spray can and a lighter as a makeshift flame thrower to frighten it off. Worst of all, his feet were causing him terrible pain – they looked like raw meat.

Once, a plane flew overhead, but it didn't spot him in the thick jungle. 8 ___ They had been looking for days and were about to give up when Yossi saw their boat. He waved his arms and tried to shout, but he had lost his voice. By chance, Kevin turned around for a last look and saw him.

Marcus and Karl were never seen again.

Glossary

raft (n) a simple boat made by tying pieces of wood together

LISTENING

A PREDICT Imagine that you have been shipwrecked on an island in the middle of the ocean. How will you survive? Put these tasks in order of priority.

___ getting rescued
___ building a shelter
___ creating a safe space
___ finding food
___ finding water

B LISTEN FOR GIST (3.4) Listen to the first part of the talk. How does the speaker prioritize the tasks in Exercise A?

C LISTEN FOR DETAIL (3.5) Listen to the full talk. Are these sentences true (T) or false (F)? Correct the false sentences.

1 Having a positive attitude will help you to survive. T / F
2 A minor medical problem could kill you. T / F
3 You must find a stream to have access to drinking water. T / F
4 A shelter will protect you from different kinds of weather. T / F
5 Avoid fruits and berries because you cannot tell if they're poisonous or not. T / F
6 The only way to attract attention is to light a fire. T / F

D LISTEN FOR DEFINITIONS, EXAMPLES AND EXPLANATIONS (3.5) Listen to the full talk again and complete the notes with no more than three words or a number.

- Create a(n) 1 '______________' free from wild animals, rocks, spiky plants, etc – anything dangerous!
- Next step = water! Find a stream / collect rainwater from 2 ______________ or large leaves.
- Use 3 ______________ to make shelter structure > use leaves for the roof.
- Food = fish or limpets – 4 ______________ attached to rocks.
- Berry test:
  1 rub across your 5 ______________
  2 touch to lips
  3 put in mouth > spit out
  No reaction = safe to eat!
- International distress signal = 6 ______________ flashes of light.
- Use three 7 ______________ / spell out a message with braches to signal for help.

E REFLECT Do you think you would be good in a survival situation? Why/Why not?

WRITING

A Read the short story and answer the questions. Underline the parts of the text that give you the answers.

1 Where does the story take place?
2 What is the main event?
3 What possible causes are mentioned?

B Read the story again. Are these sentences true (T) or false (F)? Correct the false sentences.

1 The writer went to pick up his mom while his family was making dinner. *T / F*
2 It had just started snowing when the writer left to go to the station. *T / F*
3 The writer's mom got into the car after putting her suitcase in the back. *T / F*
4 Hitting a patch of ice on the way home caused the car to skid into the ditch. *T / F*
5 The other driver helped them out of the car, then called an ambulance. *T / F*

C USING ADVERBS Complete the story with the adverbs in the box.

desperately fortunately heavily nervously noisily slowly surprisingly violently

WRITING PRACTICE

A PREPARE You are going to write a short story about a day when something unexpected happened to you. Write notes about:

- the location
- the people involved
- the key events
- contextual details (e.g. the weather, time of year, etc)
- how the day ended.

B PLAN Organize your notes from Exercise A into a plan for a short story.

C WRITE Write your short story in 150–250 words. Use your plan to help you.

D EDIT Edit your story. Check:

- spelling and punctuation
- use of adverbs
- use of narrative tenses.

AN EVENTFUL NEW YEAR

Most of the family had already arrived for our annual New Year's Eve party and were [1] ________ chatting and preparing food. It was my job to pick Mom up from the station and I'd decided to leave early, partly to get away from the noise and partly because I was worried about the drive. We live out in the country and the roads are narrow and bordered by shallow ditches. Driving around there is difficult at the best of times, but it had snowed the night before and I knew the roads would be icy. However, despite my fears, the trip to the station was uneventful.

Mom's train was on time, we hugged, and as I was putting her suitcase into the back, she got into the driver's seat. She isn't the best driver, but she also isn't the sort of person you want to argue with, so we set off back home, with me [2] ________ keeping an eye on the road.

By now, it had started snowing [3] ________ and visibility was poor. Halfway home, we hit a patch of ice, skidded [4] ________ across the road and ended up facing the wrong way with two wheels hanging over the edge of the ditch. I was about to ask Mom if she was all right, when suddenly I felt the car begin to move. [5] ________, it rolled over into the ditch, leaving us hanging upside down.

[6] ________, neither of us was badly hurt, but we were stuck. Terrified, I was [7] ________ trying to undo my seat belt when I heard a voice outside say, 'Are you all right in there?' It turned out that another driver had seen the accident and called emergency services. [8] ________, we didn't have to wait long before help arrived. A paramedic quickly looked us over, then we were driven home in a police car.

'You took your time. We were beginning to get worried,' said my aunt, when she answered the door.

'Sorry', said Mom. 'The trains were late as usual.'

Glossary

ditch (n) a long channel dug at the side of a road or field to hold or carry water

GRAMMAR
Future forms

A **Choose the correct options (a, b or c) to complete the sentences.**

1 ___ a party tomorrow at our place. Would you like to come?
  a We're having
  b We have
  c We'll have
2 The traffic hasn't moved for an hour. ___ to the meeting.
  a We aren't making it
  b We'll make it
  c We're not going to make it
3 Mark ___ the doctor tomorrow about his back.
  a sees
  b is seeing
  c will see
4 It still hasn't arrived. ___ the delivery company now to see what's happened.
  a I'll call
  b I'm calling
  c I'll be calling
5 Both teams have a poor defensive record, so it ___ a high scoring game.
  a won't be
  b will probably be
  c is
6 Don't worry, ___ you as soon as we get there.
  a I'm going to text
  b I'm texting
  c I'll text
7 ___ tomorrow, because it's a national holiday here.
  a I'm not working
  b I don't work
  c I won't work
8 The flight ___ at 4:20 pm on Tuesday morning.
  a will be arriving
  b arrives
  c is going to arrive

B **Complete the sentences with the correct future form of the verbs in parentheses. Use contractions where possible.**

1 So my brother ______________ (*get*) married in July and I have to give a speech!
2 I haven't booked anything, but I think we ______________ (*fly*) into Paris first, then take the train to London.
3 We can't fly on December 20th; my semester ______________ ______________ (*not end*) until the 21st.
4 I'm not around this weekend. I ______________ (*visit*) a friend up north.
5 If you do the dishes, then I ______________ (*take*) the trash out.
6 They're playing next month! I ______________ (*buy*) tickets as soon as I get paid.

C **Find and correct eight mistakes with future forms in the conversation.**

Cheryl: So, that's it – we've graduated! What are you doing now, Dan?

Dan: I honestly don't know. It's just such a relief to finish! I guess I'm taking a few weeks off, just to relax and reflect on things. How about you?

Cheryl: I don't think we can afford to relax; I mean, there are so many graduates these days and not enough jobs. I've already planned ahead for a few days. I'll work on my resume tomorrow, then I'll go job hunting on Monday.

Dan: Wow, you're so proactive. You're putting me to shame! What do you mean you'll *go* job hunting? Isn't job hunting more of an online thing these days?

Cheryl: Well, yeah. I'm probably spending some time searching for jobs online next week, but I need some temp work first. You know, just to get a little money coming in. This student loan isn't going to repay itself!

Dan: Temp work? Like what?

Cheryl: Well, I read in the paper that there's some part-time work available at that new grocery store in town. You have to apply for the work through the job center. Why don't you come along with me on Monday? The work is going to start on the 14th.

Dan: No thanks. It's all a bit too soon for me. I need to chill out for a little while first. I don't have time to do that once I enter the world of work …

Cheryl: Fair enough, I get that.

VOCABULARY

Noun + preposition collocations; Nouns and verbs with the same spelling

A Complete the sentences with the correct preposition.

1. One of the advantages ___ studying in a foreign country is being able to experience a different culture.
2. If you apply early, then you'll have a better chance ___ getting a scholarship, but the competition will still be strong.
3. Another year, another rise ___ tuition fees. Something really must change.
4. You need to be pretty tough to succeed ___ the world of business.
5. Max also has experience ___ programming, so he would be an ideal candidate for the role.
6. It's only natural to have anxiety ___ performing badly; we all suffer with that from time to time.
7. Do you have a sec? I'd like to get your opinion ___ a proposal I'm writing.
8. We're sorry to see you go, but wish you every success ___ your future career.

B Complete the sentences with the correct form of the words in the box. Use each word twice and make any necessary changes.

balance benefit challenge control influence produce

1. It is often ___________ for new parents ___________ a career and family life.
2. The organic ___________ grown on the farm has many health ___________.
3. The owner of the soccer team ___________ the manager's decisions. It doesn't seem like the manager has full ___________ over transfers or tactics.
4. It's hard for artists ___________ truly expressive work and still make money. Not many artists in today's society have been able to strike that ___________.
5. One ___________ of home schooling our child was that we could ___________ what we taught her; we weren't bound by a school syllabus.
6. I am a big admirer of Stephen Hawking. I feel he ___________ society's perception of disability and he had a great ___________ and impact on modern science.

PRONUNCIATION

Nouns and verbs with the same spelling

A 4.1 **Listen to the pairs of sentences. Which of the words in bold are stressed differently when the form is changed?**

1. a You can **access** the building from both sides.
   b My key card doesn't give me **access** to all floors.
2. a They've just **produced** a new model of phone.
   b All the **produce** is home-grown.
3. a There's been an **increase** in sales this year.
   b We need to **increase** our social media presence.
4. a She's just set a new Olympic **record**!
   b It's important to **record** all new vocabulary.
5. a I think you should **challenge** the decision.
   b I just need a new **challenge** really.
6. a I didn't receive an **invite** to the meeting.
   b Did you **invite** Alex to the party?

B 4.2 **Underline the stressed syllables in each of the words in bold. Then listen and check.**

1. We had to **reject** multiple designs before we found one we liked.
2. There's been a huge **increase** in illegal downloads recently.
3. Ellen can **update** you on the latest developments.
4. The app allows you to stream or **download** content.
5. They're currently offering a 10% **discount** on all airfares.

C 4.2 **Listen again and repeat the sentences.**

GRAMMAR
Future perfect, future progressive and future perfect progressive

A Choose the correct options to complete the article.

Is climate change really a big deal?

The statistics prove that climate change is a very real problem. Based on the rate of temperature increase during the last century, we can predict that the overall temperature on Earth [1]*will be rising / will have risen* by 3.4 degrees by the year 2100. This might not sound like much, but it could have a serious impact on our lifestyle. Let's fast-forward to the end of the century and imagine what life will be like ...

In the year 2100, we'll [2]***have been eating / be eating*** less vegetables. How do we know this? Well, pests that attack plants normally don't like colder weather. However, if things heat up, then the frost-free season will extend, and this will cause significant damage to crops.

It is also likely that in around 80 years' time, we'll [3]***be traveling / have traveled*** to work equipped with both sunglasses and an umbrella. In 2100, weather patterns will have become so unpredictable that we'll need to be prepared for every eventuality.

Then there are the oceans. If you live in a low-lying city like say, Bangkok, then in 2100, you will probably [4]***be living / have been living*** underwater. That's because sea levels are estimated to rise by 65 centimeters over the next 80 years. The worst-case scenario would be terrible for any place that is currently at sea level, so I wouldn't plan a vacation in the Maldives around then. In fact, you might want to avoid the Maldives from about 2050, because people there will [5]***be living / have been living*** underwater since then. We can joke, but in all seriousness, this issue is not going to solve itself.

It gets worse. By the year 2048, the international treaty to preserve our most important continent, Antarctica, will [6]***be expiring / have expired.*** If this is not renewed, then the icy continent will be open to further tourism, development, business ventures and potentially destruction.

B Complete the sentences with the future perfect, future progressive or future perfect progressive form of the verbs in parentheses. Sometimes more than one answer is possible.

1 Oh, really? So where ______________ (*you / live*) this time next year?

2 By this time next week, I ______________ (*finish*) all my work so I'll be lying on a beach sunbathing.

3 Don't call me at 12 because I ______________ (*travel*) and the signal is terrible on the train.

4 At the end of this month, Lewis ______________ (*work*) here for ten years.

5 Do you think we ______________ (*still / have*) English lessons in five years' time?

6 There's no point in calling at six – everyone ______________ (*leave*) the office and gone home by then.

7 This time tomorrow, we ______________ (*watch*) the World Cup Final. England had better win!

8 I'm pretty sure that scientists ______________ (*discover*) a cure for cancer by 2030.

VOCABULARY
Intensifiers

A Choose the correct options (a, b or c) to complete the sentences.

1 It is ___ believed that the temperature of the Earth will continue to rise, causing more and more extreme weather conditions.
   a widely   b especially   c greatly
2 Home computers are becoming ___ cheaper year by year.
   a widely   b significantly   c entirely
3 We ___ believe that a safe, healthy future is possible.
   a undoubtedly   b significantly   c firmly
4 That's not ___ true I'm afraid as there are still several coal power plants in operation.
   a incredibly   b greatly   c entirely
5 We will need to find new sources of energy – ___ when fossil fuels run out.
   a especially   b entirely   c significantly
6 A little more money would ___ improve my quality of life.
   a greatly   b widely   c firmly
7 Jonas is ___ focused on his work and will let nothing distract him.
   a widely   b incredibly   c especially
8 It is ___ true that the climate is changing at a faster rate than ever before.
   a greatly   b significantly   c undoubtedly

B Complete the sentences with the intensifiers in the box.

entirely especially firmly greatly incredibly significantly undoubtedly widely

1 It is ______________ accepted that the airplane is one of the most environmentally damaging means of transportation.
2 She was a talented all-around athlete but was ______________ good at golf.
3 He was spotted at the crime scene, but police say he ______________ denies being there.
4 Magda is ______________ a highly qualified and talented individual.
5 Thank you for your response to our survey; it is ______________ appreciated.
6 There is a(n) ______________ higher number of cars using our roads than five years ago.
7 I like your suggestions, but I don't know whether it is ______________ possible to put all of them into practice.
8 No matter what you think, it is ______________ difficult to imagine us putting humans on Mars any time soon.

PRONUNCIATION
Intonation with intensifiers

4.3 **A** Listen to each sentence. What intonation does the speaker use on the intensifiers in bold – rising (↗), falling (↘) or rise-fall (↗↘)? What effect does this have?

1 I'm not sure that's **entirely** true.
2 This is becoming **significantly** more important.
3 This puzzle is **incredibly** challenging.

4.4 **B** Listen and repeat the sentences.

1 Some items were for sale at greatly reduced prices.
2 It's incredibly difficult to get anywhere during rush hour.
3 It's becoming increasingly important to conserve energy.
4 His proposal was entirely unrealistic.
5 I firmly believe that I'm right about this.
6 She's widely expected to win the tournament.
7 It's significantly cheaper than buying a new one.
8 It's been an especially difficult year for us.

READING

A PREDICT Look at the title of the article and the picture and answer the questions.

1 What do you understand by the phrase 'smart homes'?

2 Which of today's household appliances do you think will have evolved into 'smart' devices by 2030?

B READ FOR GIST Read *Smart homes: living in the future* and check your ideas from Exercise A. Did any of the information in the article surprise you?

C IDENTIFY EVIDENCE Read the article again. Underline the evidence used to support the arguments (1–4).

1 Smart kitchen technology may soon become commercially available.

2 Solar panels may not be the only way to generate electricity from the sun.

3 Like smartphones, houses of the future could help monitor our health.

4 Despite predictions, smart technology plays a minimal role in modern housing.

D READ FOR DETAIL Read again. Complete the sentences with no more than three words from the article.

1 It's possible that household security systems in the future will rely on ______________.

2 Experts predict that ______________ in homes of the future will be part of a single, automated system.

3 It seems likely that robots will be increasingly used to perform ______________, such as vacuuming and gardening.

4 To address the issue of ______________, houses of the future may include solar-powered windows.

5 Security is an issue in smart homes as criminals could potentially ______________ your appliances to steal your personal data.

6 The market for smart homes will increase by around ______________ in the near future.

E REFLECT Think about the answers to these questions.

1 If everything can be done from home, how will that affect people's social lives?

2 Which of the smart household devices in the article do you think would be most useful? Why?

Smart homes:
living in the future

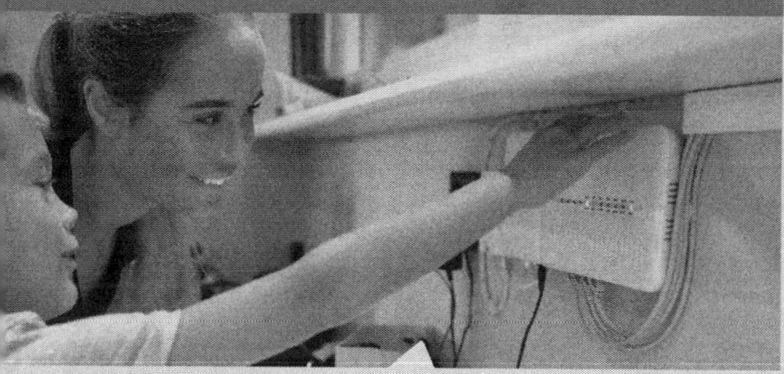

You get home from work, parking your electric car on its charging surface. On your way to the front door, a security system checks who you are using facial recognition software. You enter, and sensors connected to your smartwatch measure your physical condition and automatically play music to suit your mood …

Although this sounds like science fiction, smart homes like this might not actually be that far off. Kitchen appliances will be automated and linked into one system so that meals can be prepared and cooked remotely. Fridges will be able to monitor what food is running low and automatically generate a shopping list. In fact, one major electronics company already has fridges that can communicate directly with your local grocery store.

Robots will play a part, too. Many people already use devices, such as automatic vacuum cleaners for floors and carpets – and a similar robotic device may soon be mowing your lawn. In the future, human-like robots will be able to understand instructions and do many household chores.

Energy conservation, health and security are all major considerations in building the houses of the future. Many houses already have solar panels, but in the future, power may be generated by solar windows – a development that one expert says could be commercially available within the next few years. As mentioned before, health will be monitored and the information made directly available to the resident. In fact, a 2016 report published by the National Association of Home Builders suggested that in the future, floors and stairs within the home will be able to monitor your weight, if that is a particular concern of yours.

The level of connectivity required for these innovations is already possible. So why is it that only an estimated 1% of homes now have full smart technology? Being connected is one problem, in the sense that various companies are competing with each other, and their systems are not compatible. If you want to add or replace a device, it must be from the same company that set up your system. Security is another problem: one internet company found that eight out of ten security systems were open to hacking. Someone could hack your fridge and get ahold of all your personal data. Finally, there is the cost, though as the technology develops, many devices may become cheaper.

Despite these drawbacks, market research surveys predict a growth of about 30% by 2020. The fact that many houses are now being built as smart homes from the start will probably help the figures – and leave future homeowners with no choice.

Glossary

sensor (n) a piece of equipment which reacts to physical changes such as heat, light, pressure, etc

1

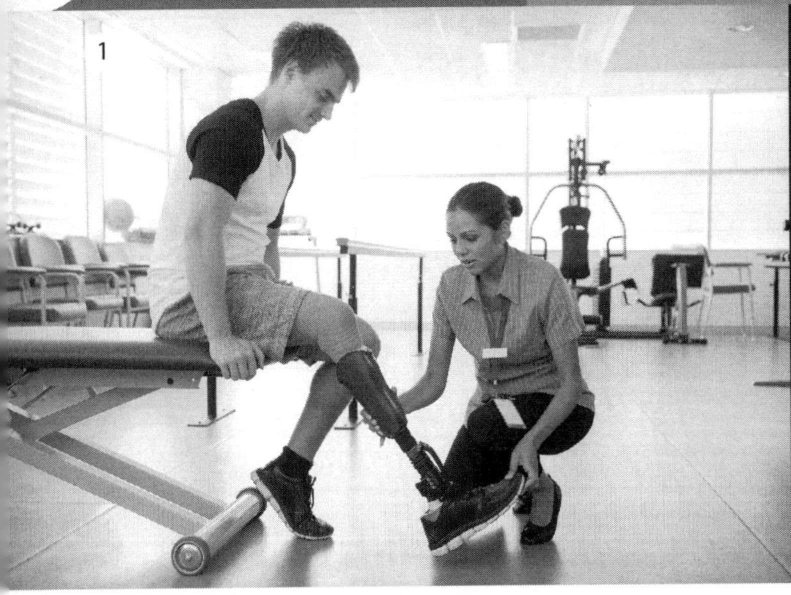

2

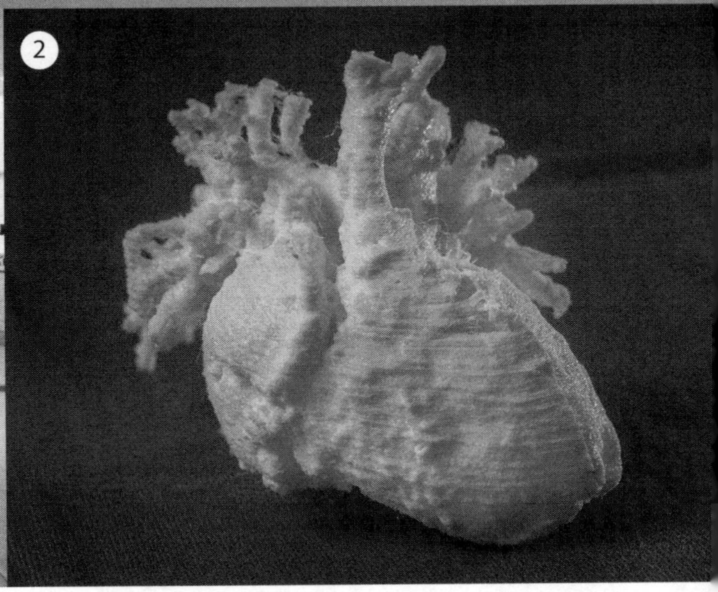

LISTENING

A PREPARE You are going to listen to a discussion about future medical technology. Look at the pictures (1–3) and list the potential advantages of each.

4.5 **B LISTEN FOR GIST** Listen to the discussion. Were any of your ideas from Exercise A mentioned?

4.5 **C IDENTIFY AGREEMENT AND DISAGREEMENT** Listen again. Check (✓) the ideas that both interviewees agree with. Write notes about any disagreements.

1. Technological advancements have improved the design and development of artificial limbs. ☐
2. Brain-computer interface technology requires complex, dangerous surgery. ☐
3. Nobody wants to expose themselves to high levels of risk, despite the potential rewards. ☐
4. It won't be long before scientists are able to 3D print organs and tissue. ☐
5. Private hospitals sometimes promote ideas like robotic surgery to get more customers. ☐

4.5 **D LISTEN FOR DETAIL** Listen again. Complete the sentences with no more than three words from the discussion.

1. Doctors first started using ______________ to replace arms and legs thousands of years ago.
2. Patients will be able to use ______________ to move their prosthetic arms or legs.
3. Dr. Scott compares 3D bioprinting to ______________ because she believes it will never become a reality.
4. Robots are better at carrying out simple procedures because they don't feel ______________.
5. Robotic surgical devices use small ______________ to carry out operations.
6. Richard believes that the use of robotic surgery has led to ______________ which have resulted in the death of patients.

Glossary

organ (n) part of an animal or plant that performs a specific function (e.g. the heart or brain)
procedure (n) a medical operation
tissue (n) the substance that animals and plants are made of

E REFLECT Think about the answers to these questions.

1. Which of the technological advances which you heard about in the discussion do you think will be 'normal' within the next ten years?
2. Can you think of any other technological advances which might be made in the field of medicine?

3

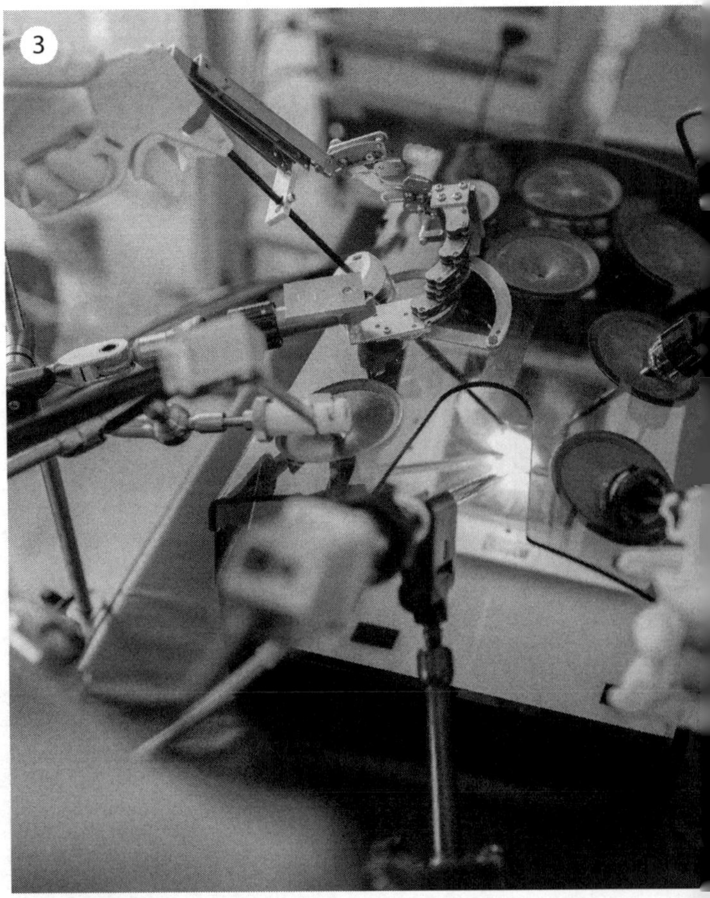

WRITING

A Read the introduction to the blog post. What issue is the writer going to discuss?

B List ideas for and against the issue.

C Scan the blog post. Which of your ideas from Exercise B are mentioned?

About Blog Contact Search

Online courses: The end of school as we know it?

1 ___ Their reasons vary – to get a degree, improve their job prospects or simply because they want to learn something new. 2 ___ They also offer a convenient way for people who have a full-time job to study on their own time or at their own pace. 3 ___ They lack personal interaction and can leave many students feeling isolated. In this article, I will explore both sides of the argument.

Perhaps the biggest benefit of online learning is the flexibility it offers students. Anyone with a computer or smart device and a good internet connection can log in and study whenever and wherever they want. 4 ___ Most courses also offer flexible deadlines, taking the pressure off students and arguably making the learning experience more enjoyable.

5 ___ Most, if not all, connection between teachers and students takes place online, via forums, chat rooms and email – something that can make the whole experience feel a little impersonal. Arguably, it also makes it much more difficult for teachers to assess each student's strengths and weaknesses, let alone their personal interests. Education should be about more than just remembering facts and figures – it teaches us social skills.

6 ___ While there are many clear benefits of studying online – indeed for some it is the ideal educational solution – it lacks the vital element of personal contact and, as such, can never fully replace the need for physical classrooms.

D STRUCTURING FOR AND AGAINST TEXTS Read the blog post again. Fill in the blanks (1–6) with the sentences (a–f).

- **a** This is particularly beneficial to people who have to fit studying around full-time jobs or family commitments.
- **b** On the other hand, many argue that online courses don't provide a complete educational experience.
- **c** In conclusion, I believe that online courses should support, not replace, traditional classroom education.
- **d** One argument against online learning is that it removes social interaction.
- **e** These days, more and more people are taking courses online.
- **f** Those in favor of online learning point out that courses are available at a very low cost.

WRITING PRACTICE

A PLAN Read the blog topic and write notes of arguments for and against.

> The benefits of increased automation in the home far outweigh the drawbacks.

B PREPARE Organize your notes from Exercise A into a plan for a for and against blog post.

C WRITE Write your blog post in 150–250 words. Use your plan to help you.

D EDIT Edit your blog post. Check:

- spelling and punctuation
- use of phrases to structure your argument
- strength of ideas.

GRAMMAR
The passive voice; Causative *have* and *get*

A Complete the sentences with the correct passive form of the verbs in the box.

add destroy donate fine publish solve

1 A report ______________ last year that strongly indicated the factory was to blame.
2 Farmers claim that their crops ______________ by the chemical and want it banned.
3 Climate change can't ______________ by people alone – we need government support.
4 Over $400 billion ______________ to charitable organizations last year.
5 The company says that meat-free burgers ______________ to the menu next year.
6 Many of the companies that were involved ______________ previously for environmental damage.

B Rewrite the sentences in the passive voice, omitting the agent where appropriate.

1 The US food industry wastes 60 million tons of food every year.
____
2 Volunteers are supporting families in need during the food shortage.
____
3 The international community still hasn't solved the water crisis in sub-Saharan Africa.
____
4 The oil spill will affect many communities of nesting birds in the area.
____
5 Most governments around the world have banned whale hunting.
____
6 Hunters have poached nearly 10,000 rhinos in South Africa in the last ten years.
____

C Complete the comment with the causative *have* or *get* form of the prompts in parentheses. Sometimes more than one answer is possible.

EmilyB
25 mins ago

Hey! Long time no speak. How's the house renovation going? Have you moved in yet?

Dan
Just now

Not yet, sadly! We [1] ______________ (*do a lot of work*), but there's still a lot more to do. While we [2] ______________ (*replace floors*), we [3] ______________ (*put in underfloor heating*). That probably wasn't the best decision we've made – we've had some pretty expensive energy bills since! After that, we [4] ______________ (*change all the doors and windows*). Normally this is really expensive, but we actually got a pretty good deal on them. We also [5] ______________ (*have to fix a few holes in the roof*). We probably could have fixed these ourselves, but it just seemed easier to call in the experts. At the moment, we're [6] ______________ (*put in wiring*) for lights and sockets, so next week, we'll [7] ______________ (*finish off walls*). We hired local businesses to help us with all the technical jobs, but I think we can manage the decorating. To be honest, I really like painting anyway. After we've moved in, we're going to [8] ______________ (*put in a swimming pool*) if we can get planning permits. But that will probably have to wait until we've saved up some more money!

VOCABULARY
Green vocabulary

A Label the pictures with the words in the box.

compost heap double glazing
energy-efficient light bulb rain barrel smart meter
solar panel underfloor heating wind turbine

1 ____________

2 ____________

3 ____________

4 ____________

5 ____________

6 ____________

7 ____________

8 ____________

B Complete the sentences with the correct forms of the words in Exercise A.

1 We have a(n) ____________ on our balcony; we mostly use it to collect rainwater which we use on the plants.

2 Good insulation and ____________ help to keep heat in and save energy.

3 I don't think we should rely on gadgets like ____________ to monitor our energy use. We should be more conscious of this ourselves.

4 Hopefully, a(n) ____________ will encourage us to think more carefully about food waste as we can see what we are throwing away.

5 There are alternatives to traditional energy sources. For example, a(n) ____________ can help supply your home with electricity.

6 If you put a(n) ____________ in every room, you won't lose light, but you will use less electricity.

7 We have ____________ which we control by setting the thermostat to the temperature we need.

8 If you have a(n) ____________ fitted on your roof, you will be saving money and helping the environment at the same time.

PRONUNCIATION
Glottal stops

5.1 **A** Listen to the sentences. Underline the words in which the /t/ sound is omitted.

1 It'll save you money, but take a while to pay for itself.

2 We'd like to start right away.

3 It'll take about a week to have it done.

4 I'm going to get a quote for a smart meter.

5 Don't worry, I bought a new light bulb.

6 He sewed a button on the energy-efficient curtain.

5.2 **B** Listen and repeat the sentences.

1 We've made a lot of changes to the house.

2 We've gotten a builder to agree to come around later.

3 I think installing a solar panel would be better.

4 She doesn't see the need for underfloor heating.

5 Do you want to buy a smart meter?

5.2 Change

Changing places

VOCABULARY
Describing areas of a city; Prefixes

A Choose the correct options to complete the sentences.

1 Providing ***housing*** / ***slums*** for the growing population is going to become a problem.

2 I would much rather live in the ***slums*** / ***suburbs*** than in the city center.

3 This is a(n) ***residential*** / ***industrial*** area, so there are no businesses here, only a few stores.

4 ***Rural*** / ***Urban*** life has its problems; there isn't much public transportation, for example.

5 Before we reached our destination, we seemed to travel for miles through a(n) ***suburb*** / ***industrial*** area filled with factories.

6 Life in the ***slums*** / ***rural*** is very hard for people – there is no running water and sometimes no electricity either.

7 There are mostly banks and insurance offices in the ***residential*** / ***commercial*** center.

8 How do you like ***urban*** / ***industrial*** living now that you've moved to New York City?

B Complete the post with the words in the box and an appropriate prefix.

developed	estimated	happy	led
populated	possible	priced	urban

PRONUNCIATION
Words that lose a syllable

5.3 **A** How many syllables are there in the underlined words? Write the number next to each sentence. Then listen and check.

1 Living in the suburbs would be preferable to being in the city. ____

2 The building is losing a lot of heat, especially without double glazing. ____

3 Our energy bills are considerably higher than I expected. ____

4 House prices in the suburbs are actually very reasonable. ____

5 I don't mind where we live. Do you have a preference? ____

6 It was traditionally seen as a poor area, but these days, it's thriving. ____

5.4 **B** Cross out the syllables that are not pronounced in the sentences below. Then listen, check and repeat.

1 Do you have an aspirin, please?

2 What's the average time it takes to do a unit in your English business book?

3 This camera's expensive, but it has a lot of different features.

4 Everyone has a favorite song, surely.

5 My mom subscribes to several general interest magazines.

6 The seats are comfortable on this plane, but what's wrong with the temperature? It's boiling!

Finding the right place

In the part of town where we most wanted to live, it was [1] ________________ to find the kind of accommodations we were looking for, and anything we did find was incredibly [2] ________________ so we couldn't afford it. We were really [3] ________________ with our current apartment because we had been entirely [4] ________________ about the amount of noise there – the people who sold it to us hadn't said a word about noise pollution! We had [5] ________________ just how badly this would affect us, and it turned out to be very hard to sleep at night, so we were forced to move. [6] ________________ living didn't really appeal to us as the places we'd seen were [7] ________________ and lacking in character – in other words, just street after street of tightly packed little houses that all looked the same. Then someone suggested looking in the old quarter, which had recently been [8] ________________. Neither of us had been there for years so we went to take a look … and fell in love with it immediately!

Richard Solomon
Poughkeepsie, New York

GRAMMAR
-ing and infinitive forms

A Choose the correct options to complete the sentences.

1 You must respect the local customs. Remember *bowing* / *to bow* when you greet the manager.
2 Annie! How great *to see* / *seeing* you! What's new?
3 Take it from me; you won't *find* / *to find* more affordable housing in Norton.
4 With no progress by four o'clock, Patrícia suggested *to take* / *taking* a break.
5 He joined the department in 2012 and went on *becoming* / *to become* the manager before he left.
6 She's pretty angry with you, so I don't think *to call* / *calling* her would be the best option.
7 *Driving* / *To Drive* just isn't an option I'm afraid – the roads are closed because of the snow.
8 Did you manage *to speak* / *speaking* to the landlord about the lock on the bathroom door?
9 I would *to pack* / *pack* a couple of sweaters if I were you – it's supposed to be pretty cold this weekend.
10 Oh, and don't forget *to pick up* / *picking up* some more tomatoes on your way home.
11 If you've finished *cleaning up* / *to clean up* the kitchen, you can give me a hand in here.
12 To be honest, I think I just wanted *to see* / *see* a little more of the world before I went to college.

B Complete the sentences with the correct form of the verbs in the box.

build chat drink fight imagine watch

1 Do you remember ______ with my ex-boyfriend in the club last night? Wow, that was embarrassing!
2 It's difficult ______ living anywhere else than New York. It's my forever home.
3 They keep ______ more and more housing projects in the area.
4 I gave up ______ coffee about four years ago. It wasn't easy at first!
5 Celebrities aren't committed to ______ climate change – they are just after publicity.
6 I wouldn't bother ______ it. I can't see how it was nominated for an Oscar.

C Rewrite each sentence to express the same meaning in a different way.

1 He won't tell me what's wrong with him.
He's refusing ______.
2 They filled up with gas on the way.
They stopped ______ on the way.
3 She let me listen to heavy metal in the car.
I was allowed ______.
4 They really don't want to work on a Sunday.
They want to avoid ______.
5 It was a very difficult climb, but they reached the summit.
They managed ______.
6 He said I could borrow his car.
He offered ______.

READING

A PREDICT Look at the picture and the title of the article. How do you think melting ice in the Arctic might affect the following?

- sea levels
- economies
- plant and animal life
- local populations

B READ FOR GIST Read *Arctic disaster as ice melts* quickly. Were any of your ideas from Exercise A mentioned?

C IDENTIFY CAUSE AND EFFECT Read the article again and complete the sentences using the causes in the box.

change in its chemical balance
coastal erosion
cost of extreme weather events
destruction of their natural habitat
erosion of sea ice global warming
rising sea levels rising temperatures

1 Ice in the arctic region is melting as a direct result of ______________.

2 The ______________ is gradually destroying the natural habitat of large mammals in the area.

3 As a result of the ______________, polar bears are being forced to look for food in local towns and villages.

4 The ______________ in the Arctic have encouraged grizzly bears to leave their homes in the south.

5 Due to a ______________, sea water is having a dramatic impact on the ocean's ecosystem.

6 Many towns and villages by the sea are at threat due to ______________.

7 ______________ are likely to lead to increased flooding in many areas outside the Arctic.

8 The ______________ will have a hugely negative impact on the global economy.

D REFLECT Think about the answers to these questions.

1 What kind of an impact do you think global warming will have on your country?

2 Are the economic interests of a country more important than environmental concerns?

Arctic disaster as ice melts

No environment on the planet is changing as fast as the Arctic. Sea ice, glaciers and even the permafrost are melting because of warmer temperatures. This not only affects the physical environment – the wildlife, people and plants of the Arctic – but has serious consequences for the rest of the planet, too.

Sea ice reflects the sun's heat back into the atmosphere, and until recently, a balance had been kept. But global warming is causing the ice to melt, which exposes more ocean, which absorbs more heat, which melts more ice – and so on, in a never-ending cycle. This steady erosion of the sea ice leads to the disappearance of the natural habitat of seals and polar bears. As a consequence, animals are having to adapt to new environmental conditions faster than they are perhaps able to. More polar bears are seen on land and close to human settlements as a result, and in some areas, animals such as grizzly bears that are used to a warmer climate are moving north as the Arctic becomes less cold.

The whole ecosystem is at risk, right down to the smallest creatures. Sea ice is also important in the production of plankton, which is the main food source for many fish, seabirds and whales. Fish, particularly Arctic cod, are the main food source for seals, and seals form a large part of the polar bear's diet. Freshwater ice melting into the sea has the effect of altering the chemical balance in the sea water, which in turn can harm organisms: so due to global warming, the delicate balance of the Arctic food chain is threatened.

Arctic ice is melting faster than the snowfall in the winter months can replace it. The sea ice provides protection to coastlines from the destructive power of waves, but the disappearance of the sea ice will bring about coastal erosion and land will be lost to the sea. Already, some coastal settlements have had to protect their coasts with rocks and bags full of sand to try and reduce the effects of erosion.

The consequences of these Arctic changes will not be felt only in the Arctic region but will have a global impact. Rising sea levels will have an impact on coastlines in Europe, the UK and America, with low-lying areas seeing an increase in flooding. It will also affect temperatures and changes in climate worldwide.

As well as environmental and climatic consequences, there are also economic ones: for example, countries whose economies rely on fishing or tourism could be badly affected, while the cost of cleaning up after extreme weather events – which are predicted to become more frequent – can be enormous.

Now that the dangers cannot be ignored, let's hope that there will be a global effort to prevent matters from getting worse.

Glossary

erosion (n) the process by which soil, ice, etc are damaged by water, wind, etc

permafrost (n) a thick layer of soil which remains frozen throughout the year

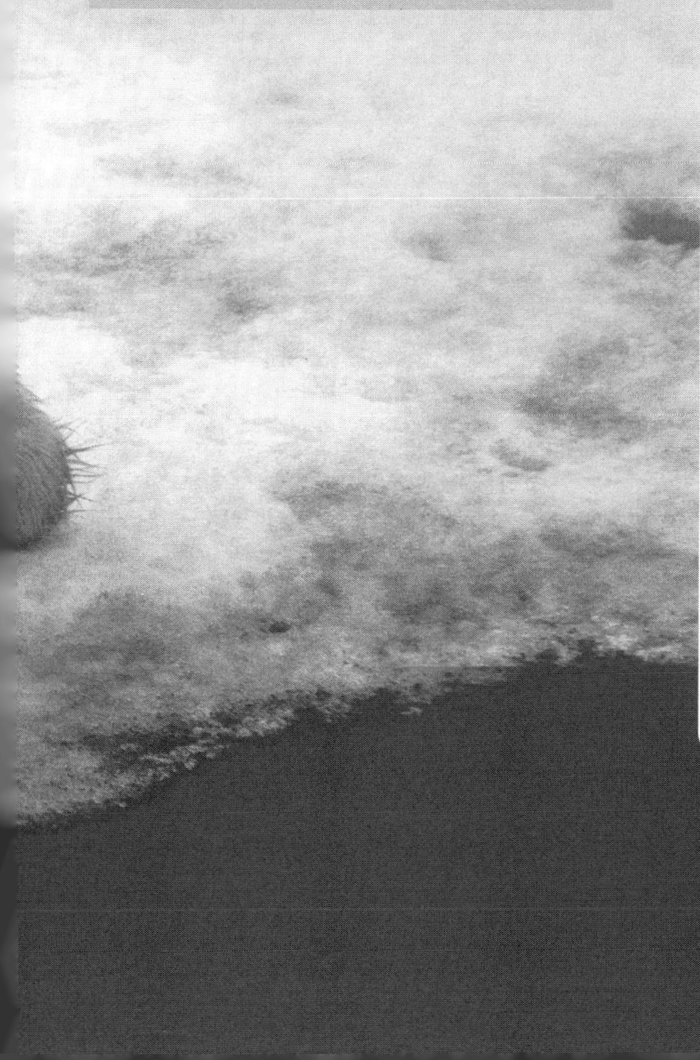

LISTENING

A LISTEN FOR GIST Listen to a radio program about two different projects related to rural areas of Europe. Choose the correct options (a, b or c) to answer the questions. 5.5

1 What is the main topic of the program?
- a encouraging people to appreciate rural life
- b problems faced by the elderly in rural areas
- c overcoming rural depopulation

2 Who will benefit from the two projects?
- a older residents in rural communities
- b village residents and newcomers to the villages
- c mostly tourists

3 What will both projects focus on improving?
- a traditional houses and hotels
- b local schools and businesses
- c the natural environment

B LISTEN FOR RHETORICAL QUESTIONS Listen again and check (✓) the questions used rhetorically. 5.5

1 Who doesn't enjoy a challenge? ☐
2 So how is this going to work exactly? ☐
3 And what are you asking in return? ☐
4 No, people had left – especially the young people, you know? ☐
5 Aren't the young people always the first to leave? ☐
6 So what changed? ☐
7 And best of all? ☐
8 Are people moving back to the village? ☐

C LISTEN FOR DETAIL Listen again and answer the questions. Write notes. 5.5

1 What are some of the consequences of rural depopulation?
2 How does Aldo hope to encourage people to move to Candela?
3 What two things does Aldo expect in return?
4 What kind of visitors come to Saint-Pierre-de-Frugie?
5 What facilities are there in the village?
6 Have the latest developments solved the original problem? Give reasons for your answer.

D REFLECT Think about the answers to these questions.

1 Which of the ideas you heard about in the interviews do you think was the most interesting? Why?
2 Are there areas of your own country which have become depopulated? Is anything being done to stop that trend?

WRITING

A Read the first paragraph of *Saving the local main street* and make a list of the problems and solutions that the writer might mention.

B **DESCRIBING PROBLEMS AND SOLUTIONS** Read the second paragraph of the article and complete the writer's notes.

PROBLEM	SOLUTIONS
rise of [1] ______ *and* [2] ______ *shopping*	• *local stores could use the same* [3] ______ • *make shopping more* [4] ______ *and relaxing*

C Read the third and fourth paragraphs. What is the second problem which the writer mentions? What solutions are offered? What is the writer's conclusion?

WRITING PRACTICE

A **PREPARE** Make a list of problems and solutions in response to the following:

Plastic waste is threatening the environment. What can be done about it?

B **PLAN** Organize your notes from Exercise A into a plan for a problem/solution article.

C **WRITE** Write your article in 150–250 words. Use your plan to help you.

D **EDIT** Edit your article. Check:

- spelling and punctuation
- structure and organization
- strength of ideas.

Saving the local main street

There has been a lot of talk about the decline of the main street recently. What are the causes of this decline, and what can be done about it? This article will first look at some of the problems and then suggest a number of possible solutions.

The biggest threat to main street stores and businesses is the rise of e-commerce and online shopping. It is far easier for consumers to buy with a click of the mouse than to make the effort to go into town. One way of dealing with this is for local stores to use the technology that is putting them out of business. Without becoming 'click-and-deliver', retailers could set up websites that allow customers to see what's available and look around the store. Another way of attracting customers would be to make shopping a more entertaining and relaxed experience. A good example of this is bookstores that provide areas where customers can sit and drink coffee and discuss books.

Another problem is access. Many main streets are busy with traffic and finding somewhere to park is difficult. One solution might be to provide more parking areas, possibly underground, and a more efficient public transportation system.

Community feeling is lost when people do their shopping at malls and big shopping centers. Shopping used to be a social experience; most people knew the staff in their local stores and would usually stop to chat. Consumers need to be encouraged to support their local stores and rediscover that visiting the main street can be a more enjoyable experience than shopping online.

Irregular Verbs

Base form	Simple past	Past participle
be	was/were	been
become	became	become
begin	began	begun
break	broke	broken
bring	brought	brought
build	built	built
buy	bought	bought
can	could	been able to
catch	caught	caught
choose	chose	chosen
come	came	come
cost	cost	cost
cut	cut	cut
drink	drank	drunk
eat	ate	eaten
fall	fell	fallen
feel	felt	felt
find	found	found
forget	forgot	forgotten
get	got	got
give	gave	given
go	went	gone/been
grow	grew	grown
have	had	had
hear	heard	heard
hit	hit	hit
hold	held	held
hurt	hurt	hurt
keep	kept	kept
know	knew	known
leave	left	left
lend	lent	lent
let	let	let

Base form	Simple past	Past participle
lose	lost	lost
make	made	made
mean	meant	meant
meet	met	met
must	had to	had to
pay	paid	paid
put	put	put
read	read	read
ride	rode	ridden
run	ran	run
say	said	said
see	saw	seen
sell	sold	sold
send	sent	sent
set	set	set
shut	shut	shut
sing	sang	sung
sit	sat	sat
sleep	slept	slept
speak	spoke	spoken
spell	spelled	spelled
spend	spent	spent
stand	stood	stood
steal	stole	stolen
take	took	taken
teach	taught	taught
tell	told	told
think	thought	thought
throw	threw	thrown
understand	understood	understood
wear	wore	worn
win	won	won
write	wrote	written

PHONETIC SYMBOLS

Single vowels			Diphthongs			Consonants					
/ɪ/	fish	/fɪʃ/	/uw/	news	/nuw/	/p/	pen	/pen/	/s/	snake	/sneɪk/
/iː/	bean	/biːn/	/eɪ/	face	/feɪs/	/b/	bag	/bæg/	/z/	zoo	/zuː/
/ʊ/	foot	/fʊt/	/ɔɪ/	boy	/bɔɪ/	/t/	tea	/tiː/	/ʃ/	shop	/ʃɒp/
/uː/	shoe	/ʃuː/	/oʊ/	nose	/noʊz/	/d/	dog	/dɒg/	/ʒ/	television	/'telɪvɪʒən/
/e/	egg	/eg/	/ju/	use	/juz/	/ʧ/	chip	/ʧɪp/	/m/	map	/mæp/
/ə/	mother	/'mʌðər/	/aɪ/	eye	/aɪ/	/ʤ/	jazz	/ʤæz/	/n/	name	/neɪm/
/ɜː/	word	/wɜːrd/	/aʊ/	mouth	/maʊθ/	/k/	cake	/keɪk/	/ŋ/	ring	/rɪŋ/
/ɔː/	talk	/tɔːk/				/g/	girl	/gɜːrl/	/h/	house	/haʊs/
/æ/	back	/bæk/				/f/	film	/fɪlm/	/l/	leg	/leg/
/ʌ/	bus	/bʌs/				/v/	verb	/vɜːrb/	/r/	road	/roʊd/
/ɑː/	arm	/ɑːrm/				/θ/	thing	/θɪŋ/	/w/	want	/wɒnt/
/ɒ/	top	/tɒp/				/ð/	these	/ðiːz/	/j/	yes	/jes/

UNIT 1

Lesson 1.4, Listening, Exercise C

1.5 **P = Presenter Y = Yasmin**

P: We're all used to hearing about the effects of social media. Even on this show, we often remark how it's possible to have hundreds of 'friends' on Facebook but no friends at all on campus. This inevitably leads to wider issues, and not just for college students. Americans of all ages suffer from social isolation, feelings of exclusion, anxiety, and so on. In the UK, the authorities have come up with an unusual way of tackling the problem. Here to tell us all about it is Professor Yasmin Ahmed, Chair of the Sociology Department. Professor, welcome to our show.

Y: Thanks. It's good to be here.

P: So, tell us about this unique approach.

Y: Well, in 2018, the British Prime Minister appointed a 'minister for loneliness', to address social isolation in the UK.

P: A minister for loneliness? That has to be a first, doesn't it?

Y: It certainly is. It's actually the first time a national government has directly tried to address the issue.

P: So, what's the story? Where did the idea for this appointment come from?

Y: It came about as the result of a recent survey by the British Red Cross which found that more than nine million British people are frequently or always lonely.

P: That's a huge number.

Y: I know! It's a serious problem, but loneliness is often a sad reality in today's modern world, and social isolation can have a negative impact both psychologically and physically. Depression, anxiety and stress are all directly linked to social isolation, and these, in turn, can lead to an increased risk of coronary heart disease, arthritis and type 2 diabetes. And in fact, the situation is quite similar in other countries. For example, a 2018 survey conducted by the global health organization, Cigna, found that nearly half of Americans say that they sometimes or always feel lonely. Another surprising thing which we learned from this research was that the younger generation actually feels lonelier than older people.

P: Actually, that doesn't surprise me. Young teenagers can often feel socially isolated, can't they?

Y: That's true, although the report specifically found that people between the ages of 18 and 22 felt the loneliest, despite being around others a lot of the time.

P: But surely, living alone has a huge influence on loneliness, too?

Y: Absolutely. In fact, I'd say it's actually the main cause of loneliness among older people. Something like half of people 75 and over in the UK live alone, and many of them find it difficult to get out and meet people.

P: And this is why the 'minister for loneliness' has been appointed?

Y: That's right. The creation of this position is an opportunity for people to start talking. To begin a public dialogue – about relationships, communities and mental health in general. The new minister wants to commission a study into the whole issue, and she wants to bring together local councils, community groups and charities, as well as businesses and individuals, to develop a strategy which will tackle loneliness across the country.

P: So what can we do, as individuals, to help on campus and in our own communities?

Y: The most important thing you can do is to make contact – make friends. Not the social media kind! Reach out to classmates or neighbors who you've never really spoken to before. Stop and chat when you see them, instead of hurrying on.

P: What about older people? Some of our listeners might feel a little awkward about just, well, walking up to somebody and starting a conversation.

Y: Well. Something else you can do is to offer practical help – taking out the trash or changing a light bulb. Many older people find it difficult to get out at all, so you can offer the person a ride to the hairdresser's or just out to the local grocery store. These activities may seem somewhat boring to you and me, but if you don't see anyone for days on end, or even hear the sound of somebody else's voice, then these small gestures are really important.

P: Did you hear that, listeners? These are ways – very simple ways – that you can make a real difference …

UNIT 2

Lesson 2.4, Listening, Exercise B

2.5 **P = Presenter G = Gudrun**

P: Hello and welcome to *Health Beat*. Now, we all know that making important lifestyle changes can be difficult – I mean, who hasn't struggled to stick to a New Year's resolution? But why is it so tough to make a meaningful change? Here to help me answer that is well-being coach and best-selling author Gudrun Nair. Gudrun – thanks for coming on the show.

G: Happy to be here.

P: So, how can we succeed in making lifestyle changes – which actually last?

G: Well, I think the most important thing is to be realistic about what you're trying to achieve. All too often, we set ourselves vague or unmanageable goals and fail as a result. Let me give you an example. Say your goal is 'to lose weight'. What does this actually mean? How much weight are you trying to lose? When do you want to lose it by? Why are you trying to lose it? Vague goals like this can actually be pretty demotivating.

P: So, what's the alternative?

G: How about something like, *I'm going to lose three kilos in four weeks*. This is a challenging, but realistic goal, and it has a clear time frame.

P: OK, so what else?

G: Two words – start slowly. Massive lifestyle changes don't happen overnight – you have to build up to them.

P: Can you give us an example?

G: OK, let's say you want to introduce some physical exercise into your routine. If you try to do too much at once, it can all feel a little overwhelming, and this is when people give up. Allocate a particular time of day to exercise and set a time limit – say, ten minutes every morning before work. You'll soon find that it becomes part of your daily routine. After a while, you won't even think about it. Then, you can move on to your next fitness goal, using the same method.

P: Yeah, that makes a lot of sense. So, what about making a list of your goals? Is that actually helpful?

G: Uh, it can be, but not the way most people do it. We tend to just write a huge list of everything we want, then forget about it. The lists I work on with my clients are a little different.

P: How so?

G: Well, first, I ask people to write down their motivation for each goal – why they actually want to make the change.

P: So, why it's important to them?

G: Right. Next, they make a list of any obstacles they might face – anything that would stop them from making progress.

P: OK ...

G: And finally, they make a plan of action – what steps they will need to take in order to actually achieve their goal. It's much more than just 'a list' – it helps people focus their ideas.

P: OK, I see how that could work.

G: Something else which I always say to my clients is – you don't have to do this on your own. A lot of people don't want to talk about their resolutions, as it kind of highlights all of their, ..., failings, their flaws. If we tell our friends that we want to lose weight, for example, it draws attention to the fact that we might be overweight, right?

P: True. It can be pretty difficult to talk about your problems – especially with people you know.

G: Exactly. But you'll find that if you're honest with your friends or family about what you're trying to achieve, you'll actually get a really positive reaction.

P: So, what's the best way to get started?

G: Well, why not use social media to your advantage? Share your resolution on Facebook and you'll have hundreds of people to support and encourage you. Committing to the goal in such a public way means there'll be a lot of people waiting to see whether you succeed and, believe me, that really helps with motivation.

P: Yeah, I can imagine. It's nice to hear about a positive use of social media for a change.

G: Well, social media has actually helped my clients in a lot of ways. For example, I was recently working with someone who had a really poor work–life balance. He rarely got home before eight o'clock in the evening, and by that point, both of his children were in bed. He felt like he never got to see them or his wife. So, to encourage himself to leave work on time, he started posting the exact time he arrived home each day and how much time this allowed him to spend with his family. That way, he could track his progress online.

P: And did he achieve his goal?

G: He certainly did. He now leaves on time every day and can help put the kids to bed.

P: Glad to hear it. So, do you have any final words of advice?

G: If nothing else, I think it's important to understand that you have to work hard to make meaningful lifestyle changes.

P: Gudrun Nair – thank you for talking to us. Next on the show, we ...

UNIT 3

Lesson 3.4, Listening, Exercise C

3.5 **C = Chuck**

C: Good afternoon everybody. For those of you who don't know me, my name is Chuck Adams and I'm a survival expert with over 30 years' experience in some of the harshest environments on the planet. Now, I'm sure many of you heard on the news this week about the very lucky man who survived for 38 days after being shipwrecked on a remote Pacific island. He was spotted by a passing ship, rescued and is now safely home and recovering from his terrifying experience. Well, today, I'm going to be explaining what you should do if you ever find yourself in a similar situation. I think the most important piece of advice I can give – and this is true of many situations in which we find ourselves – is don't panic! Panic is your worst enemy. Provided you stay calm, you have a good chance of surviving. You need to believe that you'll be rescued. Your priorities should be safety, water, shelter and food – in that order. And rescue of course, but that comes later.

So, first of all – safety. The first thing you need to do is to establish what I like to call a 'safe zone'. Start by asking yourself if there are any immediate dangers in the area. For instance, are there any wild animals? Are there rocks or spiky plants which could injure you? You need to be aware of these things. It's extremely important to avoid injury. Out in the wild – with no medication – even a small cut can be fatal.

As soon as you've done that, the next thing to do is to look for water. As long as you have a supply of fresh water, you can actually survive for quite a long time with very little food. Obviously, if you find a stream, then you're very, very lucky! If not, then you need to find a way to collect water – this means collecting rainwater or finding water dripping down cave walls. You could also try to collect water from the leaves of any large plants you can find. It's important that you stay warm and dry and away from insects that might bite you. In other words, you need some kind of shelter. Find a fallen tree. Then collect some large branches and lean them across the fallen tree. Cover these with leaves and smaller branches to protect you from the wind and rain.

On an island, the ocean is an obvious source of food. As well as trying to catch fish, look for limpets – those small shellfish that attach themselves to rocks on the seashore. You will probably find some berries and fruits, too, but how can you figure out if they're safe to eat? Well, first, rub the berry or fruit across your skin. Then, touch it to your lips without eating it. Finally, put a piece of the berry or fruit in your mouth and then spit it out again. Provided there is no strong reaction, it should be safe to eat.

Obviously, getting rescued is your ultimate goal. It's important to remember that somebody is probably out there looking for you, so don't give up hope. An example of this is the man I mentioned at the beginning of the talk. He lit a fire on the beach and the smoke was seen by a rescue ship which had been sent to look for him. So, you need to make some kind of signal in case a plane or ship passes by. A distress signal is simply a pattern of three, such as three blows on a whistle, three flashes of light or even three piles of rocks. You could also use tree branches to spell out a message. Although, remember, it needs to be really big if it's going to be seen from the air or by a passing ship. Three sailors were rescued in that way a couple of years ago. They wrote the word 'Help' using tree branches on the beach.

So, while I hope that none of you ever do find yourselves alone on a desert island, I hope that the tips I've given you today will help prepare you if you do.

UNIT 4

Lesson 4.4, Listening, Exercise B

4.5 **P = Presenter DS = Dr. Scott R = Richard**

P: Good morning. You're listening to *Future Talk* on Radio 106.7 FM with Nadia Hussein. On today's show, we'll be discussing the use of technology in medicine. My guests are Doctor Anna Scott, of Long Island City Hospital, and Richard Driver, a research scientist at the University of Ohio.

DS and R: Good morning.

P: So Anna, technology is changing the way doctors diagnose, treat and care for their patients. Tell us a little about the developments we can expect to see in the future.

DS: Well, this idea doesn't come from the future – but from the past! Since ancient times, medical practitioners have tried to replace missing body parts using artificial devices. Since then, there have been huge advances obviously, especially in the design and manufacture of artificial limbs.

R: That's true – designers are able to use lightweight plastics and carbon fiber to create the most incredibly lifelike arms and legs which don't look artificial at all.

DS: The really interesting part comes with the *control* of the limb though. Scientists are working on a brain-computer interface which will allow the patient to control his or her artificial limb using brain power alone.

R: Yes, but what you're not explaining is that this development has met with a lot of resistance from patients themselves. The kind of technology you're talking about requires far more complicated and dangerous surgery than that which is currently used to attach a prosthetic arm or leg.

DS: Well, that's true, Richard, but what's your point? We all know that these procedures are delicate, and, yes, they can be dangerous.

R: By definition, somebody who's lost a limb has already had a horrific experience. Many patients just don't want to expose themselves to another extreme procedure.

DS: I agree, Richard, but while there may sometimes be objections from a few patients, I think you'll find that most people want to improve their quality of life as much as they can. They've survived life-changing accidents – they're very brave people – and they're prepared to go that little bit further.

R: I don't know if you would say that if you were in their position.

DS: You're right, but that's why I believe we need to invest more money in this technology, so that we can be sure it's completely safe and 100% successful for every patient before we make it available.

R: Well, surely that's true of every new development, isn't it?

P: OK. Let's move on, shall we? Richard?

R: Well, Nadia, with people living longer than ever, being able to replace parts of the human body when they cease to function is going to become vital. We hope that one day we'll be able to 3D print replacement organs. Organovo, a US-based medical research company, is currently developing an incredible 'bioprinting' process . Layers of cells called 'bio ink' are built up into carefully calculated designs to create new structures.

DS: Oh, come on. For most people – medical professionals included – the idea of 3D printing new organs is just science fiction.

R: Well, you're obviously wrong, because it's happening – here and now.

DS: You're talking about 3D printing new tissue. We're still years away from what you're suggesting.

R: It's undoubtedly true that this technology is in the early stages, but researchers have already printed small sections of liver tissue in the lab. I don't think it's actually all that unrealistic. Don't forget that medical procedures which are perfectly normal today were just a dream 20 years ago.

P: Anna, can you predict any other ways in which technology will transform patient care?

DS: I remember being terrified the first time that I had to take blood from a patient. Today, robots – which are not affected by anxiety or fear – can easily perform this procedure without making any mistakes. And of course, they will soon be carrying out much riskier, surgical procedures.

P: Maybe so, but a robot isn't the same as a doctor, is it? Patients may not *want* to have an electronic doctor taking their blood. Isn't it possible that the patient's fear may significantly impact their physical well-being?

DS: When I say 'robot', we're not talking about a *Star Wars*-style android! A surgical robot is a mechanical arm to which tiny sensors and cameras are attached. A *human* doctor actually controls the entire procedure – a screen allows him or her to view enlarged 3D images of the inside of the patient's body.

R: I know that, Anna, but the level of risk is crazy! I believe that researchers are trying to develop robotic surgery too fast. There have been a lot of reports about robotic surgical devices making fatal mistakes. While I accept that in some cases these techniques are safe and useful, I just think that people have a tendency to admire anything 'new'. In some cases, the traditional surgical procedure is actually much safer. I, for one, think that some hospitals – especially private ones – are promoting these kinds of technologies in order to impress their patients and get more 'customers', if you like.

DS: Definitely! That *is* an issue, but I don't see why the unethical practices of a few private clinics should stop us from developing life-saving new techniques …

UNIT 5

Lesson 5.4, Listening, Exercise A

5.5 **P = Presenter A = Aldo M = Mark**

P: Across rural Europe, young people are leaving small towns and villages by the hundreds and possibly even thousands. They leave behind them empty streets, closed schools and cafés and an elderly population. Fields which have been farmed for generations have been abandoned and houses are falling down because there is nobody there to repair them. According to EU statistics, as many as 22% of rural European populations are elderly. However, some areas and towns are trying to change this trend of rural depopulation.

One person hoping to bring life back to their empty streets is Aldo Conti – a resident of Candela, a small town in south-east Italy. Aldo recently moved back to Candela after living in the UK for ten years, and was devastated to find it much emptier than when he left. I met Aldo last year, when he took me on a tour of the town.

A: … and this is the main square.

P: Wow! It really is empty, isn't it?

A: Yeah. When I was growing up, the square was full of people on the weekend, but now, everyone's just gone.

P: And you want to repopulate the entire village? Sounds a bit ambitious.

A: Haha! Well who doesn't enjoy a challenge? We all know that people are leaving the countryside and heading to urban areas. Here, in Candela, we hope to change that trend and bring life back to our village by encouraging city dwellers to relocate here.

P: So how is this going to work exactly?

A: Just think about it. Although most jobs and houses are in urban areas, there are a lot of people who are fed up with their hectic, stressful lifestyle in the city, people who are longing to get away and to live at a slower pace, closer to nature.

P: Sure. But that's where the jobs are. Why would people want to move here?

A: Well, for one thing, we are willing to pay people to come and live in Candela! We are offering a fee of between $800 and $2,000 to single people and families who are willing to join our community. Six new families have moved in already!

P: That's incredible! And what are you asking for in return?

A: New residents will have to commit to living permanently in the village. We will expect them to rent a house here, and we also require them to have a job with a minimum salary. So, they must work and have an income. We especially welcome families with young children as we're hoping to reopen the village school if we have enough students. The reopening of the school, local stores and businesses will create jobs for local people, too, which we hope will also encourage some of our own young people to stay here and not to head for the city.

P: A similar project is taking place in Saint-Pierre-de-Frugie, in the Dordogne region of south-western France. I spoke to one of the project leaders, Mark Henderson, about how he hopes to breathe life back into the village. So you're not actually from here, are you?

M: Uh, no. My wife and I moved here about four years ago for a bit of peace and quiet.

P: Well, you've certainly gotten that!

M: True – although I didn't think it would be *this* quiet! Our house was pretty cheap and it didn't take long to figure out why. There was no school, no stores, the farms and fields were abandoned, people were leaving. No, people had left – especially the young people, you know?

P: Aren't the young people always the first to leave?

M: Absolutely.

P: So, what changed?

M: Well, as you can see, our village is beautiful.

P: True – the countryside around here is amazing.

M: Right – so we decided to concentrate on that – the natural environment. A team of volunteers started to work in the village – we fixed the fountains and public monuments; we cleared the footpaths and created walking trails. Suddenly we had nature lovers, walkers, campers, all wanting to come and visit our village and stay.

P: That's great. But what about local businesses?

M: Well, we restored one of the bigger, older houses and converted it into a hotel. We've also opened a village store that sells organic produce and the restaurant is open again. We've even created an eco-center which has educational resources and information for visitors. And best of all? We've installed several wind turbines and are now generating our own electricity!

P: Wow! So has it worked? Are people moving back to the village?

M: Well, let me give you a few stats – the population of the village has risen from 360 in 2008 to over 400; 22% of our farmland is used for organic farming – that's compared with 3% in the rest of France; and our school has reopened – there's even a waiting list.

P: That's amazing. I hope it all continues.

Answer key

1.1 Personality

VOCABULARY

A

1 c **2** b **3** a **4** a **5** c **6** a **7** b **8** c **9** c **10** a

B

1 thrilled **2** impressed **3** tense **4** frustrated **5** stunned **6** relieved

GRAMMAR

A

1 Could you tell me where the nearest bank is?
2 Can I ask what your name is?
3 What are you thinking about?
4 What happened when you got there?
5 What didn't you like about the meal?
6 Who is taking the class today?
7 Do you know where he lives?
8 Would you mind repeating that?

B

1 the test is
2 me (what) your name (is)
3 how old you are
4 where we have to go
5 where I sign my name (, please)
6 sitting down over there (, please)
7 what your address is
8 what time it is / what the time is

C

1 didn't you tell
2 are you talking about
3 happened yesterday
4 Do you know
5 didn't you like
6 did you grow up
7 were you talking to
8 Who are you going

PRONUNCIATION

A

1 ↗ **2** ↘ **3** ↗ **4** ↘ **5** ↘ **6** ↗ **7** ↗ **8** ↘

1.2 Who we are

GRAMMAR

A

1 were you doing **2** I'd **3** he's working **4** have to **5** was traveling **6** I've **7** was raining **8** grew

B

1 hasn't finished **2** was; leaving **3** had sold out **4** closes **5** 'm seeing **6** lived

C

1 've faced **2** had burned **3** sounds **4** had **5** wasn't **6** was looking **7** 'm going **8** hadn't thought

VOCABULARY

A

1 d **2** g **3** e **4** a **5** h **6** b **7** f **8** c

B

1 confidence **2** arrogance **3** determination **4** optimism **5** loyalty **6** responsibility **7** difference **8** stubbornness

PRONUNCIATION

A

1 You can't‿always get what you want‿in life.
2 Alex isn't‿an‿easy person to get to know.
3 Actually, he's not‿at‿all like his brother.
4 Marco will support‿us whatever we end‿up doing.
5 Everyone‿at work has been really understanding‿about‿it.

B

1 How far‿is‿it to your house – will‿it take long to walk?
2 My job‿is much better now that‿I work from home‿on Wednesdays.
3 He was generally thought‿of‿as lazy and disruptive.
4 I think‿I've done the best‿I can‿on this project.
5 I think‿it's‿important to talk to people we don't‿agree with.

1.3 Reading

READING

B

They all overcame serious problems before they achieved success in their chosen fields.

C

1 d **2** a **3** f **4** b

D

1 It made him work harder. ('… criticism just made him more determined.')
2 He practiced speaking with small stones in his mouth and with a knife between his teeth. ('It is said that he would fill his mouth with small stones and practice speaking with a knife held between his teeth to get rid of his stammer and improve the strength of his voice.')
3 It wasn't a great success. ('… his first commercial movie made a profit of only $1 …')
4 Being asked to direct the movie *Duel* ('… if he hadn't then been given the chance to direct the movie *Duel* …')
5 He worked on the family farm. ('His mother died when he was nine years old and Lincoln was immediately put to work on the family farm.')
6 Working as a lawyer ('It was when he decided to become a lawyer and later to go into politics that he finally found his life's work.')
7 To hide her physical disabilities ('When she was just six years old, she caught polio which left her right leg shorter and much thinner than the left – something she wore long skirts to disguise.')
8 No. Her first choice was to be a doctor. ('… Kahlo dreamed of becoming a doctor, but her ambitions were cut short …')

1.4 Listening

LISTENING

B
2

C
1 British government appoints a minister for loneliness.
2 The decision came about because of recent research.
3 Young people are lonelier than older people.
4 The new minister will develop a strategy based on input from many groups.
5 Try to develop new relationships with your neighbors.
6 Give practical help to those in need.

D
1 b 2 b 3 c 4 b 5 c

1.5 Write a formal letter asking for information

WRITING

A
1 To ask for information about the robotics club.
2 The person who runs the robotics club.
3 Because the letter is formal and the writer doesn't know the name or gender of the person he is writing to.

B
1 salutation or greeting
2 purpose of the letter
3 request for information
4 request for a response
5 sign-off

C
1 b 2 e 3 d 4 a 5 c

WRITING PRACTICE

C
Model answer
Dear Sir/Madam,

I am writing to inquire about joining your sailing club. I would be grateful if you could answer one or two questions about the club and how it operates to help me decide if it is suitable for me.

I would like to know when and how often the club meets, as I need to know if the times fit in with my schedule. Could you tell me whether I need to have any previous experience with sailing and if instruction is provided for beginners? I have never sailed before and would need help and guidance in the beginning. I was also wondering what measures are in place to ensure the safety of the members. Finally, do I need any special equipment, such as my own lifejacket?

If you could let me know as soon as possible, I would be grateful, as I am excited to get started and hope your club suits my requirements. Thanks in advance for your help.

Sincerely,
Lucas Nilsson

2.1 A full life

VOCABULARY

A
1 stress 2 anxiety 3 depression 4 calories 5 obesity 6 cholesterol

B
1 Mental 2 processed 3 life 4 reduces 5 aging 6 level 7 suffer 8 under

GRAMMAR

A
1 been reading 2 been staying 3 lost 4 been calling 5 been 6 been trying 7 spent 8 been doing 9 haven't been sleeping 10 has written

B
1 I've finished 2 have you been doing 3 I've put on 4 I've given up 5 We've been working 6 I've stopped 7 Mía's been biking 8 he's already been

C
1 've/have broken 2 've/have been calling 3 haven't finished 4 've/have been going 5 's/has cleaned 6 've/have been waiting 7 's/has been 8 've/have been staying

PRONUNCIATION

A
1 a 2 b 3 b 4 a 5 a

B
1 They've been 2 I've been 3 We've been 4 She's been 5 He's been

2.2 Change

GRAMMAR

A
1 correct
2 He didn't use~~d~~ to have such long hair.
3 We would ~~to~~ sit out on the balcony and talk all night.
4 I found it really difficult to get use**d** to wearing contact lenses at first.
5 You'll have to ~~be~~ **get** used to working longer hours now that you have your new job.
6 Being the youngest in the family, I soon **got** used to being told what to do.
7 correct
8 correct
9 I think I'm slowly getting use**d** to such a long commute.
10 correct

B
1 used to 2 be used to / have gotten used to 3 get used to 4 got used to 5 would 6 used to 7 didn't use to 8 to get used to

PRONUNCIATION

A
/d/

VOCABULARY

A
1 Naturally **2** Sadly **3** undoubtedly **4** merely **5** frankly
6 Admittedly **7** apparently **8** simply

B
1 Admittedly, **2** Frankly **3** merely/simply **4** Naturally
5 apparently **6** Sadly

C
1 ridiculous
2 disappointed
3 concerned
4 easy
5 likely

2.3 Reading

READING

C
2

D
1 'But as we all know, advice is always easier to give than to follow …'
2 'I think we can all agree that knowing how others have coped in similar situations can give you the strength to keep going.'
3 '… many are, without a doubt, full of unscientific nonsense.'
4 'If you have the time and the money, a nice home and a loving family, then it becomes that much easier to make positive changes in your life.'
5 '… we only seem to turn to self-help when the economy is bad.'

2.4 Listening

LISTENING

B
1 Set realistic goals.
2 Focus on one change at a time.
3 Make a detailed plan of action.
4 Ask friends and family for support.
5 Use social media to log your progress.

C
1 a **2** a **3** c **4** b **5** a **6** c

2.5 Write an article giving advice

WRITING

C
1 c **2** f **3** b **4** e **5** a **6** d

D
1 make a plan before you start
2 to do some physical exercise
3 using your cell phone after 10 pm
4 break tasks down into stages
5 forget to reward yourself

WRITING PRACTICE

C
Model answer
Fear of speaking in public, whether in front of a large audience or even a small group, is one of the top ten fears most people have. At school, in college or at work, you might be asked at any time to speak to an audience or give a presentation. How will you manage the nerves, the anxiety, the thumping heart? If you want help, read on.

Prepare
- It's a good idea to start small. Practice your speech on your family or a few friends.
- Make sure you know your material inside out. Knowing your topic gives you confidence, and you'll be ready for any questions.
- Remember to practice your speech several times before the big day. Time yourself and make sure you have extra material in case you finish early.
- Whatever you do, don't try to memorize your whole speech; it will sound unnatural and tense. Memorize the key points and use cards as prompts for examples you want to make.

Beat stress
- Remember that it isn't you but what you have to say that people have come for. If you've done your preparation, there's nothing to fear.
- Meet some of the audience before you speak. You'll see they are normal friendly people.
- Don't forget to add some humor into your talk. Involve your audience, ask questions, get them to participate.
- Let your knowledge and passion for the subject shine through.

3.1 Staying alive

GRAMMAR

A
1 had already eaten
2 was trying
3 packed
4 had been decorating
5 hadn't studied
6 knocked
7 was pouring
8 had been walking

B
1 had already left
2 was leaving
3 was looking forward
4 rushed
5 had locked
6 had been working
7 remembered
8 was getting

C

… he had a funny feeling that someone ~~followed~~ **was following** him; … he ~~wasn't seeing~~ **didn't see** anyone; … until the moment he ~~had been arriving~~ **arrived** at the office; … remembered how he **had** felt eight hours earlier; Surely now he would notice if someone ~~watched~~ **was watching** him; … he ~~was having~~ **had** one last anxious look around; … ~~did he work~~ **had he been working** too hard for the last few weeks?; … his phone ~~had rung~~ **rang** and made him jump

VOCABULARY

A

1 smashed
2 growled
3 creaked
4 crackling
5 crunched
6 rumbled

B

1 b 2 a 3 b 4 a 5 a 6 c 7 c 8 b

3.2 Fear and danger

GRAMMAR

A

1 in case 2 unless 3 As soon as 4 as long as
5 Provided

B

1 our flight unless we hurry up
2 the money provided you pay me back next week
3 in case it gets cold later
4 don't call me unless there's a problem
5 let you know as soon as I arrive
6 as long as you follow these instructions

PRONUNCIATION

A

Sentences should have rising intonation on the first clause, falling intonation on the second.

VOCABULARY

A

1 talk over
2 figured out
3 straighten it out
4 went through
5 weigh out
6 put up with
7 deal with it

B

1 straighten it out
2 put up with
3 deal with
4 weigh out
5 figure out
6 talked it over
7 go through

C

1 I'm sick ~~about~~ **of** listening to him telling us how brilliant he is.
2 correct
3 It's very important to be sensitive ~~of~~ **to** the feelings of others.
4 correct
5 correct
6 Aren't you envious ~~for~~ **of** Marco? He gets to travel all around the world!
7 correct
8 It seemed that the man wasn't aware ~~from~~ **of** anyone following him.
9 I'm just so sick ~~from~~ **of** him telling me what to do all the time!
10 correct

3.3 Reading

READING

C

1 f 2 d 3 b 4 h 5 a 6 i 7 c 8 g

D

1 Colombia ('… he hitchhiked to Colombia, where he met fellow taveler, Marcus Stamm. They became friends and decided to travel to Bolivia together, where two more men, Karl Ruprechter and Kevin Gale, joined the group.')
2 They didn't have enough supplies and couldn't source enough nearby ('… they didn't have enough supplies and that the local villages couldn't provide all they needed.')
3 They didn't trust each other, particularly Karl. ([Karl] '… decided that he didn't want to continue because the river passed over dangerous rocks and waterfalls. He also told them he couldn't swim. This led to suspicion and distrust in the group …')
4 He lost them during the incident with the raft. ('… all the supplies had been lost with the raft.')
5 He made a flame thrower with a lighter and a spray can. ('He improvised, using a spray can and a lighter as a makeshift flame thrower to frighten it off.')
6 Kevin turned around and saw him. ('By chance, Kevin turned around for a last look and saw him.')

3.4 Listening

LISTENING

B

1 creating a safe space 2 finding water 3 building a shelter
4 finding food 5 getting rescued

C

1 T
2 T
3 F (The speaker talks about different methods of collecting water.)
4 T
5 F (The speaker explains how to decide if something is poisonous or not.)
6 F (You can also make a pattern or message with rocks or branches.)

D

1 safe zone 2 cave walls 3 branches 4 small shellfish
5 skin 6 three 7 piles of rocks

3.5 Write a short story

WRITING

A

1 somewhere out in the country ('We live out in the country …')
2 a car accident ('Halfway home, we hit a patch of ice, skidded across the road and ended up facing the wrong way with two wheels hanging over the edge of the ditch.')
3 the narrow roads ('… the roads are narrow and bordered by shallow ditches.'); the bad weather ('Driving around there is difficult at the best of times, but it had snowed the night before and I knew the roads would be icy.'); his mother's driving ('She isn't the best driver …')

B

1 T
2 F (It had snowed the previous evening.)
3 F (She got into the car as the writer was putting her suitcase into the back of the car.')
4 T
5 F (They called an ambulance when they saw the accident.)

C

1 noisily
2 nervously
3 heavily
4 violently
5 Slowly
6 Fortunately
7 desperately
8 Surprisingly

WRITING PRACTICE

C

Model answer

My friends and I all knew the story of how Shaka, Chief of the Zulus, had thrown his treasure into a waterfall as his enemies approached. For us though, the waterfall was just a beautiful place for a picnic and a swim on the weekend.

There were five of us who set off that Saturday morning: me, my cousin Rose, her boyfriend Jack and his brother and sister. We had prepared our food the night before as we wanted an early start.

The sun was shining brightly and we were feeling hot and dusty when we arrived at the waterfall after the long drive. We scrambled quickly down to the water – all except Jack who, as usual, dove from the top of the waterfall. Then we ate and lay in the sun. Jack decided it was time for another swim and climbed back up and dove again. This time, he did a somersault before hitting the water. We waited for him to rise triumphantly from the pool. A minute that seemed like an hour passed as we peered anxiously into the pool. His brother and I dove into the pool to look for him, staying under until our breath ran out. We surfaced, gasping desperately for air, then dove down again. At last, we found him and got him out of the pool. He had hit his head and was bleeding heavily. Fortunately, his sister knew what to do. She performed CPR and patched up his head and we carried him back to the car and got him to the nearest hospital. He doesn't seem to have learned his lesson, though. We still go there, and he still insists on diving.

4.1 My future

GRAMMAR

A

1 a 2 c 3 b 4 a 5 b 6 c 7 a 8 b

B

1 's getting 2 'll fly 3 doesn't end
4 'm visiting 5 'll take 6 'm going to buy

C

What are you ~~doing~~ **going to do** now, Dan?; I guess ~~I'm taking~~ **I'll take** a few weeks off …; ~~I'll~~ **I'm going to** work on my resume tomorrow, then ~~I'll~~ **I'm going to go** job hunting on Monday; What do mean ~~you'll~~ **you're *going to go*** job hunting?; ~~I'm probably spending~~ **I'll probably spend** some time searching for jobs …; The work ~~is going to~~ start**s** on the 14th; I ~~don't~~ **won't** have time to do that …;

VOCABULARY

A

1 of 2 of 3 in 4 in 5 in 6 about 7 on 8 in

B

1 challenging; to balance
2 produce; benefits
3 influences; control
4 to produce; balance
5 benefit; control
6 challenged; influence

PRONUNCIATION

A

produce; increase; record; invite

B

1 reject 2 increase 3 update 4 download 5 discount

4.2 What will life be like?

GRAMMAR

A

1 will have risen
2 be eating
3 be traveling
4 be living
5 have been living
6 have expired

B

1 will you be living 2 will/'ll have finished
3 will/'ll be traveling 4 will have worked / will have been working
5 will/'ll still be having 6 will have left
7 will/'ll be watching 8 will/'ll have discovered

VOCABULARY

A

1 a 2 b 3 c 4 c 5 a 6 a 7 b 8 c

B

1 widely 2 especially 3 firmly 4 undoubtedly 5 greatly
6 significantly 7 entirely 8 incredibly

PRONUNCIATION

A
rise-fall; it adds emphasis to the sentence

4.3 Reading
READING

C
1 'In fact, one major electronics company already has fridges that can communicate with your local grocery store.'
2 '… in the future, power may be generated by solar windows – a development that one expert says could be commercially available within the next few years.'
3 '… a 2016 report published by the National Association of Home Builders suggested that in the future, floors and stairs within the home will be able to monitor your weight, …'
4 'So why is it that only an estimated 1% of homes now have full smart technology?'

D
1 facial recognition software
2 kitchen appliances
3 household chores
4 energy conservation
5 hack
6 30% / thirty percent

4.4 Listening
LISTENING

C
The interviewees agree about statements 1, 2 and 4.
3 Dr. Scott disagrees, saying that people who have survived life-changing accidents are 'prepared to go that little bit further'.
5 Dr. Scott disagrees, saying that for most people, 3D printing organs is 'science fiction' and that we're 'years away' from such technology being used.

D
1 artificial devices
2 brain power
3 science fiction
4 anxiety or fear
5 sensors and cameras
6 fatal mistakes

4.5 Write a for and against blog post
WRITING

A
Online learning

D
1 e 2 f 3 b 4 a 5 d 6 c

WRITING PRACTICE

C
Model answer
These days, we don't need to cross the living room to change channels on the TV or wash all our clothes or dishes by hand. Many chores are already done by machines, giving us more free time to do the things we enjoy.
If – or when – we have walking, talking robots in our homes, what more will they do and what will be left for us to do? Some people argue that this is the future, that all our needs will be catered to and that we will have more time to work or enjoy hobbies. Others think that we'll have the opportunity to become more creative with our time and talents.
On the other hand, not everyone knows what to do with their leisure time and many people hate not being occupied by meaningful work. One argument against widespread use of robots in the home is that by having our meals cooked, beds made, lawn cut, etc by robots, we will become lazy and unhealthy. Some people argue that there is also the possibility we will lose control of them – that robots will learn how to act on their own. And who knows where that will lead?
In conclusion, I believe that while robots (or machines) can be useful labor-saving devices, we can choose how much more free time we need , and how much we use them. I think we'll have to learn, with robots in the workplace and at home, how to use our increased leisure time more productively and enjoyably.

5.1 Changing environment
GRAMMAR

A
1 was published
2 are being destroyed
3 be solved
4 was donated
5 will be added
6 had been fined

B
1 60 million tons of food is wasted by the US food industry every year.
2 Families are being supported by volunteers during the food shortage.
3 The water crisis in sub-Saharan Africa still hasn't been solved.
4 Many communities of nesting birds in the area will be affected by the oil spill.
5 Whale hunting has been banned by most governments around the world.
6 Nearly 10,000 rhinos have been poached in South Africa in the last ten years.

C
1 've had a lot of work done
2 were having/getting the floors replaced
3 had/got underfloor heating put in
4 had/got all the doors and windows changed
5 had to have/get a few holes in the roof fixed
6 having/getting the wiring put in
7 be having/getting the walls finished off
8 have/get a swimming pool put in

VOCABULARY

A

1 solar panel
2 double glazing
3 rain barrel
4 energy-efficient light bulb
5 compost heap
6 smart meter
7 underfloor heating
8 wind turbine

B

1 rain barrel
2 double glazing
3 smart meters
4 compost heap
5 wind turbine
6 energy-efficient light bulb
7 underfloor heating
8 solar panel

PRONUNCIATION

A

1 It'll save you money, but take a while to pay for itself.
2 We'd like to start right away.
3 It'll take about a week to have it done.
4 I'm going to get a quote for a smart meter.
5 Don't worry, I bought a new light bulb.
6 He sewed a button on the energy-efficient curtain.

5.2 Changing places

VOCABULARY

A

1 housing 2 suburbs 3 residential 4 Rural 5 industrial 6 slums 7 commercial 8 urban

B

1 impossible
2 overpriced
3 unhappy
4 misled
5 underestimated
6 Suburban
7 overpopulated
8 redeveloped

PRONUNCIATION

A

1 3 2 3 3 4 4 3 5 2 6 4

B

1 asp~~i~~rin
2 av~~e~~rage; bus~~i~~ness
3 cam~~e~~ra; diff~~e~~rent
4 fav~~o~~rite
5 sev~~e~~ral; gen~~e~~ral; int~~e~~rest
6 comf~~or~~table; temp~~e~~rature

GRAMMAR

A

1 to bow
2 to see
3 find
4 taking
5 to become
6 calling
7 Driving
8 to speak
9 pack
10 to pick up
11 cleaning up
12 to see

B

1 chatting 2 to imagine 3 building 4 drinking 5 fighting 6 watching

C

1 to tell me what's wrong with him
2 to fill up with gas
3 to listen to heavy metal in the car
4 working on a Sunday
5 to reach the summit
6 to loan me his car

5.3 Reading

READING

C

1 global warming
2 erosion of sea ice
3 destruction of their natural habitat
4 rising temperatures
5 change in its chemical balance
6 coastal erosion
7 Rising sea levels
8 cost of extreme weather events

5.4 Listening

LISTENING

A

1 c 2 b 3 b

B

1, 4, 7

C

1 empty streets; closed schools and cafes; an aging population; abandoned fields and houses
2 By paying them - between '$800 and $2,000 to single people and families'.
3 They must commit to living permanently in the village and have a job.
4 nature lovers, walkers and campers
5 a hotel, a store, a restaurant, an eco-center, a school
6 Yes – the population of the village has increased and some farm land is back in production.

5.5 Write a problem solution article

WRITING

B

1 e-commerce
2 online
3 technology
4 entertaining

C

Second problem – lack of parking facilities; Solution = provide more (underground) parking areas; improve public transportation; Conclusion = that people should rediscover the social side of shopping on their local main street

WRITING PRACTICE

C

Model answer

One of the biggest threats to the environment, both on land and in the ocean, is plastic waste. And if the environment is at risk, so are we. Modern lifestyles demand single-use, easily disposable products, such as water bottles, coffee cups, take-out food packaging and the plastic bags we are given in grocery stores.

The main issue with plastic is that it is made to last and it does not break down as easily as other materials. It also contains toxins that are harmful to plants, animals and humans. If you burn it, toxic gases are released into the air; if you bury it in landfills, toxins seep into the water system. One way for us as consumers to tackle the problem is to shop more responsibly. For example, we can reuse the plastic water bottles we buy, carry our own cup for our coffee on the way to work, refuse to buy products that have plastic packaging and take our own reusable, non-plastic bags when we shop. In fact, some governments have addressed the issue by making grocery stores charge customers for plastic bags, and this had the effect of greatly reducing the use of plastic bags.

The truth is, these individual actions aren't enough. You may be an avid recycler, but the current methods of waste disposal don't help much. However, we may be able to persuade companies by our actions to cut down on plastic and also force our governments to take action.

Notes

Notes

Notes